INITIATING ETHNOGRAPHIC RESEARCH

ETHNOGRAPHER'S TOOLKIT
Second Edition

Jean J. Schensul, Institute for Community Research, Hartford, Connecticut
Margaret D. LeCompte, University of Colorado, Boulder

PURPOSE OF THE ETHNOGRAPHER'S TOOLKIT

The second edition of the **Ethnographer's Toolkit** is designed with the novice field researcher in mind. In this revised and updated version, the authors of the **Toolkit** take the reader through a series of seven books that spell out the steps involved in doing ethnographic research in community and institutional settings. Using simple, reader-friendly language, the **Toolkit** includes case studies, examples, illustrations, checklists, key points, and additional resources, all designed to help the reader fully understand each and every step of the ethnographic process. Eschewing a formulaic approach, the authors explain how to develop research questions, create research designs and models, decide which data collection methods to use, and how to analyze and interpret data. Two new books take the reader through ethical decision-making and protocols specific for protection of individual and group participants in qualitative research, and ways of applying qualitative and ethnographic research to practical program development, evaluation, and systems change efforts. The **Toolkit** is the perfect starting point for students and faculty in the social sciences, public health, education, environmental studies, allied health, and nursing, who may be new to ethnographic research. It also introduces professionals from diverse fields to the use of observation, assessment, and evaluation for practical ways to improve programs and achieve better service outcomes.

1. *Designing and Conducting Ethnographic Research: An Introduction, Second Edition*, by Margaret D. LeCompte and Jean J. Schensul
2. *Initiating Ethnographic Research: A Mixed Methods Approach*, by Stephen L. Schensul, Jean J. Schensul, and Margaret D. LeCompte
3. *Essential Ethnographic Methods: A Mixed Methods Approach, Second Edition*, by Jean J. Schensul and Margaret D. LeCompte
4. *Specialized Ethnographic Methods: A Mixed Methods Approach*, edited by Jean J. Schensul and Margaret D. LeCompte
5. *Analysis and Interpretation of Ethnographic Data: A Mixed Methods Approach, Second Edition*, by Margaret D. LeCompte and Jean J. Schensul
6. *Ethics in Ethnography: A Mixed Methods Approach*, by Margaret D. LeCompte and Jean J. Schensul
7. *Ethnography in Practice: A Mixed Methods Approach*, by Jean J. Schensul and Margaret D. LeCompte

INITIATING ETHNOGRAPHIC RESEARCH
A Mixed Methods Approach

Stephen L. Schensul, Jean J. Schensul,
and Margaret D. LeCompte

A division of
ROWMAN & LITTLEFIELD PUBLISHERS, INC.
Lanham • New York • Toronto • Plymouth, UK

Published by AltaMira Press
A division of Rowman & Littlefield Publishers, Inc.
A wholly owned subsidiary of The Rowman & Littlefield Publishing Group, Inc.
4501 Forbes Boulevard, Suite 200, Lanham, Maryland 20706
www.rowman.com

10 Thornbury Road, Plymouth PL6 7PP, United Kingdom

Copyright © 2013 by AltaMira Press

All rights reserved. No part of this book may be reproduced in any form or by any electronic or mechanical means, including information storage and retrieval systems, without written permission from the publisher, except by a reviewer who may quote passages in a review.

British Library Cataloguing in Publication Information Available

Library of Congress Cataloging-in-Publication Data

Schensul, Stephen L.
  Initiating ethnographic research : a mixed methods approach / Stephen L. Schensul, Jean J. Schensul, and Margaret D. LeCompte.
    p. cm. — (Ethnographer's toolkit ; book 2)
  Includes bibliographical references and index.
  ISBN 978-0-7591-2201-7 (pbk. : alk. paper) — ISBN 978-0-7591-2202-4 (ebook)
  1. Ethnology—Methodology. 2. Ethnology—Research. 3. Ethnology—Fieldwork.
I. Schensul, Jean J. II. LeCompte, Margaret Diane. III. Title.
  GN345.S3624 2013
  305.80072—dc23
                                                       2012037984

∞™ The paper used in this publication meets the minimum requirements of American National Standard for Information Sciences—Permanence of Paper for Printed Library Materials, ANSI/NISO Z39.48-1992.

Printed in the United States of America

CONTENTS

	List of Tables and Figures	ix
	List of Examples	xiii
	Introduction	xvii
Chapter 1	**Initiating Ethnographic Research: Models, Methods, and Measurement**	1
	Introduction	1
	Ethnography Is Both Inductive and Deductive	4
	Ethnography Is Both Qualitative and Quantitative	7
	Ethnography Operates at the Micro and Macro Level	10
	Ethnography Examines Reported and Observed Behavior	13
	Ethnography Involves Discovery and Representativeness	14
	Ethnography Is Both Theory and Description	16
	Objectivity and Subjectivity	18
	Basic and Applied Research	19
	Summary	21
Chapter 2	**Selecting a Research Site and Focus**	23
	Introduction	23
	The Researcher Personal Interest and History	24
	Researcher Identity	27
	Researcher Positionality	34
	Requirements of Institutional Affiliation and Funding Sources	37
	Perspectives, Needs, and Priorities of the Study Population	42
	Summary	43
Chapter 3	**Preparing for Challenges in the Field**	45
	The Research Game Plan or Proposal	45
	Formal Permissions and Approvals; IRBs and Other Review Bodies	55
	Logistics: Support, Housing, and Other Needs	57

	Sponsoring Institutions in the Research Site	60
	Time and Timeline	68
	Personnel: Hiring and Supervision	74
	Preparing for the Collection, Transcription, and Management of Data	76
	Planning for Writing Up Preliminary Results in the Field	77
	Summary	78
Chapter 4	**The Ethnographer as Theorist: An Introduction to Modeling Midrange Theory**	**81**
	Introduction	81
	The Ethnographer as Theorist	84
	Selecting a Paradigm	92
	Defining Research Questions and Building a Formative or Local Theory	93
	Summary	101
Chapter 5	**Constructing Formative Research Models**	**103**
	Introduction	103
	Developing a Formative Model: Top Down/Bottom Up Construction	104
	Dependent and Independent Domains	110
	Diagramming and Modeling the Formative Research Model	125
	A Note on Generating Hypotheses	129
	Summary	130
Chapter 6	**Operationalization and Measurement**	**133**
	Operationalization	133
	Using the Research Model to Frame Research Goals, Objectives, and Hypotheses	145
	Linking Stages in Research Design with Stages in Data Collection	149
	Summary	153
Chapter 7	**Mixed Methods Models, Measures, and Case Examples**	**155**
	Introduction	155
	Definitions of Mixed Methods Research	156
	When Should Qualitative and Quantitative Methods Be Used?	159
	Integrating Qualitative and Quantitative Methods	161

CONTENTS vii

	Relating or Sequencing of Multiple Methodologies: Models, Methods, Measures, and Case Examples	171
	The Role of Secondary Data in Mixed Methods Ethnography	181
	Summary	184
Chapter 8	**Modeling Ethnographic Intervention Approaches**	185
	Introduction	185
	Definitions of Intervention	188
	Ethnographic Intervention Designs	192
	Guidelines for Modeling Interventions	193
	Steps in Designing Interventions: A Systems Analytic Approach to Using Modeling Techniques	198
	Linking Resources for Change to the Independent Variables: Systems Analysis as a "2 × 2 Table"	204
	Operationalizing the Intervention Model	210
	Summary	214
	References	217
	Index	229
	About the Authors and Artists	243

LIST OF TABLES AND FIGURES

Figure 1.1: Kuznar's Model	4
Table 3.1: An Example of a Project Timeline for Conducting an Intervention Study in Maharashtra, India	69
Table 3.2: Timeline for Intervention Study to Improve Oral Health Self-Management among Low-Income Older Adults	70
Table 3.3: A One-Year Budget for a Three-Year Small Grant	73
Figure 4.1: A Shell to Use for Linear Modeling	87
Table 4.1: The Continuum of Levels of Abstraction	91
Table 4.2: Examples of Paradigms and Associated Guiding Concept Choices	93
Figure 4.2: A Model of Predictors of Depression and Access to Care in Older Low-Income Adults in Senior Housing	94
Figure 4.3: Description of a Phenomenon	98
Figure 5.1: Defining Domains at the Same Horizontal Conceptual Level	106
Figure 5.2: An Initial Draft of a Model	109
Figure 5.3: A Revised Version of a Vertical Model	109
Figure 5.4: A Direct Relationship between Independent and Dependent Domains: Pre-pregnancy Health Status and Infant Health	111
Figure 5.5: Prenatal Care: Intervening Domain Affecting Infant Health Status	112

Figure 5.6: A Diagram Illustrating the Placement of the Dependent Domain in a Formative Research Model 114

Figure 5.7: An Inverse Relationship between an Independent and a Dependent Variable Domain 116

Figure 5.8: Another Inverse Relationship Introducing a Second Independent Variable Domain 117

Figure 5.9: Relationships among Independent Variable Domains 117

Figure 5.10: A Formative Research Model Showing Hypothesized Strong and Weak Relationships among Independent and Dependent Variable Domains 118

Figure 5.11: Constructing a Model using Organizational Domains Believed to Be Associated with the Dependent Domain: Lack of Teen Stop-Smoking Programs 126

Figure 5.12: Constructing a Model Using Community or Population Level Domains Believed to Be Associated with the Dependent Domain: Adolescent Smoking 127

Table 6.1: Operationalizing—Transforming Information from One Level of Abstraction into Another 135

Figure 6.1: Operationalizing—Organizing Information into Hierarchical Taxonomies by Degree of "Abstraction" or Inclusion of the Concept 139

Figure 6.2: Identifying Factors Associated with the Domain FAMILY 143

Figure 6.3: Operationalizing the Factor "Economics" 143

Figure 6.4: Operationalizing the Variable "Material Goods" 144

Figure 6.5: Locating Concepts at the Domain, Factor, and Variable Levels of Abstraction 145

Table 6.2: Purpose Statements Based on a Theoretical Research Model 146

Table 6.3: Constructing a Research Design Using the "Domain, Factor, and Variable" Framework: An Example from Mauritius 147

Figure 6.6: Generating Hypotheses about Relationships among Variables within Factors and Domains: Mauritius Study, FAMILY Domain 147

Table 6.4: Conceptual Taxonomy (Tree Diagram) for FAMILY Domain and SEXUALITY Domain: Mauritius Study	148
Figure 6.7: A Tree Diagram: Conceptual Taxonomy for the Domain FAMILY	149
Table 6.5: Links between Components of Research Design and Conceptual Source Using Tree Diagrams	149
Table 6.6: Stages in Research Design, Selection of Research Methods, and Study Objectives	150
Table 7.1: Principal Differences between Qualitative and Quantitative Research	157
Table 7.2: Purposes and Rationales for Different Approaches to Mixed Methods Research	158
Table 7.3: Linking Conceptual Levels and Types of Data Collection	164
Figure 8.1: Iterations in the Research and Intervention Process	192
Figure 8.2: Modeling the Dependent Variables in a Systems Model	201
Figure 8.3: Independent Variables at the Organization and Population Levels	202
Figure 8.4: "2 × 2 table"	204
Figure 8.5: Resources at the Organizational and Population Level That Could Ameliorate the Problems Signified by the Independent Variables	206
Figure 8.6: Linking Resources to Organization and Population Problems	209

LIST OF EXAMPLES

Example 1.1: Following the trail of smokeless tobacco from the local to the international level in India — 12

Example 1.2: Discovering a new sexual risk behavior in Mauritius — 15

Example 2.1: Entering a low-income community in Lusaka, Zambia, as an American-raised Zambian young adult researcher — 29

Example 2.2: Building trust by following ethical rules — 30

Example 2.3: A Latino researcher studying the informal economy in a Latino community overcomes distrust — 32

Example 2.4: Implications of religious identity in framing research relationships — 36

Example 2.5: Encountering and addressing institutional barriers with differential success — 39

Example 3.1: Abstract for proposed study of smokeless tobacco use among women of reproductive age in Mumbai — 47

Example 3.2: GOALS/AIMS section from study of smokeless tobacco use among women of reproductive age in Mumbai — 48

Example 3.3: An example of appropriate language to use in the description of analysis related to a study goal, aim, or question from a study of smokeless tobacco use among women in Mumbai — 53

Example 3.4: A more elaborate example of an analysis section for the formative phase of a five-year study of women and HIV — 53

Example 3.5: Achieving involvement in the Chicano West Side community of Chicago — 61

Example 3.6: Gaining entry to the Puerto Rican community
in Hartford   62

Example 3.7: Gaining access to low-income communities in Mumbai   62

Example 3.8: Gaining access to the CBO and voluntary community
organization network in Hartford   63

Example 3.9: Gaining entry by accident: How a vacation turned
into the NGO Teach Cambodia   64

Example 3.10: Gaining access to a study community in Lusaka
to do AIDS prevention research with women   64

Example 3.11: Doing the preliminary fieldwork required
for interventions   65

Example 4.1: Transforming facts into theoretical propositions   85

Example 4.2: Reformulating theory in the National Teen Action
Research Summer Training Institute   89

Example 4.3: Understanding the "problem"—identifying sexual
risk behaviors among young women in Mauritius   97

Example 4.4: Finding an intervention theory through evaluation 100

Example 5.1: Defining domains horizontally: Related domains at the
same conceptual level   105

Example 5.2: An example of modeling from the bottom up   106

Example 5.3: An example of recursivity in vertical modeling   108

Example 5.4: Identifying variability in the dependent domain   114

Example 5.5: Locating new independent domains   121

Example 5.6: How study participants can help to identify
theoretical propositions   121

Example 5.7: Considering organizational and population domains
in a study of adolescent health and sexual risk   124

LIST OF EXAMPLES xv

Example 6.1: Operationalizing the FAMILY domain among young Mauritian women in the workforce 142

Example 7.1: Coding at the domain, factor, and variable levels 165

Example 7.2: Operationalizing the factor "spousal violence" 167

Example 7.3: A mixed methods approach using qualitative and quantitative data to assess success in The Learning Circle program 168

Example 7.4: A sequential mixed methods design with qualitative/quantitative equivalency 172

Example 7.5: Convergence of qualitative and quantitative methods in the evaluation of changes in gender-equitable norms in a study population in Mumbai 174

Example 7.6: An embedded design where qualitative data supplement the results of quantitative evaluation data 176

Example 7.7: Long-term urban research in Detroit 179

Example 7.8: The nutritional health research, education, and advocacy program of the Hispanic Health Council 179

Example 7.9: A long-term program of AIDS-related research in Hartford, Connecticut 180

Example 7.10: Multistage research on HIV risk prevention among married couples in Mumbai communities 180

Example 7.11: The use of a national data set in India to compare correlates of anemia in slum communities in Mumbai with a local study community 183

Example 7.12: Using previously collected qualitative and quantitative data to shed light on a new topic 184

Example 8.1: Using the 2×2 table to create a multilevel intervention focused on reducing sexual risk among married men in Mumbai 212

INTRODUCTION

INTRODUCTION TO THE *ETHNOGRAPHER'S TOOLKIT*

The *Ethnographer's Toolkit*, a mixed methods approach to ethnography, is a series of texts on how to plan, design, carry out, and use the results of applied ethnographic research. Ethnography as an approach to research may be unfamiliar to people accustomed to more traditional forms of research; however we believe that ethnography will not only prove congenial but also essential to many researchers and practitioners. Many of the investigative or evaluative questions that arise in the course of answering basic questions about ongoing events in a community or school setting or in the context of program planning and evaluation cannot be answered very well with other approaches to research, such as controlled experiments or collection of quantifiable data alone. Often there are no data available to quantify or programs whose effectiveness needs to be assessed! Sometimes the research problem to be addressed is not yet clearly identified and must be discovered. In such cases, mixed methods ethnographic research provides a valid and important way to find out what *is* happening and to help research-practice teams plan their activities.

NEW IN THE SECOND EDITION OF THE *ETHNOGRAPHER'S TOOLKIT*

In this second edition of the *Toolkit*, we have updated many sections of the books and, based on feedback from our colleagues, we have clarified many of the concepts and techniques. Book 1 of the *Ethnographer's Toolkit* remains an introduction and primer, but it includes new material on data collection, definition, and analysis as well as new chapters on research partnerships and using ethnography for a variety of applied purposes. In Book 1 we define what ethnographic research is, when it should be used, and how it can be used to identify and solve complex social problems, especially those not readily amenable to traditional quantitative or experimental research methods alone. Book 2 now is devoted to the process of developing a conceptual basis for research studies and to more detailed questions of research design, modeling, and preparing for the field experience. Books 1 through 4 emphasize the fact that ethnography is a peculiarly human endeavor; many of its practitioners have commented that, unlike other approaches to research, the *researcher* is the primary tool for collecting primary data. As we demonstrate in these books, ethnography's principal database is amassed in the course of human interaction: direct observation, face-to-face interviewing and elicitation, audiovisual recording, and mapping the networks, times, and places in which human interactions occur. Further, the personal characteristics and activities of researchers as human beings and as scientists become salient in ethnography in ways not applicable in research that permits the investigator to maintain more distance from the persons and phenomena under study. Interpretation of ethnographic research results emerges only from the process of engaging researcher understanding with direct, face-to-face field experience.

Book 4, a collection of individually authored chapters, now includes new chapters on cutting-edge approaches to ethnography. Books 6 and 7 also are entirely new to the *Toolkit*. The former provides extensive detail on the burgeoning field of research ethics and the latter approaches the dissemination and application of ethnographic research in new ways.

We have designed the *Toolkit* for educators, service professionals, professors of applied students in the fields of teaching, social sciences, social and health services, communications, engineering, the environment, and business, and students and professionals working in applied field settings who are interested in field research and mixed methods ethnographic research. The examples we include throughout the books are drawn from these fields as well as our own research projects and those of our colleagues.

INTRODUCTION TO BOOK 2: INITIATING ETHNOGRAPHIC RESEARCH

Book 2 of the *Ethnographer's Toolkit* is unique in the literature on research methods, as it makes clear that ethnography, far from being simply a qualitative and descriptive approach, is preeminently a mixed methods approach to investigation. Built on teaching tools that the authors have honed over several decades, Book 2 transforms the difficult process of conceptualizing a research project into a step-by-step approach based on conceptual and operational models and accompanied by illustrative examples that are straightforward and simple to use.

Chapters 1 and 4 of Book 2 define the differences between inductive and deductive, micro and macro, and qualitative and quantitative approaches to research and describe how all are integrated in the construction of a competently executed ethnography. These chapters highlight the importance of using theoretical models and conceptual understandings as guides for conducting research. Chapter 1 also defines and lays to rest misconceptions about the concepts of objectivity and subjectivity in research, while chapter 4 describes how the ethnographer, as a theorist, makes use of both local and more global theoretical formulations of phenomena in the field. This chapter also provides guidance in the formulation of formative or local theories that are designed to precede and guide field research and data collection.

Chapter 2 discusses initial concerns and preparatory steps related to site selection and negotiation and ways of formulating initial research foci, addressing how both researcher characteristics and interest, and the priorities and requirements of funding agencies and institutional affiliations, can affect the direction a project takes. Chapter 3 details how to construct research proposals and describes the often-ignored logistical planning needed for survival and effective conduct of research in the field. It also provides valuable information on how to obtain the formal approvals needed prior to entering a field setting and how to begin data collection. While chapter 4 concentrates on the importance of building formative theory, chapter 5 provides a step-by-step explanation of how to construct a formative research model for research projects and how to generate hypotheses for exploring phenomena in the field. Chapter 6 describes how to make operational each stage of the project. Chapter 7 describes how and when to make use of qualitative and quantitative data in a research project and how to organize their collection into efficient and parallel or nested stages. An important feature of this chapter is instruction on how to base the collection of both types of data on the same theoretical model so as to facilitate their integration into a powerful portrayal of the phenomenon under investigation. It is in chapter 7 that triangulation, using a well-organized and staged mixed methods approach based on the prior chapters, is fully formulated and illustrated with case examples. Finally, chapter 8 is unique in the literature in clarifying the use of mixed methods research in both basic and applied intervention research and in showing how systems analytic approaches can transform research into culturally and situationally driven models for facilitating social change.

Throughout each chapter, we draw on examples from our own research in communities and organizations in the United States and other countries, as well as from the work of other researchers. These vignettes and extended examples illustrate each of the concepts, models, and stepped approaches covered in the book and provide a rationale for the methodological strategies advocated.

1

INITIATING ETHNOGRAPHIC RESEARCH: MODELS, METHODS, AND MEASUREMENT

> Introduction
> Ethnography Is Both Inductive and Deductive
> Ethnography Is Both Qualitative and Quantitative
> Ethnography Operates at the Micro or Macro Level
> Ethnography Examines Reported or Observed Behavior
> Ethnography: Discovery and Representativeness
> Ethnography: Theory and Description
> Objectivity and Subjectivity
> Basic and Applied Research
> Summary

INTRODUCTION

Prior to 1965, anthropologists and their students received little training before heading off to the field to do their research; they learned to do research on the job. Novice researchers were sent off to the field or simply "dropped off" in small communities in, for example, northern Minnesota, the Pacific islands, or rural Mexico, with little research preparation and no guidance other than a sketchy thesis proposal, or a general plan for somehow producing a dissertation. Today, such practices are untenable. The world no longer is available for such experimentation, and the practice of simply dropping or sending novice researchers off to learn how to do their work by trial and error no longer is desirable, feasible, appropriate, healthy, or ethically acceptable. Instead, it is now recognized that good research requires much preparatory work prior to entry to the research setting and initiating data collection. Book 2 focuses on this preparatory stage in the field experience. In doing so, we argue for the use of mixed methods approaches so as to better resolve epistemological differences and disagreements in ethnography. We elaborate on the discussion in Book 1 of how to develop research questions and formulate initial or formative research models. We discuss how to identify appropriate study locations, what to do if they do not work out, how to build and sustain relationships that make research easier while in the field, and ways to ensure that local people can use the research results. Since the focus of this chapter is on what field-based ethnography is and is not, we also discuss certain myths and misunderstandings that characterize ethnography as a field-based science.

Ethnographic research sometimes is defined as distinct from other forms of research because of its heavy use of qualitative data collection. However, one primary guiding principle of ethnography is its commitment to direct experience with a population or community of concern. It is this continuous exposure and engagement with a research setting, rather than the specifics of methodology alone, that distinguishes ethnography from other research approaches. Ethnography always is conducted in naturalistic settings (organizations, institutions, communities) conducive to face-to-face interaction with the people, events, and social phenomena that constitute the research setting. Moreover, ethnography seeks to understand the human world and its internal and external phenomena from the perspective of the people being studied rather than solely from the researcher's own perspective or a specific theoretical lens. Ethnographic research has developed a variety of perspectives, methods, tools, and logics that help ensure that ethnographers truly learn to understand the world through the eyes of a specific population. Putting these tools to use is referred to as the *field experience*, in which the "field" becomes the locality where the work is taking place.

"Going into the field" embodies a meaning more profound than simply walking into a location where data are being collected. Rather, "the field" is a complex notion rooted in scientific epistemology; it implies that researchers leave the world of the familiar to enter into a new sphere, one with which they are not familiar and where they are not customarily actors. To function in this new sphere, researchers must learn the rules of behavior prevailing in the particular field and come to understand the reasons for those behaviors. Even when the world into which a researcher steps is somewhat familiar, researchers must "make it strange" by suspending their prior beliefs and understandings to ensure that they do not inappropriately impose their own views on the setting.

When an ethnographer enters into the field, that presence adds a "new person" to the scene under consideration. This person, the ethnographer/stranger, will be unfamiliar with the norms for behavior in the scene and therefore will have high potential for disrupting ordinary activity and interaction. Although people in the field site will naturally be curious about the new person, they also may be suspicious, self-conscious, or surprised at the researcher's appearance; they also will be aware that a stranger might violate taboos or principles of proper relationships, pollute the environment, or create many other situations that lead people to change or modify their typical conversations, or even to hide information or change their customary routines.

Ethnographers endeavor to overcome these problems by being present in the environment for long periods of time so as to provide ample opportunity for engendering respect and affection among at least some people in the research setting and gaining sufficient trust so that people will go about their daily business without regard for the presence of a stranger. This takes time. Once the initial phase of language and culture learning and rapport building is over, researchers can turn to research methods and tools that can be used relatively unobtrusively in the "field setting." It is at this time that they can begin to identify people who can serve as guides for their work and start collecting data that reflect the ordinary beliefs, attitudes, regular practices, behaviors, and cultural patterns of residents. Methods for locating such guides (key informants, cultural experts) and collecting these data make up the content of Books 3 and 4 of the *Ethnographer's Toolkit*. However, to really understand what it means to be immersed in the lives of the people who live and interact in real communities, it is important to reflect upon what epistemological logic underlies immersion. Basically, immersion means learning to learn as a child does (Brennan and Schulze 2004; Hill-Burnett 1979; Willett 1995), by patiently being taught by local people how to live in and understand local culture. Ultimately, the goal is to learn how to think and to some extent, to behave as the local people do. We now discuss some common misconceptions about what ethnography is and is not.

ETHNOGRAPHY IS BOTH INDUCTIVE AND DEDUCTIVE

In his book, *Reclaiming a Scientific Anthropology*, Kuznar states that "in reality, scientists are never purely deductive or inductive" (45). He proposes a "cycle of science" in which "one can begin anywhere, but before knowledge can be scientific, it should pass through . . . all stages of the cycle (Kuznar 2008, 27). Kuznar's cycle is displayed in Figure 1.1.

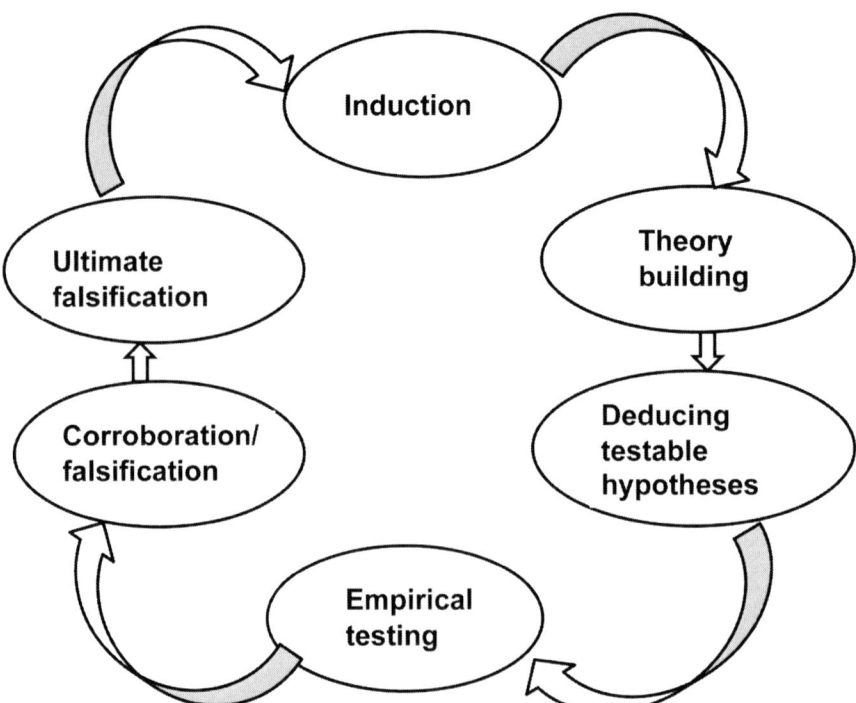

FIGURE 1.1   Kuznar's Model

This cycle is reflective of processes of micro- and macro-level inquiry described in Books 1 and 5. Theoretical statements can be generated at different levels of abstraction, from the smallest and most concrete (buses advertise cigarettes) to the largest and most abstract (inadequate transportation systems result in more health problems in a disaster situation). The ultimate goal of ethnographic research is to come as close as possible to representing and predicting "reality" both as viewed and understood by the researcher and as experienced by members of the study community. The process of testing and retesting to approximate consistency of observation can be applied to all forms of data, from observational materials to survey data. In a complex research effort, the dynamic interplay represented in Figure 1.1 is repeated over and over again until a satisfactory "model" or representation of reality is achieved.

Many people believe that ethnography is purely inductive; that is, that it emphasizes inductive reasoning by postulating that patterns, structures, and theories "emerge" from data that are collected in the field. They distinguish between this kind of ethnography and other approaches to science that emphasize "deductive" reasoning in which postulates (hypotheses) are generated based on externally derived theories that are then tested by collecting data drawn from the "field" as a laboratory. From our point of view, the only reasonable position for a social scientist to take is that the ethnographic enterprise involves both induction and deduction. No ethnographer enters the field (or institutional) setting without at least some ideas, theories, hunches, and hypotheses and a research question of some sort. Usually, an ethnographer's initial approach to research in the field setting is of necessity guided by the ethnographer's lived experience, prior knowledge, and understanding of the study topic and the location; by one or more scientific paradigms guiding how he or she position themselves as scientists; and even by some initial hunches, hypotheses, and biases that need to be examined.

The "things" ethnographers carry with them to the field thus include:

- Ideas from their life experience, personality, and accumulated knowledge

- A specific theoretical orientation
- The results of research conducted on the same or similar topics in the same or similar setting
- An initial study question
- Initial hunches, hypotheses, and biases requiring examination

Definition: A model is a diagram that illustrates a set of integrated ideas or cultural or conceptual domains and the hunches, hypotheses, and guesses that link or characterize the relationships among them

With this material, as we will describe later, the ethnographer can build an initial **model** or set of integrated ideas, hunches, and guesses about the main dimensions of a study related to the research question. The framing of this initial model is very different from the development of a deductive theory to be systematically tested. Instead, an initial model makes explicit the way in which the researcher draws upon a personal, professional, and experiential knowledge base to guide the first steps in the research process. It is very likely that the model will be incomplete, incorrect, or otherwise in need of elaboration. But it provides a starting point. In addition, the very process of specifying a model makes explicit what the researcher believes, and by situating researcher bias "on the table," the model makes beliefs and potential biases explicit. Thus the advantages of a theory, a model, and hypotheses include:

- Identification of *a priori* assumptions and hypotheses/hunches and associations
- An initial guide for where to start looking and what to start asking about
- The opportunity to test one's knowledge in dialogue with others and the literature to see if one is on the right or wrong track

Both inductive and deductive reasoning are used in ethnographic research. Inductive reasoning in ethnographic research focuses on the ability to discover patterns through ethnographic data collection that can validate or contradict elements of an *a priori* theoretical model, or to identify new elements not initially conceptualized by the researcher. One of the key strengths of ethnography is the discovery process, in which the ethnographer remains open to observing through field research new elements and patterns that were hitherto unrecognized. A researcher may identify a pattern in data collected in the field setting and seek meaning for that pattern in the literature and in theory. For example, Stephen Schensul noted that risky sex in Sri Lanka seemed to occur more frequently when sexual partners were greater than five years apart in age, with the older individual dominating the younger. This observation was reaffirmed in the literature and from data from other countries. It suggested there was an association between older age with concomitantly more economic stability and disposable income, higher educational status, *and* a desire for a wider range of sexual experiences outside of marriage. This in turn was associated with greater exposure to sexually transmitted infections, including HIV. The combination of local observations and literature review led to the development of a National Institutes of Health (NIH) grant proposal to try to understand the meaning of this association of age discrepancy with power differentials, and the ways in which it promoted pathways to risky behavior.

One could argue that this first step in the inductive/deductive process that typifies ethnography—and should characterize any scientific enterprise—could be undertaken after a few months in the field. Certainly such models can be developed and reformulated at any time during the research enterprise. However, we advocate developing an early and very general model prior to entering the field research period. The key to using such *a priori* models is recognizing in advance that subsequent ethnographic data are likely to show that many elements of the model do not completely match with reality in the field. However, the fact that models and hypotheses do not effectively capture *all* of the elements of the phenomena that have been observed does not invalidate them. Rather, it justifies using them as a starting point. As fieldwork continues, ethnographers will refine their models as more complete and more accurately reflective of the study situation or problem.

ETHNOGRAPHY IS BOTH QUALITATIVE AND QUANTITATIVE

Ethnography typically is defined as primarily focused on qualitative text-based data collected through key informant, semistructured, and in-depth interviewing and through unstructured or semistructured face-to-face or audiovisual observation and recording. While text data is indeed an important component of ethnography, ethnography is not by any means exclusively qualitative. Cutting-edge ethnographic research now calls for and includes a mix of qualitative and quantitative methods that are triangulated to build on the strengths of both approaches to conceptualizing and collecting data. In Books 3 and 4 of the *Ethnographer's Toolkit*, for example, we refer to many different approaches to the collection of ethnographic data. Some involve collecting text-based data that can be quantified; others, including spatial data, are essentially qualitative but are treated as both qualitative and quantitative when they represent degrees of variation on a visual or spatial plane. Still others are strictly numerical, as is the case with survey or observational data with fixed, closed-ended responses.

Cross Reference: See Book 4, chapter 2, on secondary and archival data

Researchers can begin their data collection by starting with either qualitative or quantitative data. One way to begin with quantitative data is to use national data sets to explore initial hypotheses and then to explain them through qualitative data collection in the field. National data sets are available on many topics, usually tracked for changes in key variables over time. These data sets may cover studies of the labor force (the National Longitudinal Survey) and of educational attainment (Barro and Lee 2010), food availability through the Food and Agricultural Organization of the United Nations (http://faostat.fao.org/), adolescent health (National Longitudinal Study of Adolescent Health: Add Health), substance use (Monitoring the Future, a National Institute on Drug Abuse–funded surveillance system for monitoring substance use of high school students), or oral/dental health (National Health and Nutrition Examination Survey—NHANES 2005 to 2006—available from the Centers for Disease Control). Internationally, a well-known source of data on national health status around the world is the Demographic and Health Surveys (DHS), supported by USAID, the U.S. Agency for International Development, and carried out in more than seventy-five countries. In

India, the DHS is referred to as the National Family Health Survey. Analysis of the National Family Health Survey (NFHS) data on reproductive health was used to identify a predicted relationship between pregnancy and intimate partner violence (IPV); reading articles about pregnancy and IPV identified this relationship. While finding such a correlation in the India NFHS is useful and informative, it does not tell us *why* such a relationship exists in the Indian context, or why it varies by state or region of the country. A qualitative investigation involving pregnant women and their husbands, community health volunteers, and the police, carried out in local settings, is needed to provide the kinds of descriptive data that would be helpful in explaining the association in a specific place and time.

Often ethnographers begin with qualitative data that are clarified and extended with a representative survey sample. Qualitative interviews conducted with Indian women, for example, show that many women report vaginal (white) discharge, a phenomenon that appears to be associated with negative events in a woman's life. The interviews show that these negative life events include intimate partner violence, low self-esteem, and sexual coercion (Kostick et al. 2010). Qualitative data from more than fifty in-depth interviews with married women helped to discover such a pattern and create a formative model, but the sample size was both too small and not necessarily representative to test whether these associations were generalizable to the wider population of married women. Developing a survey instrument based on the ethnographic data with a random or otherwise representative sample of married women produced quantitative data that made it possible to test statistically the relationship of white discharge to negative life circumstances. The two sets of results complemented each other by establishing a statistically valid relationship and by providing possible explanations through the in-depth interviews as to why such a relationship exists. We discuss the interaction of qualitative and quantitative research in Book 1, and the construction, analysis, and triangulation of ethnographic surveys in Book 3, chapter 9, and Book 5, chapter 9.

Cross Reference: See Book 3, chapter 9, on structured approaches to the collection of ethnographic data

Cross Reference: See Book 3, chapter 8, for approaches to sampling in ethnographic research

Cross Reference: See Book 3, chapter 9, and Book 5, chapter 9, for more information on ethnographic surveys

ETHNOGRAPHY OPERATES AT THE MICRO AND MACRO LEVEL

Many researchers erroneously believe that ethnographic studies can illuminate only local phenomena. The terms *micro* and *macro* refer to the points in a continuum that begin with the individual (micro), and end with the "global" (macro). A social ecological model or diagram that situates individuals in the context of social settings, institutions, and resources that are a) linked to the individual either directly or indirectly through other entities; and b) interact with each other independently, can illustrate this. Uri Bronfenbrenner was the first social ecologist to refer to an ecological model (1979, 1989), although anthropological studies as early as Robert Redfield's work in the 1940s described how local communities were affected by external factors and reacted to them in return (Redfield 1930, 1956). Bronfenbrenner used the term *micro* to refer to an individual's family or peers, *meso* to refer to the social organizations and resources at the community level, *exo* to refer to larger institutions with potential influence on the individual, and *macro* to refer to larger contextual social forces such as policies that affect the other levels. It is clear that ethnographers can and do engage in work at each of these levels.

Some ethnographers "study up"; that is, they examine the factors at the exo or macro level that have either positive, negative, or complex effects on other processes and organizations in a dynamic system, generally with a critical perspective (Nader 1974; Gusterson 1997). But linking the individual (micro) to the community (the meso/exo levels) is where most ethnography is situated because community-based ethnographic research is geared for face-to-face interaction with communities and their residents, through in-person interviewing, participant observation, and immersion in the social context. However, most ethnographers, as well as other social scientists, recognize that what transpires at the local (micro/meso/exo) level is affected by broader dynamics, regional and national political processes and policies, environmental factors, migration flows and other events, even in the smallest and most remote communities (Amselle 2002; Inda and Rosaldo 2008, Lewellen 2002; Appadurai 2001; Wasson et al. 2011).

There are many examples that illustrate the effects of global processes on local economic and other factors. One good one shows how the effect of global economic factors on health became apparent in Uganda in the 1960s. In this coffee-growing region, USAID was encouraging the addition of food and subsistence crops to promote improved nutrition. Simultaneously, a bumper crop of Colombian coffee affected world coffee prices. The result was a slump in the prices Ugandan farmers received for their coffee. This in turn led to a reduction in the quality of their diet that could not be compensated for by the efforts of USAID to improve nutrition through new food crops.

Another example involves the imposition of high-stakes educational achievement testing and performance-based pay for teachers in the United States. Such testing has been adopted by countries worldwide, with the consequence that subjects not tested, such as native languages, local history, and techniques for native subsistence, find no place in the curriculum. The result is accelerated loss of culture and language among indigenous peoples (Aguilera 2003).

Another example involves the increasing demand among more affluent people worldwide for gold products, not only for high-status jewelry but also as important components in high-technology industries. Increased gold mining has meant destruction of Amazonian forests, riverine habitat, and agricultural lands by strip mining, bulldozing, and separating out gold from base rock with cyanide. Villagers are left with no lands suitable for food production, and entire villages in the mining areas are displaced (Barbieri et al. 2009; Guimarães and Mergler 2012; Mertens et al. 2005). The demand for land suitable for industrial monocultural agriculture has led the government of Ethiopia to forcibly move entire Anuak communities off their ancestral land in the fertile river valleys in the Gambella region into state-created settlements lacking any arable land or service infrastructure. The government has subsequently leased the arable land out to multinational corporations housed in Saudi Arabia, India, China, and other countries (Gagnon 2005). Even quite local, special cultural events can become global happenings, as is the case with the celebration for *Oxlajuj B'aqtun,* the end of the Mayan calendar cycle in December 2012. Tourists, Armageddon enthusiasts, and doomsayers alike flocked to tiny Mayan communities that were ill prepared to handle hordes coming to watch what they believed would be the end of the world, inspired by Hollywood movies that capitalized on the theme (DeLuca 2012). The following more elaborated example describes a process of extrapolating and extending from local-level data to national policies and processes influencing tobacco distribution in India.

EXAMPLE 1.1

FOLLOWING THE TRAIL OF SMOKELESS TOBACCO FROM THE LOCAL TO THE INTERNATIONAL LEVEL IN INDIA

Researchers Jean Schensul and Saritha Nair studied the availability and uses of smokeless tobacco products in a low-income community in Mumbai. In the first part of their mixed methods study, the field team noticed that there were many tobacco shops of various types scattered or clustered throughout subareas in the study community of about seventy thousand people. They mapped the outlets, and interviewed the shop owners about the types and brands of tobacco they were selling. They also obtained samples of the tobacco in packets and photographed bulk and other forms of stored loose tobacco. In the process they found that the suppliers were purchasing their goods from a tobacco bulk wholesale market elsewhere in the city. The field team also heard about the representatives of manufacturing firms that went about the community marketing their products to shop owners. The study team then began to examine the locations of manufacturers and to explore their products and their networks on the Internet. They found that most of the manufacturers posted information on the Internet and identified themselves as situated within India, although not in Maharashtra. Further exploration revealed that Indian tobacco manufacturers, among the largest in the world, constituted a significant commercial and legislative lobby, able to influence the implementation of tobacco policy and decisions to allow foreign manufacturers to market or even produce new tobacco products such as *snus* (snuff) in the country. At the same time, the field team began to learn about India's tobacco control laws and regulations. They found that India not only had participated in the World Health Organization Framework Convention on Tobacco Control (WHO FCTC) but also was one of more than 140 countries that had agreed to sign its protocol. Further investigation identified a number of Indian tobacco control activist researchers who were well known both in India and internationally. By following these steps from the local "block grid" to the national and international level, the research team was able to see how international tobacco politics, both for and against smokeless tobacco, were manifested at the national level, and to understand in what ways control legislation might or might not penetrate to the local level (Schensul, Nair, Bilgi et al. 2012).

These examples illustrate how national and international processes such as worldwide recession, trade imbalance, the value of Chinese currency, armed conflict, the influence of international corporations and industries, worldwide demand for luxury goods, the entertainment industry, the media, and many other factors can be linked through ethnography to the behavior, knowledge, circumstances, and attitudes of a local community. And they make it clear that ethnographers cannot complete their descriptions of local community dynamics without describing the contextual forces that act upon local communities and institutions.

ETHNOGRAPHY EXAMINES REPORTED AND OBSERVED BEHAVIOR

Most quantitative research and some forms of qualitative research that rely on in-depth interviews focus on what respondents report in terms of behavior, attitudes and knowledge, and activities going on in their lives and their community. There are many ways of validating the results of reported information, including the use of social desirability scales (scales that measure how likely a respondent is to answer questions to please the researcher) and validation of reported responses by comparing them with clinical or other forms of interactional or observed assessments or against biological markers. For example, measuring the enzyme cotinine in urine is an established way of detecting the presence and amount of tobacco in the body (Peyton et al. 2011; Behera et al. 2003). Other ways to reduce possible response bias included assuring privacy of response through means such as paper and pencil tests, computer-assisted data entry, and interactive voice-response telephone-based data entry (IVR).

Ethnography, however, involves personal involvement in the study context. Thus there are continuous opportunities to observe behavior, to observe the ways individuals communicate, to listen to what they say to each other, and to experience rituals, activities, gatherings, birthday parties, and other events. Ethnographers document all of these in detail with field notes and sometimes with photographs, film, and videos. They also conduct informal in-the-field group and individual interviews to collect information about behavior that is reported in other ways. Immersion, like other forms of triangulated data collection, does not ensure the collection of accurate data, and it is time-consuming. Even energetic researchers cannot be everywhere or know everyone in a site. But constant exposure to community and cultural processes makes it possible for researchers to make accurate guesses about what might or might not be an appropriate response to a question. Further, the use of surveys and other ways of obtaining reports of beliefs, behaviors, and activities can often provide both breadth and representativeness of information that concentrated experience and observation cannot.

ETHNOGRAPHY INVOLVES DISCOVERY AND REPRESENTATIVENESS

A key strength of ethnography is its ability to discover new behaviors, attitudes, and knowledge that may be shared by a study group or community, but that for the most part are not well documented in the literature or known by many outside of the groups. They may not even be widely known or shared by each and every member of a group. In the following example, young women who were concerned about maintaining their virginity and thus their marriageability used terminology that justified their having limited penetrative sex without the threat of virginity loss. Most adults did not know or use this vocabulary, and it was not part of the HIV and pregnancy prevention vernacular in Mauritius. Conducting listing exercises with project staff uncovered new information that could be used later on in the context of a reproductive health risk avoidance intervention.

EXAMPLE 1.2

DISCOVERING A NEW SEXUAL RISK BEHAVIOR IN MAURITIUS

In a study of sexual behavior and sexual risk among young women workers in the Export Processing Zone in Mauritius, Schensul and Schensul worked with the staff of a family planning agency to list all of the behaviors associated with sex. The list included two specific sexual behaviors with specific Creole names that involved unprotected sex with partial penetration. The first was referred to as *faire la-haut*. *La-haut* refers to rubbing the penis on the surface of the women's genitals and the edge of the vaginal opening. The second, *mette dans bord dans bord*, refers to the insertion of the penis into the opening of the vagina, just past the labia. These behaviors, translated as "light" sex, were considered safe in a context where AIDS was not viewed as a problem but preserving the virginity of the woman was essential for marriage. These two behaviors did not penetrate far enough to "break the hymen" or cause the pain associated with the loss of virginity. Thus they were believed to keep women safe from the loss of virginity, but they were not free of risk from pregnancy, exposure to infection, and the potential of HIV transmission. The recognition of this and other locally identified risk behaviors were integrated into a survey designed to reflect representativeness and generalizability; they later became an important part of HIV/STI intervention efforts in Mauritius.

The example above describes the process of discovery in detail but it does not address **representativeness**. Representativeness is the capacity to generalize to a given population findings based on data collected from a random or representative sample of members from the study community or a designated group within it that is the focus of the research. Quantitative research, and specifically, systematic or probabilistic sampling from a population, is the most effective way to ensure representativeness of specific behaviors, beliefs, knowledge, and attitudes of a group under study because surveys reach a large (and representative) number of people in the study community and because respondents are selected in a way that allows researchers to assume that all sectors of the community are equally represented. Thus, results that are generated can be extrapolated to the entire community or population of study. Here we often refer to individuals when we speak

Definition: Representativeness is the capacity to generalize to a given population based on data collected from a random or representative sample from the study population

Cross Reference: See Book 3, chapter 10, on issues of sampling and selection

of a population, but representativeness can apply to organizations (for example, service organizations or tobacco shops, or schools), and even to specific types of activities (playground interactions), where large numbers of similar activities can be observed. Designing surveys or observational tools requires prior discovery in order to identify the unique social and cultural features of the group that are to be measured. In this way discovery and representativeness intersect; in ethnography, each requires the other, but discovery must come first.

In sum, the objective of *qualitative research*, including observation of behavior and interviewing to generate reported behavior, is to discover and explain the key elements and perceptions of the group with regard to a particular topic and a group. The objective of *quantitative research*, using systematic sampling and consistency in administering a standardized data collection instrument, is to identify effectively the representativeness of patterns and variations within a group and to test hypotheses using statistical procedures. Both approaches are vital to the ethnographic enterprise, especially when working in large, urban settings.

ETHNOGRAPHY IS BOTH THEORY AND DESCRIPTION

Many researchers believe that theories designed to explain broad ranges of human behavior are generated *a priori* and only by leading scholars in their respective social science disciplines, not ordinary scholars or "ordinary others." Behaviorism, postmodernism, critical, feminist, and many other general theoretical frameworks or paradigms generate broad organizing principles and postulates for understanding the world. Within these paradigms, midrange theories (for example, social construction theory, theories of gender/power, or motivational theory) provide more specific directions and steps that guide research projects, including choice of measures. By contrast, ethnographic case studies sometimes are seen as descriptive and relatively atheoretical; they are believed to be a simple compendium of observations and perceptions that need to be documented and amalgamated into domains such as kinship and other social relations, economic activities, and other traditional topics included in ethnographic monographs.

We, on the contrary, believe that generating theory is an "every day activity" and plays a crucial role as ethnographers seek to make sense of day-to-day life in a study community or institution and to identify the elements of local research results that raise questions about human behavior in other communities and institutions. Our view of theory thus suggests that it is generated and developed at multiple levels. From this perspective, all description begins with theory, because the ongoing sorting out of what is important from what is not typical of ethnographic research requires the kind of guiding framework or set of concepts that theory provides. Theory provides guidelines for engaging in the distilled ethnographic description that is culled and constructed and generalized from multiple instances and sources of information about cultural rules, procedures, beliefs, meanings, and behaviors. For example, documenting the techniques farmers use to till the land requires an amalgamation or summary of the individual and subgroup variations used by a range of farmers in a community. Integrating these variations into a complete description along with explanations for the variation is, in fact, developing a theory of farming in a particular local area.

Global theories have relatively poor predictive or explanatory power in a local community or institution. So we must ask, "How we can we link large-scale global or macro theories with ethnographic understanding at the micro level?" In our view, global theories are best for raising and framing initial questions, selecting research domains to study, and delineating some general hypotheses. By contrast, ethnography generates theories at the local level that create a composite picture of local reality. It also may introduce new domains, hypotheses, and perspectives that differ substantially from those reflected in "global" or even second-level, less abstract but related, theories. The bridge that is needed to connect global and local theories has been termed *middle-range theory* (Merton 1967; Pelto and Pelto 1978), a concept that we use to link descriptive theory gen-

Cross Reference:
See Book 1, chapter 3, for a discussion of main broad theoretical paradigms used by ethnographers and other social scientists

erated inductively and locally with global theory based on paradigms and their application.

OBJECTIVITY AND SUBJECTIVITY

Ethnographers collect information through participation in the daily life of the study setting. A key to that participation is the development of relationships with individuals in the study context. Some believe that these relationships may contribute to a researcher's loss of objectivity, regardless of their intimacy. By this we mean that the more intimate the relationship, the more likely the researcher is to be influenced by the beliefs, perspectives, opinions, and interpretations of the local resident, and the less likely he or she is to be able to question freely or take the multiple perspectives that constitute empirical "objectivity." Further, it could be said that local relationships could affect or interfere with the way data are interpreted or disseminated to the public.

Notwithstanding, ethnographic researchers build their research on the basis of relationships in the field in order to learn and understand local culture. In the context of the field experience, researchers almost always generate empathy for and with the individuals and families they meet in the field. While they constantly struggle to obtain the richest, deepest, and most balanced information, they also simultaneously have personal, political, age, and other relational preferences, and opinions about what would improve the quality of life in their study communities. The latter could act to influence or shape and even to limit or bias their data collection and interpretations. In shaping their results, they necessarily project a perspective or direction after taking all their evidence into consideration. Researchers *use* their subjectivities (Peshkin 1986) when they select among theoretical and interpretive frameworks to guide their interpretation of data—as, for example, when they choose between a psychological versus a structural explanation for physical suffering among workers in a factory (Bourdieu 1993). Researchers *maintain* objectivity when they adopt a stance of purposeful disinterest in the *outcomes* of the study. Maintaining objectivity requires that researchers select the best interview, observation, survey, and other instruments to measure their constructs and then explain why they chose to use those specific measures and not others. The advantage of developing initial formative theories, models, and research questions is that they highlight researcher beliefs (in the form of initial hypotheses or hunches) and provide transparency in researcher thinking. The constant interplay between reflection and inquiry is what marks ethnography as different from the other social science research approaches.

BASIC AND APPLIED RESEARCH

We conduct ethnographic research to answer three important kinds of questions: theoretical, methodological, and practical. Basic research addresses the first two domains, and all basic research may have implications for practice. Basic research refers to research that answers social, theoretical, or methodological questions but has no direct link with practice or policy formulation and does not include practice or policy components. Some basic research is conducted because there is insufficient information available to influence policy or practice, or because the theories that guide these activities must be framed. We often refer to this type of research as **formative** because it is used to "form" or forge the next steps in the research-practice-research dynamic.

Applied research is directed to solving practical, real-world problems. Like basic research, applied research also is designed to answer pressing questions, and, in contrast to basic research, applied research always includes a practical or policy component. Applied research can be highly complex and sophisticated, requiring clearly operationalized theoretical frameworks, large samples, comparison groups, and elaborate measures. Good applied research may be even more challenging than basic research because it often takes place in hard-to-control natural settings, and it involves defining and evaluating "interventions" that may take place at multiple levels simultaneously. Good ethnographic research practice always should be theoretically informed

Definition:
Formative research is used to shape the subsequent steps in the dynamic that links research and practice

and integrated with research for formative, process, and outcome assessment. Applied ethnography should:

- Describe a problem in a local population
- Assist in understanding the causes (and therefore the prevention) of a particular problem
- Assist members of the group under study to clarify and document their needs
- Provide information that can identify resources supportive of change
- Assist in formulating intervention program models
- Help to assess the efficacy of an intervention
- Modify interventions so they will be more effective

Unfortunately, many ethnographers differentiate between research and practice, implying that research is a different kind of activity from practice. Often, too, practice is valued less in research worlds, because it is considered both theoretically unsophisticated and devoid of elaborate forms of research methodology. However, we believe this distinction is incorrect; it creates a false dichotomy.

Our approach strongly endorses the integration of research *and* practice in ethnography. The results of ethnographic research can decrease the turnaround time between the generation of knowledge and its translation into policy and program development. The integration of research and practice is ideal for the development of intervention studies, for evaluation of programs (program-oriented ethnographic evaluation), and for the development of further iterations of programs as they are applied in local settings. Such locally researched and evaluated interventions can become the basis for the development of intervention models to be tested in other times and locations. Ethnographic research is an important means by which understanding *and* improving conditions faced by local communities, organizations, and individuals can be achieved.

SUMMARY

In this chapter we have introduced and attempted to resolve a number of seeming contradictions in ethnography. Doing so has paved the way for arguing for several key points, in particular the importance of preparing for field research by establishing local theoretical frameworks and conceptual models based on prior knowledge, and as well, the importance of linking etic perspectives of the researchers with local or indigenous theoretical frameworks and "practice" or intervention. In the next two chapters we turn to a closer examination of how to prepare for the field by selecting a research site and focus and engaging in the necessary conceptual, practical, political, and relational tasks that help to ensure a good field experience.

2

SELECTING A RESEARCH SITE AND FOCUS

> Introduction
> The Researcher Personal Interest and History
> Researcher Identity
> Researcher Positionality
> Requirements of Institutional Affiliation and Funding Sources
> Perspectives, Needs, and Priorities of the Study Population
> Summary

INTRODUCTION

Ethnography once was thought of as going to distant locations to find communities that differed significantly from Western culture and societies and describing their behavior norms and epistemological assumptions. Ethnographers have since moved beyond that approach to a view of communities and cultures as globalized (Burawoy 2000; Wasson et al. 2011). They have redefined their focus of interest to include a wide range of settings across many countries, geographically defined areas (villages, neighborhoods, and communities), and specific organizations and institutions. In addition, anthropologists study groups and populations with special interests and concerns that are not geographically based, such as drug users, high school dropouts, environmentalists, Internet users, and Bosnian war widows. Ethnographers also focus on institutions and their cultures (for example, corporations and schools) and community-based or constituency-based organizations, such as youth advocates and labor unions (Cefkin 2009; Durrenburger and Reichart 2010; Heath et al. 2009). The most important factors that enter into decisions with respect to where to conduct studies include:

- The researcher's personal interests and history
- Researcher identity

- Researcher positionality
- Requirements of institutional affiliation and funding sources
- Perspectives, needs, and priorities of the study population

In the pages that follow, we discuss each of the above categories in turn.

THE RESEARCHER PERSONAL INTEREST AND HISTORY

Many personal and professional reasons explain why researchers become intrigued by particular populations, geographic areas, topics, events, and other aspects of human behavior. Specific interests and passions of ethnographers are transformed into concrete topics for investigation. In applied ethnography, the dedication of the researcher also generates the energy required to move a project or policy forward and the patience required to wait while research partners make decisions that can influence the direction of the project.

How do these passions and affinities develop? The researcher's life experience plays a key role. A family member's addiction to drugs may undergird a researcher's interest in the reasons for learning to use illegal drugs. A special relationship with a teacher or unhappy experiences in elementary or secondary school might serve as an avenue for interest in understanding high school pedagogies and processes of inclusion and exclusion. A desire to learn a particular craft might lead to study of that art form's practitioners. Negative or positive experiences with an illness may create an interest in understanding the relationship between patients and the health care system and ways of improving it, or an interest in studying the illness and its sufferers. Studies of pregnancy and breastfeeding became more popular as more female ethnographers had children and began to study the factors that affected the dynamics of child rearing and nursing. Conducting research in the field, with research partners or alone, is a challenging enterprise helped greatly by passion for the topic, the location, and/or for the desire to ameliorate the social problem toward which the research is directed. No matter how the interests arise, the emotional commitment and involvement they generate is critical in carrying the ethnographer through the rough and rocky periods that inevitably emerge while collecting data on human beings in the locations where they live and work.

Ethnographic researchers also may be called upon to figure out how to address and ameliorate difficult social or health problems. For example, ethnographers and other social scientists were drawn into HIV research in the late 1980s when two things became clear. First, it was obvious that no immediate medical solutions in the form of medication or vaccines were forthcoming, and preventing risk behaviors was central to HIV prevention. But many risk behaviors were not known, and some such intimate sexual behaviors were not directly observable and were difficult to describe in sufficient detail to detect sources of risk of infection or transmission. Second, people who were discovered to be HIV positive engaged in risky behaviors that other disciplines were not equipped to understand very well or to investigate properly. For example, the behaviors that transmitted HIV between people who injected drugs together and shared needles were unknown at that time. The other social sciences did not have methods that would facilitate observing such behaviors in context, nor were most researchers in psychology or public health prepared to enter settings to observe occasions when drug users actually shared drugs and worked together, because they perceived such settings to be dangerous or risky.

Typical approaches to malaria prevention such as the use of bed nets (nets that surround sleeping locations at night to keep out mosquitoes that carry the malaria parasite) appeared to be ineffective because village people continued to contract malaria despite free bed net distribution programs. Field researchers were asked to find out why the nets failed to work, and where and how people, especially children, were encountering mosquitoes. Timed observations and interviews showed that children left their nets at night, and sometimes slept with adults outside of them (Okoko 2005; Snow et al. 1988). More recent observations and focus groups have shown several significant misunderstandings regarding the use of bed nets; specifically, that people did not know that everyone, not just women and children, should use them. And even if they did know that bed nets should be used, people who had insufficient sleeping space and had to sleep outside, as well as people who used bed nets for other practical purposes instead of protection from malarial mosquitoes, failed to use bed nets regularly for mosquito prevention (Lover et al. 2011).

A third source of interest may come from the ethnographer's job responsibilities or educational program. Students and junior faculty may be inspired by the work of an advisor or senior faculty member and want to participate in existing fieldwork or to start their own projects in that area. Anthropologist Peter Guarnaccia initiated research on asthma among Puerto Rican children while he was a student at the University of Connecticut, and he continued for many years to conduct research with Puerto Rican communities on a variety of different topics (Guarnaccia et al. 1985, 1989, 1990).

Ethnographers employed by research centers and nonprofit organizations rather than universities may find that their job responsibilities determine their topical and population focus. Categorical funding that requires addressing a particular health, development, or education problem often drives specific research assignments. An ethnographer may be hired specifically to study new types of tobacco, drug, or alcohol use in a community setting or may be asked to shift topics in order to keep a job. Through these pursuits, he or she may discover a commitment to pursue research in a new area different from the topic for which he or she was hired. Once an interest is formed, continuing to pursue it makes sense both from the point of view of personal commitment and as a way to demonstrate prior experience with the topic when looking for funding. The degree to which an interest inspired by work in a specific topic area can be continued once a specific project is completed depends on how committed the ethnographer's organization is to the topic and how able the researcher is to obtain independent funding for research in this area. As we have indicated, the strength of an ethnographer's passion for the topic often governs the desire to raise funds and goes a long way toward furthering additional research in the preferred direction.

Some ethnographers and other social scientists are committed to working in a specific field or line of work over a long period of time. Others may shift topics as they can or as opportunity offers. Two primary factors keep ethnographers engaged: a) the commitment to continue work related to the "dependent variable" or the study "problem" (for example, substance use, HIV, chronic diseases, adolescent pregnancy, climate change, school dropouts, arts education, and functional problems associated with aging); and b) the structural, social, and psychological variables that drive those problems or the "dependent variables." In other words, ethnographers may be committed to the specific health problem that drives the research, or they may find that what is most important to them is not the specific problem but the structural or other factors that drive multiple common problems. Ethnographers may also be inspired by methodological innovations required to investigate either the problem itself or its causes. Epidemiologist Jianghong Li and anthropologist Margaret Weeks, for example, are pursuing a methodological study of the factors that may bias or interfere with the representativeness of respondent-driven sampling, a systematic form of network-based sampling that is said to be generalizable. Finally, researchers may also be driven by an interest in policy or practical change at the grassroots level. The holistic or ecological approach to community life that ethnographers take suggests that they are likely to include "upstream" or structural and social causal factors, and the changes required to address a problem, in studies of individual behavior and the psychosocial factors that may shape it. This structural approach makes ethnography a flexible medium through which to conduct research on social problems.

RESEARCHER IDENTITY

The study of any human group involves engaging with the perspectives and behavior of a great many individuals who differ widely by age, gender, religion, socioeconomic status, ethnicity, occupation, political orientation, belief systems, and a myriad of other factors. Even ethnographers who share one or more of these characteristics with people in the study site will find that most people in the site differ from themselves. One of the most important requirements of ethnography is to understand the perspectives and behaviors of groups and individuals who are obviously different from the ethnographer, or who may share superficial similarities with researchers, but hold quite different perspectives and behave in very different ways.

How ethnographers identify themselves and how a study population identifies them is a complex matter and has many implications for the research process. In the initial approach to a community, for example, ethnographers who share ethnicity and physical appearance with the research population may have certain advantages. Sharing a common language, common historical experience, and appearance may help the ethnographer to blend more easily and quickly into the study community group and learn more, initially, about the people who live there. Likeness may engender more positive and trusting initial responses at the moment when ethnographers enter a new field setting and their intentions may be questioned less. On the other hand, if ethnographers come from a particular sector of the study population, likeness may lead residents to question researchers' abilities to maintain confidentiality in the research site. Trust may be reduced rather than enhanced if the researcher is perceived to be from an ethnic, class, or educational group believed to have a known negative bias toward the study population. For example, Latino researchers with PhDs may come from an urban, middle-class background and may be working in a rural poor community. Regardless of any factors that constitute a "match," all ethnographers must cross many sociocultural and even biological boundaries. They cannot at the same time be male and female, old and young, more and less educated, or more and less affluent. Thus, although some aspects of shared identity can serve to make the first steps in ethnographic entry easier, the long-term process of building relationships with diverse groups in a study community group require all ethnographers to demonstrate their ability to develop rapport, maintain confidentiality, and see multiple perspectives in order to overcome relational differences. This also explains why, especially during the early stages of the fieldwork, working in teams composed of a variety of individuals can be very useful in building trust among a study population.

EXAMPLE 2.1

ENTERING A LOW-INCOME COMMUNITY IN LUSAKA, ZAMBIA, AS AN AMERICAN-RAISED ZAMBIAN YOUNG ADULT RESEARCHER

Researcher Lwendo Moonzwe spent her teen years in southern California, where her parents emigrated from Lusaka when she was a preteen. Her parents maintained close contacts with relatives and friends in Lusaka, and Lwendo visited several times before she decided to go to Lusaka to do research on the risk of HIV infection. She had some trepidation because she had not done field research by herself in another country and did not speak the local language. Though her family was well established and she had many professional contacts in Lusaka, they were not involved in HIV-related work. So Lwendo had to find ways of making contacts with local service organizations and community leaders, and to find research assistants who spoke English and the proper local languages for the community in which she planned to work. Her primary challenges were learning the language and explaining that although she "looked" Zambian, she had not grown up in Lusaka, and she had much to learn about local cultural practices and practical issues like obtaining cash, finding transportation, obtaining food, and washing her clothes. Her identity as Zambian was helpful, but her "difference" (being raised in an American young adult environment) required that she explain herself and her work continuously in the field and learn how to become "more Zambian" in thought and behavior.

Some anthropologists and other researchers have argued that there are advantages in being new or "strange" to a group under study. People new to the study community enter it free of expectations by local residents and with less personal **baggage**. Baggage refers to the characteristics that researchers bring with them to their work. These can include the study community's negative or positive perceptions of their organizational affiliations or sponsors, and stereotypes held by the community about researchers and aspects of their identity. Once ethnographers have moved beyond the status of stranger, members of the study community might respond to other more profound characteristics—for example, their perceived socioeconomic status, ignorance of the community, or their perceived potential for bringing in needed resources. Usually residents' initial reactions to difference rapidly give way to the appreciation of researchers' more consistent and valid identities. These

Definition:
Baggage refers to the characteristics that researchers bring with them to their work. These can include the study community's negative or positive perceptions of the researcher's organizational affiliations or sponsors and stereotypes held by the community about researchers and aspects of their identity

identities have more to do with the researchers' personal characteristics and ways of conducting themselves in the field (including their social skills and willingness to help, their ethical stances, and their personal opinions) than what makes them different. Over time, with luck and perseverance, researchers can come to be seen as members of, similar to, supportive of, or advocates for and with the communities in which they do their research. There also are specific strategies that ethnographers can use to break down barriers of class, race, and foreign nationality, such as being "adopted" into a household as a member of the family. Some researchers become godparents to children, and a few marry their key informants. In Example 2.2, researcher Sherri Ludwig was at first viewed with suspicion, but as she pursued her interest in Mayan weaving and learned how to weave, she was integrated into a group of Mayan women, and accepted as one of them, which both helped her immensely with her study of the meaning of weaving and meant a great deal to her personally.

EXAMPLE 2.2

BUILDING TRUST BY FOLLOWING ETHICAL RULES

Sherri Ludwig's passion for Mayan weavings and the women who make them grew out of her first trip to Guatemala, where she participated in a Spanish-language immersion for her doctoral program. There she met a family of expert women weavers who had formed a cooperative in their home, forming a safe venue for production and sale of their textiles. The women had been hired by the local language school to provide some lessons in Mayan cultural practices, and they also provided a traditional Maya lunch to the Spanish-language students. Ludwig was fascinated by how the women taught their children to weave and the differences among those pedagogies and both teaching and learning in the village school and in U.S. schools. Ludwig had struggled to teach Guatemalan immigrant children in the United States, and she decided to study indigenous pedagogy by being taught how to weave.

She arranged an apprenticeship with the eldest daughter of the weaving cooperative family, whose matriarch was renowned throughout Guatemala and the anthropological literature on Mayan weaving for the quality and design of her work. In the cooperative, Ludwig believed that she not only could learn to weave (a secret passion), but she would be able to document how it was done as *she* was taught, and as well, observe how the women taught each other and their children. Gaining initial entry as a student from the language school was easy. However, working out permission to study weaving daily for more than a year and to actually study the women themselves was another matter. This family had provided subject matter for any number of anthropologists interested in the technology, designs, and meaning of Mayan weaving. But few researchers were very interested in Ludwig's topic: the women themselves and why they continued to weave when doing so had marked them for oppression in a genocidal war on the Maya for over five hundred years. In the process of getting to know the family and local educators from the village school, Ludwig developed a detailed research plan, transformed it into written consent forms in Spanish and English, and asked a native Kakchiquel speaker to read the form aloud to women whose Spanish was insufficiently fluent. She spent a number of days explaining to family members what she wanted to do and why, she promised to share all her work with the family, and she gave them authority to reject any of her photographs of which they did not approve. Ludwig's university's Institutional Review Board was scrupulous about protecting human subjects who were children, who did not speak the native language of the researcher, or who were being asked about potentially sensitive subjects. They also were particularly concerned about obtaining informed consent and protecting the privacy of subjects, especially with nonliterate populations. After Ludwig's explanations, Carlos, a son of the family and a university student, took all of the forms home. When he returned them, he explained that they had had a long family discussion about her work. The family members argued that they were quite tired of being used to foster the careers of anthropologists whom they never saw again after their studies were complete. But Ludwig seemed different. Never, he said, had any other researcher explained what they really planned to do to the family. None even so much as asked formal permission to study the family, or to disclose that they planned to publish information about the family and their pictures, which currently adorn the covers of some significant coffee table books. Nobody had asked to *learn from* them, rather than just *study* them, as objects. Nobody had seen them as partners in an investigation. Because she took their participation in the study as equals seriously, this time, the family granted permission for the study. As the months went by and Ludwig's skill in weaving grew and her integration into the complex family dynamics became more secure, trust grew. When Dona Marisela, the family matriarch, introduced Ludwig to visitors to the cooperative as "a real *tejadora* (weaver) of San Carlos del Lago," Ludwig began to feel a part of the community (Ludwig 2006).

The next example is a mirror opposite of the previous one. In this instance, a researcher of the same ethnic/cultural group is treated as an outsider because of his appearance and presentation of self. Like Ludwig's experience, however, he too became integrated into the study community over time and was able to collect very sensitive data about illegal activities on a main thoroughfare in the Puerto Rican community of a small northeastern city.

EXAMPLE 2.3

A LATINO RESEARCHER STUDYING THE INFORMAL ECONOMY IN A LATINO COMMUNITY OVERCOMES DISTRUST

While a graduate student at the University of Connecticut, ethnographer Jose Garcia received a minority supplemental grant through the Institute for Community Research to study the interaction of the formal and the informal economy on the main commercial avenues in a Puerto Rican community in Hartford. His study was a supplement to Jean Schensul's parent grant funded by the National Institute on Drug Abuse exploring pathways to hard drug use among older teenagers and young adults aged sixteen to twenty-four. The researchers in the parent study were interviewing young men involved in various types of hustling on the main avenues, and Garcia had some idea of how products such as pirated music and videos, clothing, diverted goods, and drugs were obtained and sold to generate income and what types of drugs youth in that area were using. Garcia's work involved two dimensions: engaging in dialogues with mainly male youth in both English and Spanish who were involved in purchasing, using, and selling drugs in the study area to understand the structure of the drug trade on the street; and learning from these young men and shop owners about commercial activity on the avenues and the interaction of small businesses with drug users and the street drug economy.

Garcia was at the time a tall, fair, young Puerto Rican man of approximately twenty-two years of age. A student, he carried a backpack and wore a ponytail. At the time he had recently arrived in Hartford from Puerto Rico and had limited familiarity with the Latino community. He had to establish fresh relationships and build trust from the ground up with merchants on the main avenues and with young vendors and buyers. He did not readily fit into the stereotyped representations of Puerto Rican young men on the street, and people were not forthcoming when he introduced himself as a researcher studying the economy of the avenues. After several weeks of limited success, one merchant who was more open than the others mentioned that people thought he was a "narc" (a "narc" is defined as a law enforcement officer or a person who may not be a member of law enforcement but turns people into the police for drug dealing). Given his presentation of self and the ubiquity of the drug trade in the neighborhood, this was not surprising. The question for Jose became how to counter this image so as to establish authentic relationships with the people from whom he wanted to learn. After an open discussion with the merchant in which he described his real interests, the merchant agreed to help him. Little by little, the other merchants in the area began to know Garcia. As time passed, and there were no police arrests or stings associated with him, they came to feel confident that they could share their knowledge of illegal and semilegal activities in the area in safety. He was very successful in uncovering the complex interactions between merchants and substance users, the structure of the drug trade in his study area, and what factors contributed to risk exposure and safety in the sale and use of illegal substances in the street environment. In Garcia's case, ethnic/national identity conferred no benefits, and at first, when combined with his self-representation, actually impaired his rapport-building activities in what in any case was a very challenging field situation.

Some topics and situations require homophily or congruence between ethnographers and participants along specific dimensions such as gender or marital status. For example, in most cultures, a male ethnographer might have difficulty discussing gynecological and/or sexual issues with a female respondent. Where sex before marriage is at least theoretically unacceptable, young interviewers who are not married may have difficulty interviewing married adults on this topic. A nonbeliever or a Jew might have a problem accessing members of a group of orthodox Jews, fundamentalist Christians, or Muslims (Peshkin 1986). People who have always been uninvolved in social revolutions may find it difficult to be convincing enough to gain access to the leaders of national or even international social movements, whereas the opposite is true for those who have been involved (Gillan and Pickerill 2012). In such cases, "authenticity" of identity may be important in gaining access and trust. It also may be crucial in determining what questions to ask that simultaneously make sense to participants and have the potential for advancing knowledge. Regardless, it always is important to ask about which interviewer/researcher characteristics might lead to the most effective data collection both before and during the implementation of a study. In a study of sexual behavior associated with the drug Ecstasy, for example, the study design required researchers to ask detailed questions about sexual and relational intimacy, including explicit comparisons of feelings and behaviors with and without the use of the drug. Screeners always asked the study volunteers whether it made a difference if a male or a female interviewed them. Most respondents said it didn't matter, but some, males in particular, preferred to be interviewed by females.

In sum, the selection of a topic and a group to study requires a consideration of researcher identity and experience in relation to the group and the topic under study. Nevertheless, irrespective of how carefully researchers and participants are matched, ethnography always requires the development of long-term and positive social relationships, the establishment of a legitimate role in the group under study, and demonstration that the research has value for the community or group. No one, no matter how closely their identity matches that of the study population, can avoid the challenges of relationship building in the hard work of ethnographic research.

RESEARCHER POSITIONALITY

 **Definition:** Positionality refers to both the structural relationships between the ethnographer and the people under study and the way those relationships are perceived and reflected upon by both

 **Cross Reference:** See Book 1, chapter 1, for further discussion of positionality

Closely related to "identity" is the concept of **positionality**. Positionality refers to both the structural relationships between the ethnographer and the people under study and the way it is perceived and reflected upon by both. Most frequently, ethnographers conduct studies among people who are marginalized by virtue of their ethnicity, socioeconomic status, sexual orientation, religious affiliation, illegal behavior, substance use, and other factors. Because of their educational status, institutional affiliation, ethnicity, or other factors, ethnographers almost always are viewed initially as holding "outsider" status, or as having power over the persons they are working with or studying. Addressing perceived and actual power and other status differentials is a challenge for basic and applied researchers alike, because they affect all significant relationships on an ongoing basis. Further, addressing them only once at the beginning of a study is not sufficient. Researchers must constantly reflect upon the problem of positionality and readjust their relationships over time so as to recognize and try to minimize or otherwise compensate for gaps in power, prestige, and status between themselves and members of the study community.

Ethnographers also must learn to deal with status differentials in which they are perceived by potential research subjects to be of lesser status. Increasingly there have been examples of research in which ethnographers hold lower status than members of the groups they are studying. This occurs, for example, when ethnographers are studying structures and policies of authority and power in national or state systems or commercial enterprises. Laura Nader (1974) and others have described this approach as "studying up." Studying up may focus on public or private corporations, systems of higher education, the health care system, or leadership among government officials who have decision-making power over vulnerable populations. Ethnographers have been employed for many years in the evaluation of health care innovations, educational programming, business development, the military (Fosher 2010; Gillan and Pickerill 2012) and other environments where powerful gatekeepers restrict access to participation and to data.

Holding higher status may result in limiting access to some sectors of the population and in the generation of data that at least in the beginning are not accurate representations of community life. Further, when the ethnographer holds higher socioeconomic status (e.g., is wealthier, more educated, from a prestigious institution such as a major university perceived to wield power and influence in the study community and beyond, or a member of a respected religious order) than study participants, there is always the risk that respondents may share information because they fear negative consequences if they do not. The danger in these circumstances is that the relationship could violate ethical concerns about real or imagined coercion of participants, and as well, run the risk that participants who feel coerced will either deliver falsified information or simply tell researchers what the participants think researchers want to hear.

Holding "lower status" may result in limited access to key informants and observation sites, as well as to secondary databases of importance to the study. On the other hand, it can lead powerful participants to view ethnographers as relatively harmless, and therefore as appropriate and trustworthy recipients of information. Holding higher status can open up some doors, but it may also restrict access to information or result in socially acceptable responses. Many ethnographers work in settings where they hold both statuses simultaneously, depending on with whom they are working. Some even change their personal identities during the course of fieldwork, which affects their perceived status in the study community and influences their continuing access to data.

EXAMPLE 2.4

IMPLICATIONS OF RELIGIOUS IDENTITY IN FRAMING RESEARCH RELATIONSHIPS

In Chicago, a research team working in the Mexican community included a researcher who was a student at a local high-status university and, at the same time, an ordained priest. He was an excellent field researcher and was able to collect many high-quality in-depth interviews. In the process, he wore his collar and respondents knew that he was a priest. When he left the priesthood to marry, he found that although his prior status had provided him with ready access to people, it had not required him to develop the interpersonal skills needed to obtain data from community members without that initial authoritative status. He thus encountered difficulties collecting data in his new capacity. People who had known him as a priest were very suspicious of his desire to leave the priesthood. He had to learn to connect with community members based only on his social skills and desire to learn, rather than upon the respected status of Catholic priest with the power of the confessional. He also had to justify leaving the priesthood in ways that were understandable to Catholic community residents.

Regardless of the ethnographer's status, the process of building relationships remains the same. The diversity of groups under study requires recognition that positionality shifts and is contingent on the perceived relationship *at the time of the encounter* between the researcher and the respondent. Approaching a physician whose age is the same as the ethnographer's calls for a relational strategy that is different from that required when approaching an older or younger physician. Interactions with a respected older man in the Mexican community in Chicago or a senior woman leader in a low-income community in Mumbai require more formal behavior and language than that used with people in the same context who are younger and less experienced.

Many researchers with a commitment to applying research results to facilitate social change feel that their work with more marginalized people helps to "balance the scales" in terms of achieving a fair distribution of societal resources. Social justice researchers feel that they thus are, in a sense, "giving back" to the community. Most researchers also report that working with higher-status populations can be more difficult than working with populations of lower socioeconomic status in terms of general acceptance, hospitality, openness, and accessibility. Regardless, ethnography always requires relationship building based on the personal and social resources of the ethnographer, and it always must be adapted to the cultural context and the individual statuses and personalities of key informants and respondents.

REQUIREMENTS OF INSTITUTIONAL AFFILIATION AND FUNDING SOURCES

Ethnographers' interests alone do not drive a decision to conduct research in a specific area, on a given topic, or even for use of specific research methods or designs. Where ethnographers work or who pays their salary and the social and intellectual resources available to them may also play an important role in what they can do and with whom they work. Universities and colleges probably offer the most flexible environment for doing independent research. At the same time, departments or research foundations may indicate preferences for one type of study over another. Medical schools tend to favor laboratory science, clinical trials, or medication development versus community-based research. Schools of public health prefer funding from the National Institutes of Health because of the high overhead costs that are associated with these grants. Public health scientists may be privileged over other social science researchers who work on less well-funded, nonhealth-related topics such as agricultural sustainability or community development. Often donors fund research centers to focus on very specific topics, requiring researchers to find ways to adapt their interests to funder priorities. One such donor funded a center that focused initially on prostate cancer in African American men. For a time, it was not possible to expand to other significant health problems that faced this population despite the fact that prostate cancer was not the most important health problem in that population.

Students are subject to the opinions and interests of their advisors in planning their studies. One doctoral student in Connecticut, for example, was told that a dissertation that examined factors contributing to elevated blood pressure in African American children was unlikely to be productive and she should not pursue this direction. Later research reviews showed increases in blood pressure associated with increases in obesity in children eight to seventeen years of age, with the greatest increases in Mexican American and African American children (Din-Dzietham et al. 2007). Such findings underscored the importance of the original idea, though the advisor's opinions meant that it could not be actualized.

Universities make decisions regarding the degree to which they favor or disregard community engagement as an approach. Some universities—for example, land grant universities in the United States—still focus more heavily on serving local communities. Those universities that wish to receive a Carnegie Foundation designation as community-engaged campuses provide incentives for faculty to find ways of sharing their research methods, results, and perspectives with local communities (Barker 2004; Jean Schensul 2010). Universities interested in community engagement may place more emphasis on local research and offer less financial and faculty support and encouragement for international work. Nontenure track or untenured researchers based in universities that are heavily funded by private-sector interests can run the risk of losing their jobs if their work on such topics as environmental contamination through oil spills, genetically modified crops, toxic industrial waste, or nuclear by-products threatens those interests (LeCompte and Bonetti 2010; Mooney 2005; Shulman 2006; Smith 2003; Washburn 2005). Tenure has been denied to several faculty members who have outspoken views about inequitable distribution of wealth in America and structural factors contributing to racial discrimination (Nelson 2010). There are times when researchers in this position can restructure their roles, turning a losing situation into a winning one. The following example illustrates how one researcher was able to do this in one university-community setting with very positive results, but was unable to do so in another.

 **EXAMPLE 2.5**

ENCOUNTERING AND ADDRESSING INSTITUTIONAL BARRIERS WITH DIFFERENTIAL SUCCESS

Medical anthropologist Stephen Schensul was hired as the head of a community research component of a federally funded Community Mental Health Program (CMHP) on the West Side of Chicago. The program was based in a department of psychiatry, part of a larger medical school system. The research component was created to provide guidance to the staffs of community mental health centers that were part of the federal community mental health program and serving African American, Mexican, and Middle European communities in that part of Chicago. Center personnel were unresponsive both to the needs of the populations and to results from studies carried out by the research component that suggested how service practices needed to be changed in order to serve the diverse mental health catchment area population. The center staff subsequently turned to other strategies, leaving the community research unit with the freedom to reframe its mission and link up directly with leadership and activists in the Mexican community. Fortunately, the director of the community mental health program supported this shift. The new partnership made it possible for the ethnographer, as the leader of the research team, to shift to the development of innovative prevention and community mental health development strategies to organizations based in the community rather than remaining in the government-funded clinic at a time when funding for innovative community mental health services was readily available at the federal level.

A second venture was less promising. Schensul was hired to direct a federally funded community mental health program based in a department of psychiatry at a south Florida university. The program attempted to be culturally responsive by hiring researchers with experience in or actually from ethnic/cultural backgrounds that matched the communities served by the community mental health program centers. The focus of the program—service improvement—was established before Schensul arrived. None of the research personnel were hired in line with Schensul's priorities which were prevention and advocacy for community development as a means of promoting mental health and well-being. Thus on arrival, he inherited staff that disagreed with the direction in which he wanted to move the program. Further, researchers held personal political and professional agendas in relation to the ethnic/cultural community in which they were working, which, they felt, could best be carried out by "sticking to service," a safe strategy in the complex political environment at the time. Thus efforts to move the research staff toward prevention and community development through community mobilization were unsuccessful, and as a consequence, university administrators made it clear that they did not support this direction.

Funders are guided by their mandates and their money. Ethnographers seeking funding for their research must remember that private and governmental funders as well as research centers are driven by *their* own funding sources (business and individual donors, and the Congress of the United States) as well as their missions. Both of these considerations affect what research they fund, and to whom. For example, the United Nations Population Fund (UNFPA), the United Nations, and the National Institute for Research in Reproductive Health (NIRRH), a government research center in Mumbai, India, support research on maternal and child health (MCH) and well-being. MCH is part of their mission, and the funding they receive from international donors or, in the case of NIRRH, from the Indian government, is focused on MCH research and development. These institutions will entertain areas of study less related to MCH (such as migration, HIV, and effects of tobacco on reproductive health), but negotiating work in these nonmainstream areas takes time, persuasiveness, and persistence. The National Drug Research Institute (NDRI) in New York supports and encourages the acquisition of grants that address drug use and related health consequences; AIDS is a related topic, and many NDRI researchers have obtained funding to do research on HIV-related topics, but the organization is likely to be less interested in cardiovascular disease, an area in which they have little expertise.

Key point *Researchers' track records are important in shaping their potential to obtain funding for their research.* While the Institute for Community Research (ICR), an independent community-based research organization in Connecticut, often explores new research directions, it has not conducted research on environmental issues mainly because no researchers at ICR have the experience and track record to obtain funding to carry it out. The Pacific Institute for Research and Evaluation (PIRE) is a grant-driven organization with offices in Philadelphia and Berkeley, California, well known for its long-term focus on the prevention of health problems. Among other things, PIRE's researchers concentrate on alcohol and other substance abuse, tobacco use, and HIV risk. Researchers are hired for their experience in these areas, and with the organization's substantial history of obtaining funding, they are able to help newer researchers to jump-start their research careers in these areas. However, it might be difficult to argue for the development of new areas of research at PIRE unless researchers at this organization already have shown the ability to obtain the required funding, or can find others in collaborating institutions with the appropriate experience who can help.

While these organizational, personal, and funding constraints may appear to be serious limitations, ethnography is sufficiently flexible that ethnographers often can insert many of their own interests into other specific areas of research. Because every human group is interesting, researchers should be able to find intellectual stimulation and challenges by working anywhere in the world, including at home. Further, a hallmark of ethnography is its encouragement of the discovery of new ideas and behaviors. Most intervention studies require formative or discovery research and process evaluations, both of which call for ethnography. As more and more clinical researchers testing new procedures or medications in controlled situations realize that issues such as compliance or contextual factors influence different patterns of use that can critically affect outcomes, ethnography's role in basic and intervention studies and clinical trials expands. Thus, ethnographers can find themselves working in interdisciplinary teams in many different types of research projects. By participating as members of research teams, ethnographers may find that their own interests and associations evolve, opening the door to the development of their own independent or interdisciplinary studies and projects. Ethnographers also may be hired to work in new study settings or with new populations where they can offer new research methods and approaches, and establish new contacts for researchers from other disciplines who otherwise would not have the skills or knowledge to gain access to these new settings. Finally, the importance and potential impact of the ethnographer's work is enhanced when it is linked to a larger multiphase mixed methods or controlled comparison study focused on service improvement and social change. In sum, ethnographers need to find ways to link their own interests, skills, and social capital to the needs of their institutional base, the concerns of the study population, available sources of funding for their work, and other researchers with like interests.

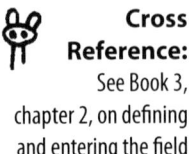

Cross Reference:
See Book 3, chapter 2, on defining and entering the field

PERSPECTIVES, NEEDS, AND PRIORITIES OF THE STUDY POPULATION

Key point

Ethnographers (and all researchers working in communities) always should seek and foster the formal and informal support of members of the population under study. Beyond that, it is important to decide together with community members and stakeholders exactly what the role of the community is or will be in the research. The degree of engagement of the community in the research will vary along a continuum from a full partnership to a mere welcoming presence. A welcoming presence is the minimum condition without which no ethnographers or other community-based researchers can do their work. Increasingly, however, communities and community organizations have begun to see themselves as partners in the research process, and ethnographers should be prepared to work with them in the design and conduct of studies.

Many communities have had prior experiences working with (or against) researchers. Even when communities want to be partners in research, ethnographers should know what prior experiences community collaborators have had with researchers. For example, communities may feel negatively about research based on their prior experience with "helicopter" researchers who came, collected data, left, and were never heard from again (Bhutta 2003; Dennis and Neese 2000). This had been the experience of the Maya family with whom Ludwig worked, described in Example 2.2. Ethnic/racial populations that traditionally have been harmed by researchers and their work, including African Americans and all indigenous peoples, may establish their own barriers and guidelines for research by creating their own institutional review boards, or establishing complex review procedures. In a few instances, these could include delays and open hostility. Groups, institutions, and communities that do not view the research topic as a priority may request that the topic be refocused or reject the research project outright. Evaluation researchers often find that evaluations that are required by the funding agency and approved by institutional leaders are deeply resented or feared by program implementers, simply because prior evaluators were highly critical of practitioners and demonstrated little understanding of the very real constraints of implementation. They also may have communicated the results of their evaluations to program staff in negative or otherwise nonproductive ways.

In earlier years, anthropologists and other social scientists simply arrived at their research sites, armed with notebooks, cameras, tape recorders, and their own research interests. Now the situation has become more complex. The researcher's interests must be integrated with the priorities of the funding source, the employer institution, and the study population. Researchers in general and ethnographers in particular need to be able to negotiate these agendas when they are defining a population and topic.

SUMMARY

In this chapter we have focused on the variety of ways in which ethnographic researchers identify their research interests and as well, the factors that they need to consider even before they devise a research strategy and plan. Four factors critical to what could be called the "preparation quadrangle" are:

- The personal characteristics and interests that ethnographers bring to the problem and to the field situation
- The ethnographer's positionality, or how the above characteristics interact with people and situations in

the field in ways that shape their relationships and access to information
- The ethnographer's ability to find and establish relationships with people in the study location
- The institutional and other resources and constraints that shape the research effort

In the next chapter we discuss the technical, institutional, and other arrangements required prior to entering a field situation, regardless of whether one is a student, faculty member, or researcher working in a nonacademic setting.

3

PREPARING FOR CHALLENGES IN THE FIELD

> The Research Game Plan or Proposal
>
> Formal Permissions and Approvals; IRBs and Other Review Bodies
>
> Logistics: Support, Housing, and Other Needs
>
> Sponsoring Institutions in the Research Site
>
> Time and Timeline
>
> Personnel: Hiring and Supervision
>
> Preparing for the Collection, Transcription, and Management of Data
>
> Planning for Writing Up Preliminary Results in the Field
>
> Summary

Entry into research sites has become increasingly difficult for many reasons. These include "overstudying" in a particular site; the proliferation both of studies in specific areas and of agencies that regulate research; research site members' increasing awareness of the value of research funding and the potential consequences of research results; the need for communication with collaborators and staff, and the complexity of field logistics. This chapter is designed to help researchers at any level prepare for research in a field setting, whether close to home or far away.

THE RESEARCH GAME PLAN OR PROPOSAL

The primary objective of classical ethnography was to describe the culture of remote or "different" peoples and communities with academic, museum, or government, or even self-support. This objective no longer suffices as the *raison d'être* of the ethnographic enterprise. Though a first trip to the field may be purely exploratory, and often is self-funded, all researchers will need to write a proposal to obtain funding for their extended fieldwork, as well as to obtain permission to enter the country and the setting in which it is to be conducted. No matter the funder or regulatory agency, a research proposal must be convincing and generally consist of several different key components:

> **COMPONENTS OF A RESEARCH PROJECT**
> - An abstract
> - A goals or aims section
> - A literature review or section stating the significance of the proposed work
> - A design and methods section
> - A data analysis section
> - A short section on how data will be stored and managed
> - An overall statement about the organization of the study
> - A section describing how the rights of human subjects will be assured

Because figuring out the appropriate language to use in a research proposal can be difficult for beginning researchers—or even more experienced ones—we provide examples for each of the components listed above. It is important to check funder guidelines, however, and to talk directly with funding officers, to find out exactly what they require and in what formats. Proposals, no matter how brilliant, can be rejected simply because they are not prepared using the correct formatting.

The Abstract

The abstract is a short and precise statement of what the proposal is about. It generally contains fewer than five hundred words. In those few words, researchers must present the purpose of the study, the goals or aims of the study, a brief rationale for the study, its anticipated outcomes, and potential uses for the research results. Each funding agency requires something slightly different for an abstract; researchers *must* make sure that they have followed the guidelines of their chosen potential funder or approving agency.

**EXAMPLE 3.1**

ABSTRACT FOR PROPOSED STUDY OF SMOKELESS TOBACCO USE AMONG WOMEN OF REPRODUCTIVE AGE IN MUMBAI

This Fogarty International Research Collaborative Award (FIRCA) application titled "Smokeless Tobacco Use and Reproductive Health among Women Users in a Low Income Community of Mumbai" proposes to explore the use of new and highly addictive forms of smokeless tobacco increasingly used by Indian women during their reproductive years. Smokeless tobacco use is increasing dramatically among women in India and has been shown to contribute to reproductive health problems including premature birth, low birth weight, stillbirth, and maternal morbidity among (low income) Indian women. The study is being conducted with Drs. Saritha Nair, Scientist, and Donta Balaiah, Deputy Director and Scientist, National Institute for Research on Reproductive Health (NIRRH), Mumbai, and is an extension of NIH Grant number 1 R01 DA020393-01A2. The five study aims are: (1) to conduct qualitative research with a sample of ninety women and twenty community experts in one large, low-income/slum area of western Mumbai on the meanings and practices associated with smokeless tobacco during three stages in reproductive history, immediately postmarriage, during first (or second) pregnancy, and between second and fourth pregnancy; (2) to understand marketing, promotion, and availability of smokeless tobacco (ST) to low-income women; (3) to conduct a survey with four hundred women in one low-income/slum area of western Mumbai known to be receptive to prevention studies, approximately 125 in each reproductive health category; (4) to use data to generate and evaluate social acceptability of intervention approaches with women in the study community and others affected by smokeless tobacco use; (5) to increase the capacity of NIRRH, the partner organization, to conduct social and behavioral intervention research on smokeless tobacco and reproductive health issues in India through capacity-building training on qualitative research methods; tobacco's implications for morbidity and mortality prior to, after, and during pregnancy; and proposal development. The research results will contribute to culturally and contextually appropriate interventions focused on smokeless tobacco prevention and cessation among women in low-income communities of Mumbai. Consultants to the study include P. C. Gupta, PhD, internationally recognized expert on tobacco use/control in India and tobacco use, pregnancy, and female morbidity and mortality; Stephen Schensul, PhD, and partners conducting intervention research in a similar community on life stress (*tenshun*), perceived reproductive health symptoms (*kamjori* and *safed pani*), marital conflict, and STI/HIV risk. Other Indian and U.S. consultants will be added to capacity-building workshops each year based on topic. Significance lies in the study's capacity to address a critical public health problem in India, the apparent increase in risky and addictive new forms of smokeless tobacco with potentially serious implications for pregnancy and morbidity and mortality of women, and to provide the basis for educational and other forms of appropriate intervention to reduce smokeless tobacco use, a practice intertwined with other aspects of their lives, among women of reproductive age.

The Purpose, Goals, or Aims Section

This section spells out the specific goals or aims of the study. Different funders and guides prefer different language when referring to purpose, aims, goals, and purpose of a study. The purpose is generally the overall statement of direction or intent. Sometimes it explains why the study is important. One example of appropriate language for a purpose statement is as follows: "The purpose of this study is to reduce emergency room use for acute asthma episodes among young men of color. Young men of color are at highest risk for limited self management and access to medication, and experience more asthma-related morbidity and mortality than other populations." Another might be the following: "The intent of this study is to identify the main facilitators and barriers to educational achievement among recent immigrants from West African countries in order to improve educational outcomes."

Goals or aims derive from the study purpose and provide details about it. Statements of goals and aims sometimes spell out methods to be used, or refer to stages or phases in the study.

EXAMPLE 3.2

GOALS/AIMS SECTION FROM STUDY OF SMOKELESS TOBACCO USE AMONG WOMEN OF REPRODUCTIVE AGE IN MUMBAI

AIM I. To use qualitative/ethnographic (interview, observation, elicitation, mapping) methods to identify patterns of smokeless tobacco use in urban, low-income women.

a. Discover and document in a group of low-income Indian women of reproductive age the individual and social patterns, meanings, and social/contextual factors associated with initiation and continuation of the use of smokeless tobacco products.
b. Identify their beliefs regarding the linkages between uses of smokeless tobacco, health in general, and their own reproductive health.

AIM II. To explore ways smokeless tobacco is marketed to and accessed by urban, low-income women.

a. Identify the outlets and strategies through which smokeless tobacco products are available and the ways in which these outlets attract female consumers.
b. Delineate the strategies used to market smokeless tobacco products to women and families via the electronic media (national and local), narrowcast (signboards, newspapers, and magazines), and radio and televideo (films and videos and advertising promoted on television and radio via prime-time programs).

AIM III. To establish the individual, social, and contextual factors; use pathways and health risks associated with smokeless tobacco use and perceptions of effects of use on reproductive health in a representative sample of low-income women of reproductive age using quantitative (survey) methodology.

AIM IV. To use study results to develop multilevel prevention or early intervention strategies tailored to the diversity-of-use patterns and stages of use of these women and to assess their acceptability.

AIM V. To enhance NIRRH capacity for conducting mixed methods research on reproductive health aspects of smokeless tobacco use among both women and men in their household and community settings.

A Literature Review

The literature review presents a scientific and social rationale for the study. It reviews bodies of research literature relevant to the study and points out how the study will add to the existing body of knowledge about the topic. The literature review answers questions about:

1. why the study has important implications for the discipline that informs it, as well as practical value for the population and specific problem under study;
2. how the study differs in approach, concept, or methods and population from previous studies;
3. why the study site is the right place for enhancing understanding of the study topic; and
4. how the researcher's approach to the topic will fill a gap in the literature and/or extend extant work.

Literature reviews cover three aspects of the extant literature on the topic. First, they review studies at the substantive level, describing all studies that address the substance of the problem under consideration. For example, researchers might search for effectiveness data on every existing study of dual-language bilingual programs. They identify the populations for which the studies were carried out, the age level and language groups for which the programs were developed, the program duration, and so on. Second, they review at the methodological level, assessing whether studies were experimental, quasi-experimental, longitudinal, cross-sectional, or long-term observational studies and what kinds of data were collected. Finally, they review at the theoretical level, determining the conceptual and theoretical frameworks that might underlie how the studies were constructed and how the data were analyzed and interpreted. For example, a researcher whose orientation was positivist might assume that effectiveness data in a Spanish/English transitional bilingual program could best be assessed from an experimental design that looked at English-language test scores alone, given that the goals of the program were to ease children into English-language instruction. Failure to examine achievement in Spanish, however, would obscure the students' growth in their native language, and as well, their overall linguistic competence. A critical perspective might also use qualitative methods to look at contextual issues beyond the mere administration of an experimental instructional program to determine what the students' prior language facility was, how accurately the program was implemented, and if the teachers themselves were trained for and believed in the experimental approach being used. By examining substantive, methodological, and theoretical aspects of prior studies, researchers can determine what gaps exist in the literature that their own study can fill. Thus, the final part of a literature review often includes a summary that indicates where this particular proposal fills gaps in the literature. Some funders, like the National Institutes of Health, actually require a description of innovative aspects of a study, including methodological and theoretical features, although innovation is not always

A Design and Methods Section

The methods section first describes the research design to be chosen, followed by research questions, research model, study hypotheses if they exist, and very specific steps to be taken to collect data relating to the aims or goals of the study. It then discusses how the researcher will define and select a population, the sampling strategies to be used, if needed, and how participants will be recruited. Books 1, 3, and 4 of the *Toolkit* provide useful information regarding the strategies to be used in devising the sampling strategies and approaches to data collection required for a strong methods section. It is always best to be as clear as possible about the data collection methods, particularly in terms of the conceptualization and collection of qualitative data. For example, instead of simply stating that data collection will include key informants, it is important to specify who the key informants will be (e.g., teachers, community health workers, local government leaders), how many will be interviewed, on what topics they will be interviewed, and when the data will be collected from them (one time only or multiple times through the course of the study). One way to be sure that the methodological steps to be taken are clearly described is to place them in a "data collection matrix." Book 1, chapter 6, illustrates how methodological material is put into a matrix that indicates how each research question will be answered by eliciting information from specific sources and using particular forms of data collection. Data collection matrices not only make very clear the researcher's plans to readers but also help researchers think through their procedures systematically.

A Data Analysis Section

This very important section of a proposal often is neglected. Many qualitative studies do not describe very well how the data collected will be analyzed to answer the research questions. Often this is because researchers may not have a clear idea of exactly what data they will end up collecting. Nonetheless, what can be anticipated should be spelled out very carefully, and very detailed attention should be paid to how the analysis strategies proposed actually will answer the questions implied or specified in the study aims and goals. With regard to analysis of qualitative data, researchers should describe the particular strategies they use for rendering the piles of field notes, interviews, and survey and other data amenable to crunching and manipulation. Books 1 and 5 of the *Ethnographer's Toolkit* clearly spell out many of these strategies and describe well-known procedures that, if cited, will assist reviewers of proposals in understanding exactly what the researcher plans to do. Book 4 does the same for additional forms of data collection, including the retrieval and use of archival and secondary data, material culture artifacts, consensus analysis, spatial data, and multimedia data. This book, as well as Books 1 and 5, also show how codes and themes emerge from and help to build the study's formative and analytic models. Researchers also should specify which specific computer-based management and analysis programs that they plan to use (e.g., programs such as ATLAS.ti or NVivo for qualitative data of all types; SPSS, SAS, or other analytic packages for quantitative data; ANTHROPAC for analysis of free lists and pilesorts; ArcInfo for management and analysis of spatial data, etc.).

A discussion of quantitative data analysis will include data cleaning strategies, plans for data management, and a variety of procedures for univariate, bivariate, and multivariate statistical procedures. This section should also include power calculations when appropriate in determining the size of a sample to be used for statistical analysis. Sometimes researchers write the analysis section specifically by aim or goal. The following is an example drawn from a very concise proposal (six pages) of the type of language that might be used to describe analysis related to a specific goal and set of data.

> **Cross Reference:**
> Chapter 6 in this book describes the coding process (including reliability checks) and details of theme identification. Book 5, chapters 4, 5, and 6, provides a more detailed discussion of ways of approaching coding, and how to code and manage coded text; chapters 8 and 9 of Book 5 discuss common statistical procedures used to analyze quantitative data

EXAMPLE 3.3

AN EXAMPLE OF APPROPRIATE LANGUAGE TO USE IN THE DESCRIPTION OF ANALYSIS RELATED TO A STUDY GOAL, AIM, OR QUESTION FROM A STUDY OF SMOKELESS TOBACCO USE AMONG WOMEN IN MUMBAI

To address AIM 2, we will analyze data from the fifty-five semistructured interviews. First, we will apply text codes that reflect components in our study model. We will also identify quotations that might be relevant to the creation of new codes. Once having read the data closely, we will classify blocked quotations and transform them into additional codes that either identify new model components or are subsets of the initial set of codes derived from the study model. After coding, we will reorganize codes into higher-order conceptual codes to help us to move to patterns and structures. We will also code at the item level to identify items that vary for use in scales to be used in the study's survey.

The larger the project, the more detailed the description must be and the more carefully it must be linked to the study purpose and aims or goals. The following example is taken from a much longer, twenty-five-page proposal for a five-year study of women and HIV.

EXAMPLE 3.4

A MORE ELABORATE EXAMPLE OF AN ANALYSIS SECTION FOR THE FORMATIVE PHASE OF A FIVE-YEAR STUDY OF WOMEN AND HIV

There are two types of qualitative data in this proposed project: (1) the formative data, which will enhance our understanding of the people, cultures, systems, and the study community; and (2) the evaluation data, which will serve to assess the acceptability, social validity, integrity, outcomes, sustainability, and institutionalization of the intervention. The results of the formative data need to be available at key points in the first year to help shape the quantitative instruments, to contribute to intervention design, to inform the intervention during the course of the project and, in the final year, to assist in the interpretation of results. The evaluation data must be available to program implementers throughout the intervention process, assisting in shaping program elements and providing interim assessments of program process and outcome. The procedures for transcription, storage, and analysis of the data must address both the richness of the material as well as the need for timely information. The procedures developed for management and analysis of qualitative data in the studies carried out in our last decade of work on sexual risk have provided the methodology to maximize the utility of qualitative data.

All observations and in-depth interviews will be transcribed, translated, entered into Microsoft Word files, and transformed into text files for storage and analysis. The key to effective qualitative data analysis is the coding system. Codes will be developed in this research using a tree diagram method in which factors will be embedded in domains, allowing analysis to occur at the domain and the factor level (Schensul, Schensul, and LeCompte 1999).

Codes will be developed collaboratively with the Principal Investigator (PI) and co-PIs in the United States and in India (see Appendix 4 for codes developed for the Women's Supplement). Once a coding scheme has been derived and consensus reached among the research team members, coders will be trained in the use of the coding scheme through guided practice. All coders will independently code the same segments of narrative text and then compare the application of the coding scheme. Discrepancies will be resolved through discussion among coders. The process of coding and comparison will continue until an acceptable level of agreement—85 percent to 90 percent—is reached (Bakeman and Gottman 1986). Coders will then work independently on different text files. To check for consistency of application of the coding scheme across the data sets, 20 percent of all text will be coded by a second coder and a numerical index of agreement will be computed. Coded segments will be reviewed for patterns, both for consistency and variation and for exemplary cases.

Text and codes will be entered into ATLAS.ti, v5.0 (Muhr 2004), a computer-based text-search program that allows multiple codes to be searched at the same time, providing the capability of qualitative "testing" of hypotheses. In addition to generating important results that can only be gained qualitatively, the textual data will be crucial to the formulation of the structured survey instruments (Nastasi and Schensul 2005; Schensul et al. 1994). First, it will allow the researchers to review the factor and subfactor coded segments to generate a further "breakdown" into variables. Second, the qualitative analysis will provide the basis for making a judgment about the worth of the variable for inclusion into the quantitative instruments in terms of importance, correlation, and variation. Third, the qualitative data can assist in identifying a range of alternative responses for purposes of structuring closed-ended survey questions. Fourth, by cross-referencing codes with individual items on the quantitative instruments, hypotheses can be tested both by quantitative and qualitative analysis.

A Human Subjects Section

Most ethnographers, folklorists, and other social scientists are required to describe ethical considerations in their study. Fundamentally, this means assessing and describing what they plan to do to and with the people they are studying. Any researcher from any field who elicits information from live human beings is required to undergo an ethics review to assure that the study conforms to obligations for the ethical treatment of human subjects of research. Typically these sections of a proposal include the following:

- A description of the study populations
- The kinds of data to be collected
- The duration and site of the study
- Whether or not participants will receive any compensation
- How participants will be recruited and procedures for obtaining their consent for participation
- How confidentiality of individuals in the study will be protected
- What risks they might be exposed to
- How those risks can be justified or mitigated

Cross Reference: See Book 1, chapter 10, and Book 6 for a description of the procedures for ethical review by institutional review boards (IRBs)

Increasingly, researchers are being asked to consider the ethical implications of their work for whole communities. In some cases, such as field-based substance abuse or violence research, the research ethics section of a proposal describes the risks and protections for study staff as well as community residents and the community as a whole.

FORMAL PERMISSIONS AND APPROVALS; IRBS AND OTHER REVIEW BODIES

Before entering the field, a variety of formal permissions are usually required. Both students and experienced researchers will need approval of Institutional Review Boards (IRBs) or Institutional Ethics Committees (IECs), the term used for ethical review committees in countries other than the United States and Canada. IRBs are bodies associated with universities and research organizations that review proposals for human subjects and research ethics concerns. IRBs usually want to review what the characteristics of the study participants will be, what researchers will do with them, and how researchers will protect them from any foreseeable harm. Thus, they are less interested in the theories and concepts behind the study than they are in the study proposal's purposes, proposed participants, and methods. They do not assess the quality of the methods *per se*, unless the quality is so flawed or the study either so risky or so trivial that it is deemed unacceptable. The IRB reviews parts of proposals related to sampling and recruitment, interviewing security and safety, and whether the researcher plans to present the study accurately and properly in field settings. They also review and approve interview schedules, both open ended and closed ended, and other protocols for collecting elicitation and geographic data, items of material culture, and local archival data. IRBs always review the written consent forms to be used with individual respondents or study participants and the conditions under which they are to be interviewed. They also consider requests to substitute oral for written consent, or in some few cases, waiver of formal consent procedures altogether. Without IRB or IEC approvals, data collection in the field cannot begin.

In joint or collaborative projects, IRBs of all the participating partner organizations and group partners usually want to review the study. Some IRBs or IECs are more rigorous and detailed than others, especially those in medical schools or clinical settings that typically review clinical trial or treatment protocols. Many Native American or First Nations groups in the United States and Canada have their own IRBs and procedures for reviewing studies, formal collaboration and cost sharing, and ethical review. Building relationships that ensure that the research is compatible with and carried out in partnership with tribal or national goals, interests, and researchers requires trust that is built through collaboration over time.

Many researchers, including students, are involved in cross-institutional collaborations. Above and beyond IRB/IEC approval, cross-institutional collaborations generally involve contracts or formal permission to work together, to collect data in the institution, and to comply with institutional ethical requirements. International work may require an additional substantive and ethical review of a study at the national level and the granting of permission through the applicant's country embassy before a project can be funded. Obtaining these formal permissions requires good contacts and relationships both at the governmental and community level, and they can take a long time to complete. It is not unheard of that a researcher may have to wait beyond the period for which a study was funded to obtain all approvals required to start. Researchers should start early to build their relationships, to identify and obtain the necessary approvals, and to prepare and submit their studies for ethics review by the proper bodies. Discussions with other researchers who have worked in a setting or country as well as project funders while in the development phase of a project should go a long way toward avoiding such problems.

LOGISTICS: SUPPORT, HOUSING, AND OTHER NEEDS

Whether or not a researcher has the ability to start a project on time, to work with a team, and to collect data efficiently calls for careful prior consideration of study logistics. If the research will take place outside the researcher's home territory, and especially if the study community is in another country or a distant, different, or marginalized area of one's own country, field logistics become even more important. Researchers need to consider where to live and what kind of place is likely to be most comfortable. They have to decide how to communicate with people within and beyond the study site, and how to ensure access to the Internet. A crucial issue is how to secure and continue to obtain money to support daily life while in the field. The possibility of encountering a serious health problem in the field should be identified, and preventive measures should be taken prior to leaving for the field. Researchers should be sure to take all regularly used medications with them, or to learn whether these medications can be obtained in the field, and how.

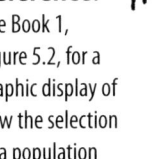

Cross Reference: See Book 1, Figure 5.2, for a graphic display of how the selection of a population affects all logistical considerations; see also chapter 6 in Book 1 about logistics and planning

Social science researchers will vary considerably with respect to their definition of and requirement for comfortable living situations in the field. However, the most basic survival needs include a comfortable, safe place to sleep, a desk, a chair or two, proper lighting, a fan, air conditioning or a heater depending on the climate, and a safe and inexpensive place to eat, buy food, or wash and cook food at home. Other needs include finding ways to clean or wash clothes, convenient telephones or Internet sites, and identification of transportation modes and transportation routes. Both individual researchers and field teams will need these amenities. Of course, needs will increase if children and other family members accompany researchers to the field. There are a number of good publications that describe family fieldwork situations (Loeffler 1998; Jean Schensul 2006; Sutton 1998; Wasson 2006; Zulaika and Zulaika 1998).

Many options are available for seeking and locating a place to live and meeting daily needs. Some ethnographers are "adopted" by and live as paying guests with a family. This has numerous advantages, including gaining cultural knowledge from home owners, help with learning the local language, opportunities to share food preparation, and access to advice in case medical assistance is needed, or social dilemmas arise, as well as for travel, and other issues. The local family can also "protect" the ethnographer and communicate with others about the advantages of working together. Living in someone's home is very important when working in rural areas where there are few other options, and the researcher might benefit from a readily available set of companions and, as well, from the presence of people knowledgeable about any dangers or pitfalls in the community. Some researchers do prefer to live in a university hostel, on a university campus, or in a nearby hotel at least for a time, if such amenities are available. Hotels are the least effective option, because they can be very impersonal, especially in the event of a health or other emergency. Local people may see some larger hotels as an alien place reserved for wealthy foreigners. Resident hotels can often "trap" the ethnographer into socializing with other customers, thus taking time and resources away from work with local people, and hotels are likely to be more expensive than other forms of residence.

Nowadays, having access to the Internet and a cell phone really are requirements in the field. There are a few locations without satellite reach in the United States—in some national parks and rural or mountainous areas and deserts—where cell phones and even the Internet are not usable. In such places, researchers must still depend upon landlines and borrowed phones. However, most locations offer Internet access if only at Internet cafes or commercial sites for searching and emailing at relatively low cost. For long stays in any very remote field site, the best option for ethnographers is a USB satellite receiver purchased or modified for in-country use, including international settings that provide Internet access in most places in the world for a reasonable monthly fee. If Internet is readily available, Skype also allows international "face-to-face" real-time communication via computer and web camera free. Notwithstanding our current level of technology, however, ethnographers often find themselves lacking the communication infrastructure to which they have become accustomed, and will have to make accommodations.

Portable computers are a must for collecting, storing, and conducting preliminary analysis on data while in the field. They require electricity and regular backups in case of loss, hard drive corruption, or other problems. Saving data on a portable computer and an external hard drive at least once a week is of the utmost importance. Having several backup locations for data, in fact, is ideal. Some researchers prefer a desktop portable for work "at home" and a small, light portable or tablet for data collection when interviewing or taking observational notes. Researchers should plan ahead to carry this equipment with them, since it can be very expensive to ship, and there is the risk of mishap along the way. Since such equipment is easily stolen, plans to safeguard it should be made.

Other considerations include obtaining visas if required, getting health and dental checkups and vaccinations prior to going to the field, and planning ahead to carry critical medications and a medical kit with sufficient supplies to last the duration of the field visit. International health insurance can be useful; it usually covers assistance in seeking trained and certified medical advice in an international setting and evacuation in case of serious illness or accident if required. Such insurance may cost anywhere from $150 to $450 for one full year, but the expense is well worth it. International insurance may be available through one's institution. The Institute for Community Research, for example, purchases international travel insurance for its employees, and it is considered part of the fringe benefit package.

A bicycle, motorbike, or even a car may be required in the field, if the research plan calls for traveling long distances between villages or neighborhoods. It's always best to have a car that is unobtrusive and that resembles local cars. Having a car in good repair is important to minimize the possibility that it will break down, thereby losing valuable time and considerable expense and hassle in the field. In most places, bus, train, and informal means of transportation (*collectivos*, chicken buses, autorickshaws, tuk-tuks, and pedicabs or other options for transporting large numbers of people) are available relatively cheaply. Using local transportation is a form of symbolic capital in much the same way as staying in a local residence. It reduces the social distance between researchers and the communities where they are working, and it offers many opportunities for making new connections and gaining new information about how local people live their everyday lives. Some dangers can accrue in traveling on local, cheap transport, including the possibility of being robbed or sexually harrassed. Communicating with local residents can help to decide when, where, and how to use local transportation comfortably and safely.

SPONSORING INSTITUTIONS IN THE RESEARCH SITE

It usually is not effective simply to appear in a community, school, corporation, or even a public setting such as a street, market, or community meetings without the permission, approval, or endorsement of sponsoring organizations. Individual researchers can sometimes negotiate entry into these settings, but in order to avoid any problems or misunderstandings, it is much better if they seek out informal or even formal involvement and affiliation with a local institution or organization. These organizations can include recognized not-for-profit, nongovernmental organizations (NGOs), institutions of higher education, governmental agencies, and private corporations. They can also include well-known individuals and local advocacy groups. Researchers should be aware, however, that these individuals, groups, and institutions all have a history, reputation, and role in the community that may both facilitate and constrain the ability of the researcher to gain access to certain sectors. Thus researchers should do their "ethnographic homework" before deciding to affiliate with a specific civic or municipal organization, community-based organization, church, or advocacy group. The following examples illustrate how involvement in two distinctly different urban communities in different parts of the country was achieved.

EXAMPLE 3.5

ACHIEVING INVOLVEMENT IN THE CHICANO WEST SIDE COMMUNITY OF CHICAGO

Stephen Schensul sought involvement in the Chicano community on the West Side of Chicago at a time when it was beginning to establish an identity and visibility on the Chicago political scene in the late 1960s. His initial contact was an individual living in the community and working for the Chicago Police Review Board, which had been created in response to charges of police brutality, particularly toward racial and ethnic minorities. This community activist provided a "tour of the community" that led to introductions to youth gang leaders, young Chicano activists, and the young staff of a neighborhood settlement house. Almost all of the people to whom Schensul was introduced were second- and third-generation residents of Chicago and in their twenties. Since Schensul also was in his late twenties, this group provided a natural "social home" for him. However, other approaches were necessary to develop entry to the much larger segment of the community that consisted of first-generation immigrants who had come either from the southwestern U.S. states or directly from Mexico. Each of these groups had a different social composition, and each played different roles in the community. In addition to these groups, the parent generation of the second- and third-generation youth constituted Schensul's primary reference group.

EXAMPLE 3.6

GAINING ENTRY TO THE PUERTO RICAN COMMUNITY IN HARTFORD

Later, when Stephen Schensul shifted his residence to Hartford, Connecticut, in the late 1970s, his entry into the Puerto Rican community was facilitated by an activist group, the Puerto Rican Health Committee of La Casa de Puerto Rico. This committee was seeking to redress inequities in the health status and health care for the growing Hispanic—and then predominantly Puerto Rican—community. Schensul's affiliation with the Puerto Rican Health Committee structured much of the research carried out in a partnership between committee members and anthropologists for the next several years. The Puerto Rican Health Committee had charged the city's hospitals with discrimination and for failing to provide appropriate resources for translation services, a situation that resulted in the death of a baby whose monolingual, Spanish-speaking mother had brought the baby to, and been rejected by, the emergency rooms of the three city hospitals. Unable to reach treatment in time, the baby died of pneumonia in a taxi. Schensul recognized that collaborating with the committee made entry into the community and its organizational structure easy; but at the same time, it hampered his entry to the city hospitals.

Schensul and medical anthropologist Pertti J. Pelto, both from the University of Connecticut, then forged a link with a tenants association made up of African American and Hispanic/Puerto Rican residents of a public housing project in Hartford concerned about health care in the community. To enhance the relationship, Schensul and students worked with the tenants to organize a protest against the city health department that had charged the tenants with throwing garbage outside rather than inside the dumpsters provided by the city, thus attracting rats. Through documentation provided by the researchers, the advocacy group was able to demonstrate that the problem of rats stemmed not from resident misbehavior but from deteriorated dumpsters. To emphasize the point, a member of the activist group placed a dead rat in a shoebox and left it in the unlocked front seat of the city health department director's car. This action drove the point home to the director, but it was of some annoyance to city officials. Moving ahead to argue for other community health needs required mending fences to reestablish relationships, which took time and effort, but eventually resulted in the creation of a federally funded community health center.

EXAMPLE 3.7

GAINING ACCESS TO LOW-INCOME COMMUNITIES IN MUMBAI

Stephen Schensul began work on HIV/STI prevention in Mumbai with the collaboration of faculty members from the International Institute for Population Studies (IIPS), a graduate-level university with a long history of conducting research in its local community as well as throughout India. While IIPS sponsorship provided an effective base for securing India government ethical and scientific approval of the project, it had little effect in securing entry to the low-income urban communities that were the focus of the research project. It was through the work of individual faculty members with extensive work in the study communities that entry was established. Further, IIPS was a quantitatively oriented institution that was slow to accept qualitative methodology and data. Finally, IIPS had little experience with intervention since its primary role was demographic research. The project called for multilevel intervention at the individual, health care system, and community levels, requiring considerable support from a medical college, community NGOs, and the health department of the Mumbai Municipal Corporation.

EXAMPLE 3.8

GAINING ACCESS TO THE CBO AND VOLUNTARY COMMUNITY ORGANIZATION NETWORK IN HARTFORD

In 1987, Jean Schensul was appointed director of the newly formed Institute for Community Research, with the task of defining its collaborative, community-based mission of research for social justice, and communicating that mission to the many community organizations and formal and informal community groups in the greater Hartford area. Though she was already known to some extent for her work in the Puerto Rican community of Hartford through another organization, the Hispanic Health Council, for the most part she had played an "inside," research administration, and development role in that organization, forgoing local external networking in support of its executive director, Maria Gonzalez Borrero. The entry process involved her own acceptance in the community, as well as the acceptance and endorsement of the new organization. She knew that many organizations knew nothing about research or evaluation, others had had negative experiences with university-based researchers, and still others were interested in research collaborations but did not know how to start. To assist her in these efforts, she used resources internal to the Institute, namely a leader in the older adult and lesbian, gay, transgender, bisexual, and questioning (LGTBQ) communities, and urban planner Marlene Berg, who had had many years of experience in the African American neighborhoods of the city, as well as with many of the development community-based organizations (CBOs) and larger agencies. With the guidance of those two key informants she was able to meet gatekeepers, organizational directors, agency staff, community activists, and school personnel by making appointments to discuss the role and direction of the new institute. She also used the opportunity to generate ideas for projects to illustrate how the new institute would work collaboratively. Finally, the Institute's strategy was to model collaborative problem solving through research by creating and obtaining funding for a number of large consortium projects. To forge these projects, ICR called together partners interested in specific projects that met the ICR's mission and concerns in the community (e.g., in HIV, changing community demographics, the status and well-being of women). Successful funding and cost sharing provided examples of ICR's collaborative style and ways of using research for social change and community well-being, making it easier to subsequently approach organizations and community groups. This entry process took nearly three years.

EXAMPLE 3.9

GAINING ENTRY BY ACCIDENT: HOW A VACATION TURNED INTO THE NGO TEACH CAMBODIA

Finding herself between jobs in 2007, educational anthropologist Yuri Wellington decided to fulfill a lifelong wish to travel around the world. The airlines would allow her only eighteen stops, so though she had to narrow her list of fifty-plus must-see countries down, she knew she had to include Cambodia, whose Angkor Wat temples she had wanted to see since childhood. Before leaving the United States, she contacted Global Tier to see if they needed any English teachers. They countered by asking her if she would conduct teacher-training workshops in progressive literacy techniques in Cambodia. Since her stopover was long enough, she agreed to do a two-day teacher-training workshop in Siem Reap, the town adjacent to Angkor Wat. Upon arrival, she found an educational system struggling to regenerate after decades of genocide and civil war. Sambour School near Siem Reap was staffed entirely by teachers who had no teacher training at all. Most had some elementary schooling at best, and because the Khmer Rouge had closed all schools and killed most educated people, including teachers, several generations of adults had never attended school at all. They were desperate for education, but adult education was impossible, given the governmental rules. By law, everyone who goes to school in Cambodia must start in kindergarten or first grade, and no one who drops out can re-enter. No alternatives to the government schools exist. So when people found out that Dr. Wellington was going to teach classes, half the town wanted to come. That the classes were for teachers and that her classes were just two-day workshops was irrelevant; if it meant a chance for education, they'd become teachers. Dr. Wellington was mobbed wherever she went by people begging her to let them attend school. So she cancelled her round-the-world trip and began the process of building Teach Cambodia, a nongovernmental organization devoted to teacher-training programs.

EXAMPLE 3.10

GAINING ACCESS TO A STUDY COMMUNITY IN LUSAKA TO DO AIDS PREVENTION RESEARCH WITH WOMEN

University of Connecticut doctoral student Lwendo Moonzwe made a decision to return to her country of origin, Zambia, to do her dissertation field research in

PREPARING FOR CHALLENGES IN THE FIELD  65

Lusaka, Zambia's capital and largest city. Her research focused on the social and structural factors that placed women in low-income communities in Lusaka (and elsewhere) at risk for HIV. She decided to visit Lusaka before actually starting to do her field research to determine in which community to conduct her dissertation research, what organizations and people could help her to do her work, and what issues women were facing. With this information, she would move forward with her study's formative model and the ability to describe the research community and the infrastructure to support her work and benefit from the results.

She knew of some of the organizations doing AIDS work in Lusaka before she left the United States because members of her family were church activists in a city where churches functioned much like NGOs, serving different sectors of the community. However, she was not certain which of them would be able to provide her with access to a community setting, how many women they served, and which sectors they represented. On her first visit she visited the University of Zambia, Lusaka, and identified a community suitable for her research using the criteria of size, socioeconomic range, and duration. She was able to talk with representatives of NGOs who acted as gatekeepers to the community, with members of the municipal council situated within the community, with the personnel at a health center that served the community, and with several community women. During her visit she was able to find a comfortable, neutral place to rent and to gain basic skills—where to shop for food, to obtain local money, how to take public/private transportation, where to find research staff, and how to communicate. Once her NIMH predoctoral research grant was funded, she returned to the field and started her formative work almost immediately.

EXAMPLE 3.11

DOING THE PRELIMINARY FIELDWORK REQUIRED FOR INTERVENTIONS

Dr. Yuri Wellington returned to Cambodia in May 2008 to begin a two-year process of exploring all available data on Cambodia, including its demographics and history, the obstacles people faced in trying to get an education, and the characteristics of the existing educational system. Because she did not want to duplicate other people's efforts or reinvent the wheel, Wellington visited the Cambodian government teacher-training school to see why few people attended it. She found it was too far away for most people, given the nonexistent transportation network. Even had it been close by, most people could not afford to pay the tuition. She then explored working through existing NGOs. However, the NGOs only wanted to teach English to Cambodians, using untrained teachers and the most traditional methods of rote memorization. They were not interested in Wellington's commitment to bring progressive teacher training to Cambodia. Some NGOs suggested creating a partnership with her to construct a central place where people could come for classes. But she already had discovered that if people could afford to come to a central place, they also could get to the government school, and that this was not a viable option. Then, a new but vacant hotel in Siem Reap went up for sale. It seemed perfect; students could live in it and attend classes. But it was too expensive for Teach Cambodia's budding budget. She then thought of building a school in a village that lacked one, but the paperwork, permits, and problems of building trust seemed overwhelming. Further, she needed not only dorms for people to stay but also a laboratory school for the teacher trainees to practice. For this, she needed a community with resources, especially space to teach.

And then, in August 2010, Dr. Wellington was contacted by one of the three villagers who had reopened the school at Sambour village after the Khmer Rouge. They offered to house her program. The teachers were already there and needed training; the director, also an untrained teacher, had visions of creating a progressive school. The government would not help; it had written the village off a few years previously when the school had been struck by lightning and several buildings were damaged. No other NGOs operated in the area.

When Yuri visited, she found a school that was "beyond the end of the road. The road ends, and then you look to the left, and a 100 yards beyond the end of the road, there's the school." The community was desperately poor. Even though Siem Reap was only ten kilometers away, the community was a decent road and a psychic world away. Technically, Sambour's school was an operating government school, but only seven of fifteen classrooms were in session. The two damaged buildings could not be used, and the remaining classrooms had no furniture, no water, no plumbing, no floor, no books or equipment, and no electricity. Cows were sleeping in some classrooms. Some rooms were used for storage; people were sleeping in others. Overall it looked abandoned. At first she hesitated. But then, she thought, the school could be a laboratory school; if they housed the program at the school, and held classes for teachers during the school day, it could function as the professional development school she envisioned. And they wouldn't have to create a group of children to have a practicum. Further, the untrained principal was passionate about making it a good school, and the three villagers who had restarted the school were determined. Wellington decided to give it a try, offering courses at the school.

She spent the next three weeks going daily from Siem Reap to meet everyone in the village because everyone had to give permission for her to start. She met with the commune chief, the school director, and the village chief because nothing could happen in school without permission from the village, nothing could happen in the village commune without permission from the village chief, and nothing could happen in the school without the permission of the school director. In the end, the villagers agreed to turn the building where the locked-up library was housed over to Wellington's program for ten years rent free, to be used for teacher training. She in

PREPARING FOR CHALLENGES IN THE FIELD

turn agreed to train the Sambour teachers for free and promised that Teach Cambodia would renovate the building. That started with moving the animals out and removing the anthills.

At the end of the three weeks, Wellington received a summons from the Minister of Education to appear at his office at 3:00 the next day. She had not contacted the Ministry about the school and her plans earlier, because she and the villagers were still trying to figure out exactly what they wanted to do. But the village chief, in whose notebook was recorded all official meetings, had reported about her to the government, which in turn was reported to the Ministry of Education. She immediately called friends and told them that if they had not heard from her by the next morning, they should call the United States' embassy. Dressing formally for her visit, and expecting a grilling from the Minister, she appeared for her meeting, in which the Minister spoke to her in Khmer through a translator.

"Who are you?"

"I am an educator; I work in schools, helping teachers to do a better job."

"Why did you come to Cambodia?"

"I was asked by many people if I could help train teachers because they had no way to go to provincial training schools here in Cambodia."

"What was your purpose in being here?"

"To train teachers. I have read your national curriculum, and I was impressed with how great a plan it is. I am offering my services to help you achieve the goals of your national curriculum."

"Well, what courses would the teachers be taking in your school?"

"We will teach how to teach literacy, math, social studies, science, how to assess student progress, and how to plan lessons."

"No sociology classes?"

"Sure, we could have that . . ."

"No psychology?"

"Yes, we could have that too."

"What religion will you be teaching?"

"We aren't teaching any religion. We are just trying to help teachers teach."

"What ideology will you be teaching?"

"We don't have a particular ideology; we want to help the Cambodian government achieve its goals for education."

He smiled. "I like this. I'll sign the paper."

Wellington thought, "What paper?? I didn't know there was a paper to be signed."

The Minister then told her that if she would bring him a list of all the courses, who would teach them, and so on, he would "sign" it by putting a stamp and a thumbprint on it. And then, he said again—in English!—that he would sign it.

"Oh," said a surprised Wellington. "So you speak English!"

The Minister smiled lightly, "A little bit . . ." and gave her a post-it with his number on it. "Call me any time."

And she left, thinking, "I guess we are starting a program!"

TIME AND TIMELINE

Timelines

Thinking through in advance how much time will be required for each stage of the research project, and in particular determining how much time each type of data collection will take, is of utmost importance. First of all, IRBs will want to know how much time research participants will be required to devote to the study activities; excessive time away from work, home, the classroom, and other duties can be considered a risk. In addition, since researchers never have unlimited time to spend in the field, it must be carefully allocated so as to avoid waste and the possibility that needed data will not be collected for lack of time. Every project is time constrained, and time is a valued resource. Each field project requires a timeline to guide field implementation scheduling. Creating timelines that detail who will do what, with whom, where, when, and for how long is a useful way to do the initial planning. Chapter 6 in Book 1 displays several kinds of such timelines and timetables used in research projects.

A timeline consists of a series of activities anticipated to be carried out by the researcher, or the researcher with other project staff, scheduled by week, month, or quarter (every three months). Proposals and operational projects require that each and every step of a project be scheduled and associated with project staffing. Well-conceptualized projects will associate activities with the project budget. In this way, research administrators will know in advance whether they have the time, the staff, and the budget resources to carry out the project.

Field studies are time bound depending on the task (an MA thesis, a dissertation, a pilot project, or a larger grant with many personnel). The duration of a project can last from six months to six years or more. Before committing to a project, researchers should determine what specific tasks need to be accomplished in order to complete the study and how long they will take. Judging how long a task will take is not a simple matter. It depends on:

- The experience of the researcher to judge the complexity of the task. More experience improves the estimate
- Conditions in the field. Estimates are generally made based on current conditions in the field (community leadership, access, political and climatic conditions, social and economic resources, for example). If these suddenly change, a task estimated for a month might take four or five months, or might not be accomplishable
- How one task intersects with others. If a task depends on others that must be accomplished first, or at the same time, failure in timely completion of the other tasks may delay the one in question significantly
- Whether or not there are complications with funding, or institutional approvals

It is very important to complete an initial planning timeline and to have others check it to make sure that a project or project component actually can be completed during the time available (Table 3.1).

This timeline is organized by the three study aims—along the left-hand side—and by years and quarters (three-month periods) for the duration of the five-year study across the top. The first aim includes two activities, key

TABLE 3.1 An Example of a Project Timeline for Conducting an Intervention Study in Maharashtra, India

	Year 1				Year 2				Year 3				Year 4				Year 5			
	Q1	Q2	Q3	Q4	Q1	Q2	Q3	Q4	Q1	Q2	Q3	Q4	Q1	Q2	Q3	Q4	Q1	Q2	Q3	Q4
AIM 1																				
KII																				
IDI																				
					Medical case sheet analysis															
AIM 2																				
					Ind				Ind + Comm				Ind + Comm + Group							
					Group				Group + Ind				Group + Ind + Comm							
					Comm				Comm + Group				Comm + Group + Ind							
					Ind				Ind + Group				Ind + Group							
					Group				Group + Comm				Group + Comm							
					Comm				Comm + Ind				Comm + Ind							
													Ind + Comm + Group							
													Ind + Comm + Group							
												Analysis of intervention data								
AIM 3																				
									Mathematical Modeling											

Note – KII: Key Informant Interviews; IDI: In-depth interviews; Ind: Individual Intervention; Group: Group Intervention; Comm: Community Intervention.

informant activities (KII) and in-depth interviews (IDI). The timeline indicates that the key informant interviews will take place in the first quarter of the first year, and the in-depth interviews will take place during the first two quarters. This sequence, the researchers believe, is achievable because only a small number of key informants will be interviewed, and they are already known and listed. Researchers already know that it will be relatively easy through partner organizations to find people newly on antiretroviral treatment (ART) willing to be interviewed about their AIDS prevention needs and concerns.

This timeline (Table 3.2) illustrates three study phases along the left-hand side: formative research; preparation for the intervention and evaluation; and conduct of the evaluation, report writing, and grant submission for a larger grant. The study is to take place over a twenty-four-month

TABLE 3.2 Timeline for Intervention Study to Improve Oral Health Self-Management among Low-Income Older Adults

REVISED 4/2012	2011				2012							
Activity	Sept	Oct	Nov	Dec	Jan	Feb	Mar	Apr	May	June	July	Aug
Phase 1 – Formative Research												
Recruit formative building					X	X						
Develop focus groups guide/FAQs				X								
Recruit focus group participants					X	X						
Conduct focus groups to test approaches						X	X					
Analyze data									X	X		
Refine/adapt/review scales/measures									X	X		
Evaluate feasibility/acceptability										X		
Finalize measures										X		
Finalize protocols for campaign, AMI intervention and evaluation screenings etc.										X		
Phase 2 – Building and Individual Interventions: preparation												
Recruit Buildings								X	X			
Recruit Pro-GOH Campaign Volunteers											X	X
Training and Preparation of Volunteers										X	X	X
Pro-GOH Campaign Materials										X	X	X
Training research assistants and clinical examiners											X	X
Finalize assessment tools											X	

	2012-2013											
	Sept	Oct	Nov	Dec	Jan	Feb	Mar	Apr	May	June	July	Aug
Phase 2 – Building and Individual Interventions: implementation and evaluation												
GOH Campaign Events			X	X								
Baseline assessments	X	X										
AMI-PM intervention		X	X									
3 month follow-up			X	X	X							
Data Analysis						X	X	X	X	X	X	X
Report writing								X	X	X	X	X
Finalization of protocols								X	X	X	X	X
Write U01 application if invited								X	X	X	X	X

period (two years), 2011 and 2012, beginning in September of 2011 and ending at the end of August 2013. The timeline identifies the critical activities in each of the study phases, and when they are to take place. It helps the research team for this modest NIH-funded pilot study to know how many important activities will be taking place at the same time, so as to plan for the allocation of key staff to project tasks. Since the project represents collaboration between ICR, senior housing buildings, and the University of Connecticut, School of Dental Medicine, and will involve dentists, periodontists, and residents, the timeline is critical in order to synchronize and coordinate everyone's participation in critical events related to the intervention, such as oral health screening and oral health campaigns.

These timelines give researchers a clear sense of the feasibility of achieving project aims, staffing required, sequencing of activities, initiation and conclusion of component activities, and when activity levels might overwhelm staff resources. Like budgets, timelines are guides—they are rarely implemented exactly as planned because the "real world" intrudes on scheduling. Delays in funding, approval, access and entry, personnel changes, worker strikes, natural occurrences (e.g., blackouts, flooding, monsoons), and many other factors can delay the best-laid plans. However, timelines assist researchers to plan their studies; at the same time they provide a measure of feasibility and demonstration of capacity for the benefit of funders.

Budgets and Budgeting

Ethnographic fieldwork can be a costly venture, especially when it involves employees/staff and a field team. Expenses may include:

- The cost of living (housing, transport to and within the field site, food, and other expenses)
- Supplies (books, paper, pads, software)
- Equipment (laptop, backup computer battery, camera and video, audio recorder)
- Respondent incentives (money or small gifts, if necessary)

- Staff (e.g., research assistants, translators, data enterers, coders)
- Transportation (car purchase, rental, gas, or bus/train/plane fares)
- Socializing in the field (dinners, entertainment, purchasing others' lunches, tea, etc., in the course of negotiating the study or doing interviews)

Funders always want a detailed budget and a budget rationale. Typical budget categories are personnel, consultants, travel (international, in-country), supplies (including computer software, paper, etc.), equipment and other (rent, administrative costs, incentives, etc.). Some budgets include a category for administrative overhead. In federal research applications this is called *indirect*. Whether overhead, or indirect, both terms refer to the assignment of money to the cost of administering the proposal. Most student proposals are considered training and do not include a lot of indirect or overhead. The field costs are covered in the project budget, and few administrative costs are incurred. Larger proposals may include indirect or overhead costs up to over 80 percent depending on the grant program, and the indirect cost rate that the grantee institution has negotiated with the federal government. State budgets include overhead in the direct cost of a project and do not include additional overhead. Foundations pay between 5 and 20 percent overhead rate over and above the direct cost. Most, but not all, federal agencies pay an institution-negotiated indirect cost rate, but some grant programs (for example, training programs) do not come with indirect. The NIH R25 is an example of a training grant program that includes a flat 8 percent indirect cost (8 percent of the direct cost total).

The example in Table 3.3 uses the budget categories and line items typical of a federal NIH budget. All budgets must be justified. Justifications are explanations of all of the line items within the categories identified as pertinent to the project. For example, the salary and associated costs for each of the key personnel (researchers) listed in a grant must be justified by explaining the salary times the amount of time staff spend on the project, % fringe

PREPARING FOR CHALLENGES IN THE FIELD

TABLE 3.3 A One-Year Budget for a Three-Year Small Grant

Principal Investigator/Program Director (Last, First, Middle): Ms Aruna Lakhani

DETAILED BUDGET FOR INITIAL BUDGET PERIOD DIRECT COSTS ONLY					FROM	THROUGH	
PERSONNEL *(Applicant organization only)*		TYPE APPT. (months)	% EFFORT ON PROJ.	INST. BASE SALARY	DOLLAR AMOUNT REQUESTED *(omit cents)*		
NAME	ROLE ON PROJECT				SALARY REQUESTED	FRINGE BENEFITS	TOTAL
Ms. Aruna Lakhani	Principal Investigator	24	15%	$4582			$4582
To be recruited	Project Co-ordinator	24	100%	$5727			$5727
Ms. Sushma Parekh	MIS Co-ordinator	24	100%	$4582			$4582
Ms. Jane Reuben	Documentation Officer	24	50%		$2291		$2291
To be recruited	Data entry operator	24	100%	$2291			$2291
Ms. Tejal Yagnik	Accountant	24	25%		1718		$1718
To be recruited	4 Outreach workers	24	100%	$9164			$9164
				SUBTOTALS			$30355
CONSULTANT COSTS							$2386
EQUIPMENT computer with printer, tape recorder							$1136
SUPPLIES Stationary, Computer Stationary, Cassettes, CD, Battery Cell, Etc.							$1670
TRAVEL							$4773
PATIENT CARE COSTS INPATIENT not applicable							
OUTPATIENT gynecologist (52 visits) medicines and other surgical expenses services provided by Deepak Medical Foundation							$1241 $1909 $1145
ALTERATIONS AND RENOVATIONS *not applicable*							
OTHER EXPENSES incentive to peers (8 peers) Field transport expenses Translation Training of field staff Report writing							$2291 $2864 $716 $477 $1591
SUBTOTAL DIRECT COSTS FOR INITIAL BUDGET PERIOD						$	22199
CONSORTIUM/CONTRACTUAL COSTS					DIRECT COSTS		$52554
				FACILITIES AND ADMINISTRATIVE COSTS			$4204
TOTAL DIRECT COSTS FOR INITIAL BUDGET PERIOD *(Item 7a, Face Page)*						$	56758
SBIR/STTR Only: FEE REQUESTED							

(benefits and tax), and the activities to be performed by the person that justify the cost. The same procedure applies to other expenses including travel, supplies, incentives, and equipment.

Most projects do not spend funds exactly as initially budgeted for many of the same issues raised in relation to the timeline. However, an initial budget that matches the timeline and associated staffing and other project costs allows researchers to assess the feasibility of the project within the constraints shaped by available financial resources.

PERSONNEL: HIRING AND SUPERVISION

Most ethnographers find that they need help in gaining entry, in learning and managing the local language, in orientation to local cultural practices, and in carrying out data collection, analysis, and interpretation. Such help involves adding staff to a project, which can suddenly grow to be far larger than anticipated. When any additional team members join, it becomes mandatory for the lead researcher or project director/principal investigator (PD/PI) to pay attention to forging a cohesive, well-organized field team. Even when only one other person is added, researcher-directors or principal investigators (PD/PI) suddenly have to address staff interactions in order to develop good working relationships and a common standard of data collection. Working relationships also will vary, depending on the skills and responsibilities of staff members. Most senior researchers do not work side-by-side with field staff on site because they may not have time or the requisite skills (linguistic fluency, for example) to work in the setting, or their time and skills may be needed to meet multiple other project needs. This constrains the time they have for fieldwork. Further, senior researchers (PD/PIs) are usually not supported for enough time on a project to be able to collect data in the field. More probable and realistic team research arrangements and responsibilities include the following:

- An experienced researcher (in a university or research center), working with students who have

had formal training in ethnographic methods but no actual field experience
- An experienced researcher or an experienced senior research team (two or more PD/PIs) working with a field team of academically trained ethnographers
- Experienced researchers working with a team of nonformally trained personnel familiar with the study site who receive on site training in field research methods
- A mix of the above

Hiring the "best" people to create an effective research team can be a "hit and miss" process for anyone. It can be particularly difficult in ethnographic work because of the relationships that ethnographers are expected to develop in the field, and because the work often is "basic research" that does not offer a service of any kind to people in the community. Establishing relationships with key people in the field setting without offering them anything initially other than "rapport" or empathy and interest can be particularly difficult for people who are trained to be service providers (clinicians and social workers), enjoy being in the field, want to know more about "their clients," and want to be helpful to them. They have to find innovative ways of making themselves accepted and well received without resorting to the usual contributions associated with their disciplines.

Research administrators should pay attention to whether or not potential recruits possess the following characteristics when considering hiring members of a field team who do not have formal ethnographic or field research training.

- An inquisitive approach that avoids stereotypes and seeks to learn more about local culture and behavior without trying to change it
- Willingness to learn about all aspects of the research design and process and to go beyond simply the more mechanical aspects of data collection
- Reliability and dependability
- Willingness and ability to work at all hours including evenings and weekends

- Capacity to relate to a broad variety of members (e.g., male/female, older/younger, low/high socioeconomic status) of the study population
- Ability to use and write field notes on a computer in the local language and a global language (e.g., English, French, Spanish)
- Interest in involvement in data analysis and in learning the skills to work with others to analyze the data they collect
- Interest in presenting the results of the study to the community and to professional audiences in the form of interactive presentations, plays and performances, posters, PowerPoint presentations, and orally delivered papers and peer-reviewed written papers

Ethnographers have a responsibility to produce reliable and valid results. They also should be expected to contribute to communities they study and to the well-being and individual career advancement of individuals they work with. One way to do this is through improving the capacity of field staff in the conduct of ethnographic research. As a consequence, once members of a research team are hired, they should be trained in the argument for the research and the research and design questions. The study team should participate in reviewing and modifying them, based on their experience in the study community and professionally. Staff members also should be trained in the approaches to data collection that will be used in the study (key informant interviewing, semistructured interviewing, observation and recording, elicitation techniques, mapping, diagramming, field notes, etc.). They also should learn how to standardize transcribed field notes, engage in the joint development of survey instruments, and to the extent possible, learn about and participate in qualitative and quantitative analysis techniques.

PREPARING FOR THE COLLECTION, TRANSCRIPTION, AND MANAGEMENT OF DATA

Preparing to keep data organized is a key element in readiness for the field. It is likely that the ethnographic research

PREPARING FOR CHALLENGES IN THE FIELD

study will collect a wide variety of data that will need to be organized under the following subdirectories:

1. Key informant interviews, which may be collected over multiple sessions
2. Materials that might include newspaper articles, court, medical, or real estate records or maps, that must be collected and scanned for computer storage
3. Digital and audio recordings and photos (organized into subfiles)
4. In-depth interviews (organized by task and group)
5. Free lists and pilesorts
6. Social network analysis
7. Geographic (spatial analyses)
8. Survey data

Cross Reference: Book 3, chapter 3, on organization and management of field notes

In Book 5, chapters 2 and 3, we have included many ways of organizing different types of field data and field notes during and immediately after a study. Many types of data can be organized in and through special software programs, including: ATLAS.ti, ANTHROPAC, ArcInfo (for spatial analysis), UCINET, and other network analysis programs. Outputs usually are located elsewhere in "results" file directories.

PLANNING FOR WRITING UP PRELIMINARY RESULTS IN THE FIELD

Most researchers think of the field as the place to collect data and the home/office/university as the place to write up the data in the form of papers, presentations, theses, and dissertations. We suggest that ethnographers write up early study findings while in the field, or while study teams are in the field. There are several advantages to in-the-field write-up. The process of initial and early preliminary analysis and write up identifies gaps in knowledge that can be addressed through additional data collection in the field. In addition, writing up early results or initial analyses in the field affords the field team the opportunity to review, critique, and contribute to drafts.

Cross Reference: See Book 3, chapter 3, and Book 5, chapters 2, 10, and 11 for ways of writing up data in the field

Writing up early results and initial analyses in the field also provides the opportunity to share research progress with other researchers who may be in distant places but who feel connected to the study team and the field and would like to offer input on the initial analyses and query the field notes themselves. Sections that can be written up more easily in the field include the description of the population/setting/community, the methodology of data collection, and cases drawn from in-depth interview cases that exemplify the focal problem and its antecedents.

We encourage field researchers to begin to arrange, classify, and code their qualitative data and perform preliminary analyses in the field in accordance with those codes that are central to the study. Again, these analyses can be shared with senior members of the research team and with major advisors for students. Results of write-ups can also be shared with members of the study population through discussion with individual key informants and focus groups as a means of "member checking" and social validation.

SUMMARY

In this chapter and those preceding it, we have seen that ethnographic researchers cannot simply show up in the research or field setting. Instead, they are required to do extensive preparation that includes:

- Identification of a focal topic
- Review of the literature
- Development of a research model
- Defining and measuring domains
- Establishing sponsors and collaborators
- Development of research proposals, timelines, budgets, and human subjects sections
- Receiving permissions by official gatekeepers
- Establishing living situations and personal maintenance
- Hiring research staff
- Planning for preliminary analysis

PREPARING FOR CHALLENGES IN THE FIELD

Conducting any kind of research, whether in the laboratory or in a community, calls for anticipation of the unexpected. Examples of unexpected events are the emergence of new and contradictory findings, or a contextual problem (e.g., a policy restricting some aspect of the research, such as a ban on smokeless tobacco during a study of its use, or a teachers' strike that closes the public schools during a study of formal schooling in Central America) that temporarily or even permanently disrupts the research program. This chapter has attempted to provide insight into the level of preparation necessary to take on the unexpected. In the next chapter, we describe how researchers can develop an initial theory related to their work and display it in a formative model. We outline the reasons for creating formative models and the steps that can be taken to do so.

4

THE ETHNOGRAPHER AS THEORIST: INTRODUCTION TO MODELING MIDRANGE THEORY

> Introduction
> The Ethnographer as Theorist
> Selecting a Paradigm
> Defining Research Questions and Building a Formative or Local Theory
> Summary

INTRODUCTION

Ethnographers seek to generate useful information about culturally patterned beliefs and behaviors as well as reasons that account for behavioral and other forms of diversity within groups. While early ethnographers sought broad-based and comprehensive descriptions of non-Western peoples to highlight differences between theirs and Western cultures, current ethnographic studies depict selected and specific social and cultural domains from within a culture, community, or institutional setting because they view those domains as related to a focal problem. Interdisciplinary partners, funding agencies, institutional review boards, and supervisors/advisors require this more focused research. Planning for the implementation of research most frequently requires the development of a "proposal" as described in chapter 3. It includes an informing theory, a rationale for the study, a review of the literature, a description of preliminary studies, a description of the design and methods, and in some cases even what the results are expected to be. Some ethnographers are committed to a more "ground-up" inductive approach, finding that the demands for specificity in a proposal go beyond their level of comfort and seem to predetermine research results. We argue, by contrast, that this initial stage of conceptualization is vital to the research endeavor and provides a very important blueprint for the study. However, we also caution that the theory, models, methods, and anticipated results should be viewed as preliminary, and that some or many of the elements identified prior to data collection may be shown in the course of the study to require modification or elimination depending on ongoing review of the data in the field. *In other words, conceptualizing the various components of the research process does not "lock in" a study, but rather establishes a baseline against which discoveries can be matched and early hunches and hypotheses evaluated.* For example, Galileo was able to determine that the earth revolved around the sun only when he contrasted his own evidence with existing theory that stated that the sun revolved around the earth. Armed with an initial theory, the discovery of new phenomena provides the ethnographer with an opportunity for discovery of contrasts.

Key point

Some ethnographers are encouraged to enter the field with research questions, but without much formal conceptualization. They emphasize induction as the main way to discover conceptual domains, factors, variables, and other "things" as they emerge through interaction in the field setting. In this book, consistent with Books 1 and 5, we encourage the development of ideas, concepts, and preliminary research models as a key part of a researcher's preparation for field study. Preparatory conceptual development makes explicit the concepts that shape the ethnographer's quest for information. It helps to avoid implicit bias by asking researchers to state their assumptions, beliefs, and even their initial hunches and hypotheses ahead of time. It also creates a starting point for fieldwork. Since many researchers do not have unlimited time to spend in the field, these initial steps in conceptualization help to create a more focused data collection process. Finally, because the formative research "model" is open to exploration and inquiry, it helps ethnographers identify and clarify limitations in their original set of research ideas, hunches, guesses, and hypotheses.

We hold that theory is vital to the research endeavor, especially in ethnography. In the next three chapters we demonstrate how this is true. In fact, the first job of any ethnographer is to organize his or her questions and hunches into an initial or formative theory that will guide first the collection, and later the analysis, of data. However, the concept of *theory* has been so mystified that many novice researchers shun theoretical discussions and argue that theory is neither practical nor comprehensible. It is the intent of this chapter to "demystify" theory and to begin the process of capacitating the reader–social scientist as a "theorist."

In the pages that follow, we walk readers through the steps in the development of a formative research model or guiding theory that is built on what the researcher already knows about the study topic and the field. It constitutes a starting point for the research. In doing so, ethnographers become theorists, responding to the following questions:

- What are the research aims and objectives?
- What research question or questions drive the study?
- What conceptual model will be used for the study?
- Why is a conceptual model needed for the study?
- How will the study be situated within macro theory (see Book 1)?
- What will be the process of developing or identifying relevant "middle-range" theory?
- How will local theory be built?
- What steps will be taken in constructing models (e.g., identifying dependent and independent domains)?

The process begins with the building of a formative (baseline) theory that requires identifying a research problem (that is, a question to explore) and situating it in a research paradigm or "grand theory" (Miles and Huberman 1994, 434). The research questions must be clearly formulated; a set of initial concepts, hunches, and hypotheses must be identified; and the resulting framework used

Cross Reference: Research paradigms are discussed in Book 1, chapter 3

as a starting position for an ethnographic research project. In this process, theory has two primary functions: the first is the development of research questions, hypotheses, and proposed causal models; the second is that it provides an initial set of concepts that help to make sense of empirical data and to interpret results.

THE ETHNOGRAPHER AS THEORIST

At its simplest, theory involves the ordering of facts in a meaningful way. In other words, theory is what makes sense of a series of observations, statements, events, values, perceptions, and correlations. Theory is the glue that aggregates facts into a hypothetical description of a given time and place that can then be used to predict/explain events in another time and/or place. The degree to which theory fails to explain adequately, and to predict events in a given place and time, is the degree to which initial formative theories will require modification and further testing. Such modifications occur naturally, both during and after the period when ethnographic data collection takes place. Thus, rather than referring to "a" theory to be tested, ethnographers as well as other scientists prefer to talk about theory building, and to view the construction of theory as an ongoing and interactive process of discovery, testing, interpretation, observation, retesting, and interpreting once again. This is a little like calibration and recalibration of quantitative models in science, where the association among linked variables in a model is tested and retested against reality to arrive at the most accurate prediction/interpretation at that moment. Ethnographers, like other system scientists, know that the communities they study are dynamic; they change as a result of the interaction of many forces over time, as well as the deepening of researcher knowledge. Thus, all models must be "recalibrated" or adjusted to accommodate new knowledge and new situations as a study proceeds.

The Use of Existing Theory

Every social science field has existing theories that seek to explain human behavior across time and location.

In Book 1 we have referred to these "larger" theories as guiding paradigms or macro theories. Leading members of a discipline or historical figures who sought a global model for explaining and predicting human behavior developed these theories. They then have been refined by others or modified in significant ways (Kuhn 1996). Students spend considerable time learning these theories, and faculty frequently subscribe to a particular theory and promote it with their colleagues and students. Paradigmatic theories such as ecological, behavioral, interpretivist, or critical theories, however, are like highway signs in Charleston, South Carolina, that point to New York. They are not helpful in figuring out which of the many possible different pathways will actually get a traveler from Charleston to New York. They are too abstract or general to explain much at the local level. Even "midrange" theories that could be developed based on these larger paradigms may not be very useful when applied to a local field situation. Further, the existence of these theoretical models may inhibit junior researchers who erroneously believe that only disciplinary leaders can *generate* theory, while everyone else can only *apply* it. This situation is further exacerbated when students and junior members of the discipline are not trained to contribute to those grand theories or to construct theory that applies to their own local situation. *Every researcher must be able to generate theory that structures the design and methods they use, and to modify that theory to interpret the empirical data they collect.*

Cross Reference:
See Book 1, chapter 3, for theoretical paradigms that offer guidance when approaching a study topic

Key point

EXAMPLE 4.1

TRANSFORMING FACTS INTO THEORETICAL PROPOSITIONS

Researchers observed that over half of the young people who participated in the Summer Youth Research Institute at the Institute for Community Research, individuals who are chosen for their average or less-than-average school performance, enjoy and are skilled at some form of artistic expression (observable fact). The Summer Youth Research Institute offers a six-week program of training-in-action research methods, including in-depth interviewing, pilesorting, mapping, survey research, and visual documentation involving a variety of different social, literacy, and mathematical skills. We also noted that *the motivation of these teens, and their academic performance in the program, were higher* when *dance, music, drawing, and photography were integrated into the curriculum.* The preceding sentence is a low-level theoretical statement involving an hypothesized relationship between the three italicized ideas: *motivation, academic performance,* and *dance, music, drawing, and photography . . . into the curriculum.* We have created a preliminary or formative theory that hypothesizes that *school underachievers will do better at school if art is incorporated into their curriculum.* The preceding sentence is a midrange theory of intervention that could guide an intervention approach.

Theory is no more and no less than description. Pelto and Pelto state that "description and theory are not different kinds of logical processes" (1978, 7). All description *is* theoretical because it involves a selection and reorganization of observations of reality into a set of descriptions that seek to predict or explain future reality. Thus, a theory attempts to take textual and/or quantitative data and organize them into a description or model of individual or group behavior in a specific time and place that predicts what people will do. This description or model can then be tested at another time, or in another place.

Miles and Huberman review other ways in which theory is described in the literature (1994, 434). Theory can consist of:

- A "map aiming to generalize the story or stories told about a case" (Rein and Schon 1977, as cited in Miles and Huberman 1994)
- A predicted pattern of events to be compared with what is actually observed (Yin 1991 as cited in Miles and Huberman 1994)
- A network of nonhierarchical relationships expressed through statements defining linkages among concepts (Carley 1991). This idea is closely related to the idea of creating research models for discovery discussed in chapter 5 of this book on operationalizing
- A model consisting of a series of connected propositions that specify relations, often hierarchical among components (Reed and Furman 1992), an idea that

ETHNOGRAPHER AS THEORIST

is related to modeling associations described in chapter 6 of this book
- A diagram of a set of relationships between certain factors that are believed to impact or lead to a target condition.

Another way of thinking about a good conceptual model is that it:

- Presents a picture of the situation at the project site
- Shows assumed linkages between factors affecting the target condition
- Shows major direct and indirect relationships affecting the target condition
- Presents only relevant factors
- Is based on sound data and information
- Results from a team effort (http://portals.wi.wur.nl/msp/?page=1240)

An example of a "shell" that can be used to create a model by filling in the blanks is displayed in Figure 4.1. It is a linear "model" that reads horizontally from left to right and vertically from top to bottom, following the directionality of the arrows.

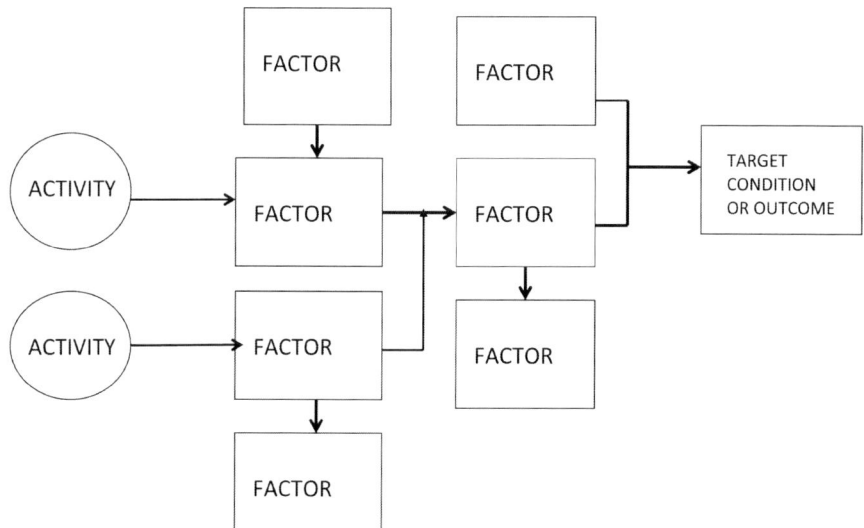

FIGURE 4.1   A Shell to Use for Linear Modeling

 **Key point** *Theory is important because it helps us to know what to consider and what to leave out of our observations.* It *never* is possible to observe all the human behavior and human-environment interaction that flows before our eyes in a field setting. Nor can we capture everything we are able to observe in our field notes and records. No matter how detailed the description of a community meeting, it is highly likely that as much will be left out as was included, simply because too much is happening for one or even several people to observe at the same time. Information left out of the description will probably include much verbal and nonverbal communication, behavior that appears to be idiosyncratic, interactions between dyads and in small groups, kinetics or body movements, and many aspects of the context. Sometimes researchers might be able to observe or hear these elements but intentionally may edit them out as less relevant to the research topic; sometimes they are missed completely (i.e., unseen or unheard), and on other occasions, they may be observed and noted but not recorded. If we were recording with audiovisual equipment, we still would miss some activity because the camera(s) were not aimed in the correct direction.

Even if it were possible to record virtually everything (and it never is, regardless of the recording medium), the facts (the observations) gleaned from a single community meeting are useful only in terms of their ability to explain and predict focal aspects of future community meetings or events in the community. Thus, in field notes, the description of a single community meeting is theoretical to some degree, because it selects from the jottings and initial write up information that is most relevant to understanding the interactional dynamics of group members and how the meeting activities relate to other ongoing aspects of community or institutional life. The description may also be a first-level attempt to describe the purpose of community meetings and how and why they are conducted across time in a single place. Such a "low level" theory based on a single description must, of course, be compared with and evaluated against many community meetings in this same location over time to assess whether the fundamental elements of community meeting conduct, and the links among these meetings and other aspects of community life revealed in the first or subsequent observations, are in fact predictive of other such meetings in the future. If they do, they can be said to constitute a *pattern*.

Theory thus helps the ethnographer to identify what to look for, ask about, and omit in the process of data collection. Theory initiates the research process by helping the ethnographer to deal with the observation of real-world complexity in the field setting, and it ends the research process by facilitating reorganization (modification) and elaboration of the initial formative theory and its explanations by virtue of concepts that have been identified and verified through repeated observation in the field. We refer to this as an iterative or recursive process. This process may appear to be complicated at first, but in our experience, people from every walk of life can readily come to understand and build theory. Theory building is, in fact, what people do in everyday thinking when, for example, they examine the weather, determine the probability of rain, and decide whether or not to take an umbrella. Or when they examine all the factors involved in leaving one job and taking another, and ultimately, decide to stay where they are. Thus, theory building is a human endeavor without which people could not come to learn, understand, and construct/reconstruct their daily life in cultures and settings.

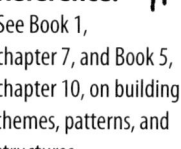

Cross Reference:
See Book 1, chapter 7, and Book 5, chapter 10, on building themes, patterns, and structures

Cross Reference:
See Book 1, chapter 7, and Book 5, chapter 4, for a more information on the iterative or recursive process in the analysis of qualitative or mixed methods research

EXAMPLE 4.2

REFORMULATING THEORY IN THE NATIONAL TEEN ACTION RESEARCH SUMMER TRAINING INSTITUTE

Youth engaged in research training in the 1998 Summer Youth Research Institute of the Institute for Community Research determined through personal experience and group discussion that a number of contextual-, social-, and individual-level factors predicted dropping out of school. They identified as salient the domains of SELF-ESTEEM and PREGNANCY (individual level) and INSTITUTIONAL RACISM (community/societal level) and explained why they thought these three domains were predictive of leaving school. To test these midlevel theoretical statements, they further defined and collected data from their peers on self-esteem, pregnancy, and institutional racism in relation to dropping out of school from surveys, pilesorts, and interviews. When they analyzed their data and discussed it in relation to their original model, they decided that, based on their interview data, two domains were still missing. These were the PHYSICAL ENVIRONMENT, which they guessed had a direct effect on dropping out of school, and MEDIATING ATTITUDES/FEELINGS through which other factors were filtered so as to lead toward or away from dropping out. The youth then modified their original model by adding these two new domains.

A similar group of youth studying factors associated with sex at an early age went through the same process, eliminating a number of unrelated domains and focusing mainly on self-esteem and the effects of the media on early initiation into sexual behavior.

To summarize, theory is a tool of science. Theory:

- Clarifies the research questions and their relationships
- Defines the kinds of data to be collected or narrows and helps to define the range of facts to be studied
- Offers a conceptual scheme by which relevant phenomena are systematized, classified, and interrelated
- Summarizes facts into empirical generalizations and systems of generalizations
- Is open at all points to explicit modification and reformulation when components are shown to not be robust (predictive)
- Predicts facts
- Points to gaps in our knowledge

A number of philosophers of science and social science have provided schema that deal with "levels of abstraction," linking research paradigms as broad lenses for viewing the world at one end of the continuum with local "facts" sifted through the lens of the researcher, the research topic, and the initial theoretical model or blueprint at the other (Kuhn 1996; Kaplan 1964; LeCompte & Preissle 1993). Table 4.1 offers one way of thinking about this continuum. This table combines the conceptual and analytic frameworks discussed in Book 1 and presented by Pelto and Pelto in their 1978 text.

In this scheme, Pelto and Pelto define modes of observation as operationalizing concepts; *propositions* as state-

TABLE 4.1 The Continuum of Levels of Abstraction

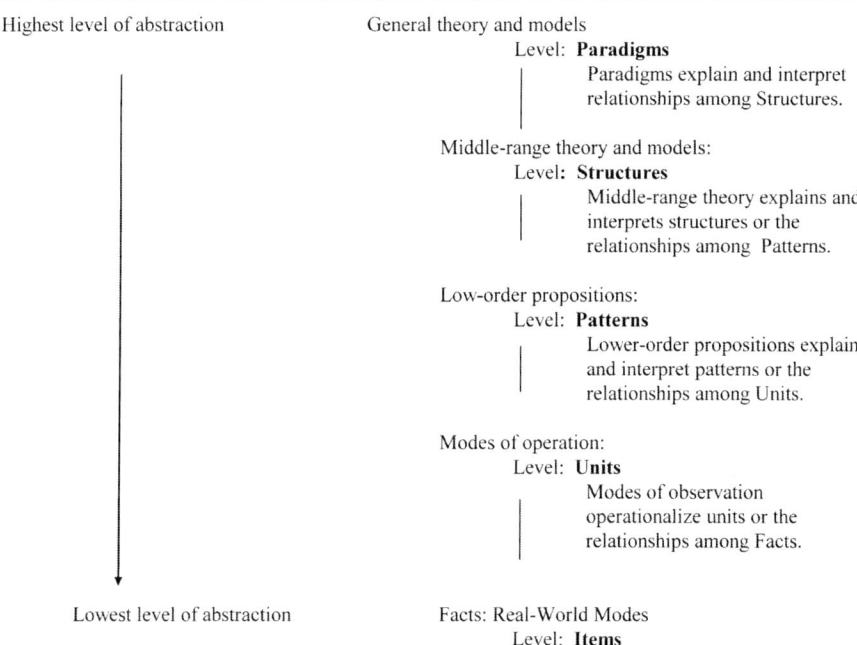

ments about the interrelationship among concepts; and *theories* as systems of interrelated propositions (Pelto and Pelto 1978). LeCompte and Schensul (2010; 2012) define modes of operation as operationalizing units as organized patterns of association among observed *facts* or *items*; lower-order propositions as explaining or interpreting patterns or relationships among *units*; middle-range theories and models as explaining and interpreting structures characterized by relationships among *patterns*, and general theory as explaining and interpreting associations among *structures* linked to *paradigms*. As ethnographers, we can move up and down the ladder of abstraction when we collect data and generate preliminary hypotheses in the field—from "facts" to units, patterns, and structures, and the other way around.

This scheme offers important guidelines for the conduct of ethnographically informed social science research, suggesting that researchers begin by selecting a paradigm and building a formative model.

Cross Reference: See chapter 6 in this book for a discussion of operationalizing concepts

Cross Reference: 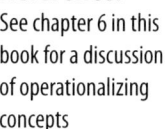 See Book 1, chapter 7, on data analysis and Book 5, chapters 5 and 8

SELECTING A PARADIGM

Cross Reference:
See Book 1, chapter 3; for a summary see Figure 3.1 in Book 1

We recommend that ethnographers begin a study by choosing an initial paradigm such as those we outlined in Book 1; for example, ecological, critical, positivist, or interpretivist paradigms. They may also use other paradigms that we do not mention here because they are used less often in anthropology and sociology, for example, scripting theory (Gagnon 1991; Tomkins, 1987) or social learning theory (Abrams and Niaura 1987; Bandura 1979, 1986). While these broad, macro, or "grand theoretical" frameworks are not predictive as such, they serve the important function of raising questions and providing perspectives that can begin to structure more locally situated theories. It is important for ethnographers to think through the relationship of their research to these frameworks, as well as why the choice is appealing to them. Thinking about their reasons for choosing a particular theoretical paradigm will identify important personal perspectives that can both guide and explicitly reveal bias. They also will identify assumptions that are embedded in the paradigm that may be incompatible with some of the researcher's goals and perspectives.

The choice of research paradigm is just the beginning of the long process of sifting through the many options ethnographers have and the decisions they make with respect to the initial models that guide their research. The researcher's socioeconomic status, ethnic membership, gender, familial structure and dynamics, disabilities, neighborhood and residence, religion, and many other factors contribute to the selection of a research question, paradigm, research model, and preference for data collection methods. We also have discussed how self-reflection can be helpful with regard to the selection of a paradigm and research model. Self-reflection helps researchers to:

Cross Reference:
See Book 1, chapters 1 and 3, and chapter 2 in this book

- Make explicit to themselves and the population under study the underlying assumptions, ideas, and perspectives affecting the research design
- Locate, for users and funders, the intellectual traditions within which the research is situated
- Formulate research blueprints, guides, and models that help to organize data collection

TABLE 4.2 Examples of Paradigms and Associated Guiding Concept Choices

PARADIGM	GUIDING CONCEPT
Critical theory	Stigma
Phenomenological	Failed identity
Ecological	Cultural conflict
Network	Social influence
Scripting theory	Sexual scripts

Once ethnographers have chosen an initial theoretical paradigm and clarified their reasons for doing so, they should select one or more **guiding concepts**. Guiding concepts form a link between the paradigm selected and the formulation of local or midrange theory. The following are some examples of paradigm and guiding concept choices that researchers have made:

The guiding concepts researchers select should be consistent with their paradigm of preference (Table 4.2). The next steps in the process are defining research questions and creating a formative or local theoretical model.

Definition: Guiding concepts form a link between the paradigm selected and the formulation of local or midrange theory

DEFINING RESEARCH QUESTIONS AND BUILDING A FORMATIVE OR LOCAL THEORY

Often qualitative researchers begin with a series of questions about a topic in which they (or their partners or both) are interested. For example, resident and building managers identified depression in older adults living in senior housing as a problem. They pointed to the fact that some residents never emerged from their apartments, and in one building a resident committed suicide. The study mounted by the Institute for Community Research and the Institute of Living, a psychiatric institute serving older adults in the Greater Hartford area, began with the following questions:

- Is depression a significant problem among residents of senior housing?
- What are the differences between people who seem depressed and those who aren't?
- Is there something about the buildings that fosters higher or lower levels of depression?

- What are the possible causes of depression among residents?
- Are there variations by ethnicity, age, or other characteristics in rates of depression?
- What kinds of problems or barriers do residents face in getting access to mental health treatment for depression?
- What kinds of treatment do they get, and does type of treatment make a difference in outcome?

The funders in this case were interested in barriers to treatment. But the study committee, consisting of researchers from the two institutions and a committee of geriatric clinicians and other mental health advocates, decided that there were other antecedent questions that could be asked. Once the study was funded, the questions were formulated into a study model based on what the team already knew from work in the buildings and the literature on depression in older low-income and minority adults. The study model that emerged is shown in Figure 4.2.

Returning to models and midrange theory, there are two main reasons for formulating initial ideas and ques-

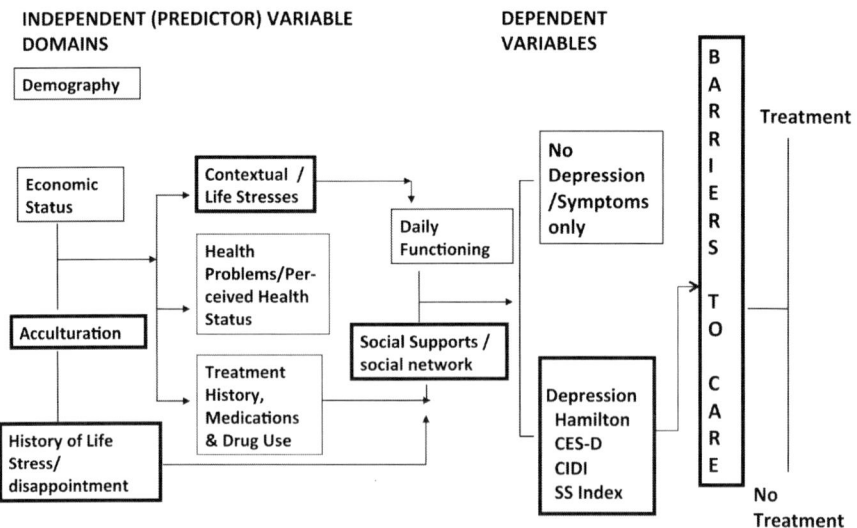

FIGURE 4.2 A Model of Predictors of Depression and Access to Care in Older Low-Income Adults in Senior Housing

tions into a middle-range theory as expressed through a formative theoretical model. First, doing so makes explicit the nature of the research objectives. At the same time, a middle-range theory along with a model provides a set of ideas that can be compared to empirical results on an ongoing basis and systematically modified. Before we begin, we must clarify what we mean by the term *formative theory*, explain why we refer to it as *middle-range theory*, and demonstrate how these two terms, though related, are different. Formative refers to the idea that research models are start points. A **formative research model** is an initial set of concepts linked by hypotheses that provides a start point in guiding field research. Formative models always change in response to data. They summarize what the researcher knows through brief introductory forays into the field, a review of the literature, and a close reading of secondary data. These activities, such as those that Yuri Wellington engaged in during her initial two years in Cambodia, allow the researcher to arrive at an initial set of questions related to a set of conceptual domains that are linked through initial hunches and hypotheses.

Middle-range theory starts with a problem or question to be addressed in a localized population in one place and time and emerges from empirical observation as a set of assumptions or locally applicable theoretical principles to be tested. The concept of middle-range or midrange theory was coined originally by sociologist Robert Merton, who saw it as an antidote to what he considered to be the widespread use of theoretical concepts that were so broad as to be useless. With reference to his own discipline, sociology, Merton noted that "sociology will advance in the degree that its major concern is with developing theories of the middle range" (Merton 1967, 9). **Midrange theory** aggregates disparate local empirical observations into a cohesive system of concepts that can be explained through the construction of explanatory hypotheses (Boudon 1991; Pelto and Pelto 1978, 2–7; Trotter, Schensul, and Kostick 2012). Midrange theories are formative when they develop around initial observations, and then become refined and consolidated over time through the accumulation and integration of additional data. They are finalized when they are able to

Definition: A formative research model is an initial set of concepts linked through hypotheses that is useful as a start point in guiding field research. Formative models always change in response to data

Definition: Midrange theory aggregates disparate local empirical observations into a cohesive system of concepts that can be explained through the construction of explanatory hypotheses

achieve a high level of predictive capacity and when they are explained based on evidence gathered in the field, using commonsense explanations that are tested against the literature on the one hand, and against the understandings of members of the study community on the other. Both formative and summative theories should make sense to study participants and the study community.

There are a number of sources for the development of local or middle-range theory. They include:

Cross Reference: See Book 1 for discussions of the importance of local meaning and perceptions with reference to framing, analyzing, and interpreting the results of a study; see also Book 5, chapter 4

- The researcher's life experience, interests, attitudes, and values
- Popular, local, or "emic" conceptions of the phenomena
- Studies documenting research results with comparable populations and issues
- Intervention, service, or policy needs of partner organizations
- The expressed views, needs, and interests of members of the local population
- Secondary data available on the study population (e.g., census data, surveys, studies conducted by other researchers, archives)

The development of a research topic and an associated middle-range theory requires some prior knowledge of the community or setting within which the study is to be done, or other setting similar to it. This knowledge may be gained through reading relevant literature; reviewing media or other popular conceptions of the topic; mulling over ideas generated through discussion with research partners, intervention organizations, or members of the research community in which the study is to be done; and prior personal experience of the researcher (cf. Stringer 1996). ***We do not recommend beginning an actual study with open-ended participant observation without going through the above steps and the initial stages of the modeling process as we describe it in the following pages.***

Key point

Once the research topic has been identified, researchers may move in one of several directions:

ETHNOGRAPHER AS THEORIST

- Description
- Association
- Evaluation

Description

First, researchers may wish to describe the phenomena better, more deeply, or in a more comprehensive and systematic fashion (cf. Carley 1991; Stringer 1996, 93, Figure 5.1). Many ethnographic studies focus on obtaining a comprehensive qualitative understanding of a specific problem or question. For example, ethnographers may wish to understand variations in the ways in which parents, teachers, and students conceive of "growing up" in the preadolescent years between the ages of nine and twelve and whether gender is associated with differences in their definitions, values, beliefs, and socializing practices related to "growing up." In other words, do they believe that gender makes a difference in how preadolescents "grow up" and what behavior is expected of them? This descriptive approach is best suited for the very early stages of research in which the ethnographer is asking a basic question about the boundaries, characteristics, and component parts of a single cultural "domain"—in this case, GROWING UP. As the research proceeds, the ethnographer will begin to want to know what connections this domain has with other domains in the group under study.

EXAMPLE 4.3

UNDERSTANDING THE "PROBLEM"—IDENTIFYING SEXUAL RISK BEHAVIORS AMONG YOUNG WOMEN IN MAURITIUS

Researchers Schensul, Schensul, and Oodit focused their work in Mauritius on the increasing opportunities for sexual behavior and exposure to sexual risk of young, unmarried women who were working outside the home for the first time, in the factories of the Export Processing Zone in the capital city of Mauritius. One early question had to do with when and where young men and women might meet and where they might have opportunities to be alone for romantic encounters. Interviews with key informants in clubs and with teachers, taxi drivers, hotel desk attendants, and people selling products on the many beaches of Mauritius and with shop crew managers and bus drivers suggested that young men and women could meet in many settings without supervision, including bus stops, in clubs and bars, at after-school "tuitions," at work breaks, on the beach, and at small hotels. This provided the context for exploring the behaviors that they engaged in that might expose women to pregnancy and both men and women to STIs and sex risk (Schensul, Oodit et al. 1994; Schensul, Schensul, Oodit et al. 1994)

The following model (Figure 4.3) illustrates how we can diagram a situation in which description is the goal. It shows that the researcher has identified four domains that might be connected with the problem to be studied, in this case, school performance. The ethnographer interested in this project will use ethnographic tools described in Books 3 and 4 to figure out the meaning of school performance, how it is enacted in and out of school, and what seems to be associated with it based on what respondents say and observation suggests. There are no linear or "causal" associations among elements in this model. It is "configurational"; that is, the elements interact with each other in complex ways that must be uncovered with more study.

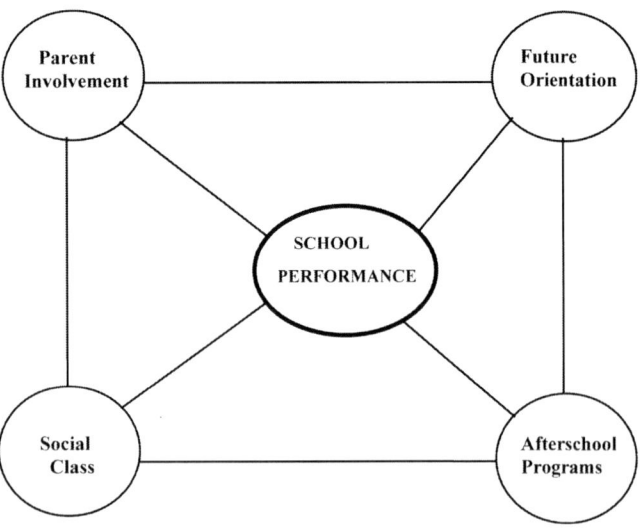

FIGURE 4.3 Description of a Phenomenon

Association

In addition to learning more about the problem or topic, ethnographers seek to identify what might be associated with it (cf. Reed and Furman 1992). Association is always important, but it becomes especially important when ethnographic work is carried out for evaluation purposes or to promote intervention or service programs. Researchers want to know what factors are likely to be associated with behaviors that people (researchers and others) might like to change. Association is what determines the most important independent domains for intervention and prevention to impact on the problems. If, for example, adolescent pregnancy or parental involvement in early education programs is the topic of interest, a researcher may be interested in what is associated with either one of them. Knowing what is associated with adolescent pregnancy can help to prevent it. Knowing what is associated with parental involvement in early education programs can help to encourage it.

Cross Reference: See Book 7 for a discussion of the application of various approaches to intervention, service delivery, and structural change

Another way of approaching association is to consider the influence of the problem selected on potential consequences for the study community (Stringer 1996, 95, Figure 5.2). For example, researchers might like to investigate the proposition that teen pregnancy influences or even predicts positive consequences, such as higher levels of self-esteem and school performance. Or, as illustrated in another youth study, teens in the Institute for Community Research Summer Youth Research Institute examined the relationship between the age of initiation of sex (which they termed "sex at an early age") and future life outcomes. They predicted that sex at an early age would result in low self-esteem, dropping out of school, and the probability of having children at a young age (J. Schensul 1998).

Evaluation

Many ethnographers are asked to conduct ethnographic descriptions or assessments of programs. Sometimes these programs are guided by middle-range theories that program developers have selected from those available in the literature. More often than not, programs are guided by unarticulated local theories of "how things work" which produce program goals and objectives. The program goals and objectives constitute the "standard" or baseline, against which ethnographers are asked to collect and compare their data. But the theoretical underpinnings are not clear. One major contribution ethnographers can make to program evaluation is helping program staff to generate their own program theory (Guba and Lincoln 1989).

EXAMPLE 4.4
FINDING AN INTERVENTION THEORY THROUGH EVALUATION

In an ethnographic and quantitative outcome evaluation of a fourth-grade diet, nutrition, and gardening program in a working-class town in the northeastern United States, interventionists introduced classroom and summer outdoor garden projects and a nutrition curriculum with interactive classroom exercises and homework. The curriculum was introduced to four treatment classrooms, and the results were compared to those obtained from four control classrooms that received the standard fourth-grade didactic nutrition and diet curriculum.

As ethnographer and outcome evaluator, Jean Schensul collected data on program events, classroom process, teacher instructional style, student products, and pretest and posttest scores on a knowledge-based assessment instrument. The experimental study design anticipated better outcomes on posttests administered to children in the treatment versus the control classrooms. The results of quantitative analysis of test scores demonstrated that improvements in the treatment classrooms were significantly higher than in the comparison classrooms. A deeper examination of outcomes in the treatment classrooms, however, showed that performance increased in only two of the experimental classrooms. A review of the ethnographic data collected through process evaluation in treatment classrooms showed that instructors in the two high-achieving classrooms used interactive, cooperative learning techniques, small-group work, and facilitated learning. Teachers in the other two classrooms favored didactic instruction and lectures. Theories of experiential and cooperative education helped to explain why the positive results concentrated in two of the four experimental classrooms.

SUMMARY

In this chapter we have made the case that theory is important in ethnographic research. We have also suggested that when proposing or describing their work, most ethnographers start with an initial set of concepts and assumptions that are drawn from their own experience, including experience in the study field as well as from the literature. Many ethnographers begin with questions about the topic they are interested in studying. In this chapter, we suggest that theory formulation really begins well before the formal period of data collection. The "formative model" is a local model that generates a local midrange theory. It provides a readily accessible way of summarizing what is already known or believed to be known about a *local* situation. In the next chapter, we describe in more detail just how to go about generating a formative model.

5

CONSTRUCTING FORMATIVE RESEARCH MODELS

- Introduction
- Developing a Formative Model: Top Down/ Bottom Up Construction
- Dependent and Independent Domains
- Diagramming and Modeling the Formative Research Model
- A Note on Generating Hypotheses
- Summary

INTRODUCTION

Research is conducted to investigate a problem, to describe a phenomenon and understand its relationship with other phenomena, to illuminate relationships between and among phenomena, to document processes, to solve problems, to develop the informational foundation for promoting approaches to change, and for many other reasons. All research needs to start with a direction, or some sense of the phenomena to be studied, however vague and undefined. In applied research these phenomena usually are social or environmental problems such as teenage sexuality, school dropouts, drug abuse, poor nutrition, smoking, low agricultural productivity, environmental pollution, poor access to water or transportation, high levels of unemployment, educational inequities, poverty, or limited health care provision. In order to study such phenomena, researchers start by creating a **formative research model**. A formative research model spells out the initial relationships among elements or concepts with regard to the topic to be studied. An excellent way to display "how things work" is to create a diagram that represents relationships among elements in a model. Such diagrams have a number of advantages:

Definition: A formative research model spells out the initial relationships among elements or concepts with regard to the topic to be studied

- They are a tool for getting ideas out of the researcher's "head" and on to paper so that they can be seen more concretely and objectively.
- They provide an opportunity to engage colleagues who can provide more effective feedback when they see the ideas visually.
- They compel researchers to envision relationships among domains that are less clearly specified in study questions.
- They draw on existing knowledge that is sometimes underused in the initial stages of formulating a study.

DEVELOPING A FORMATIVE MODEL: TOP DOWN/BOTTOM UP CONSTRUCTION

Constructing an initial explanatory formative model involves more than a unilinear and unidirectional process; it is, in fact, a complex, multidimensional cognitive process, one in which the human brain engages daily and at many levels. Human brains can receive information about phenomena in one place and one time and generate a local or "grounded theory" (Corbin and Strauss 2008) about those phenomena; they also can imagine a grand scheme or paradigmatic theory for, for example, human behavioral motivation, such as B. F. Skinner's "behaviorism," or Charles Darwin's theory of evolution that explained biological development. Human brains also can envision stepping into a research situation at a midpoint by suggesting, for example, that two cultural domains seem to be linked; researchers can then generate ideas about the characteristics of the domains and the reasons behind their linkages, both inductively and deductively. This constitutes constructing middle-range theory. Researchers even can start with a single domain or topic and rapidly expand their thinking horizontally and vertically. The set of guidelines described here for constructing formative or midrange theory produces diagrams or representations that simplify the complex phenomena

CONSTRUCTING FORMATIVE MODELS

that humans can conceptualize. These guidelines frame a system of thinking—a systematic approach to organizing thoughts, understandings, and beliefs—at the start of a study. Such theory generation involves the following conceptual and cognitive processes:

- Moving horizontally from a single phenomenon to identify related phenomena that remain at the same conceptual level or level of abstraction
- Moving vertically from bottom up (inductively) or top down (deductively)
- Moving up and down vertically in a recursive or an iterative way

In the pages that follow, we discuss each of these processes.

Moving Horizontally from a Single Phenomenon to Identify Related Phenomena at the Same Conceptual Level

By **conceptual level**, we refer to "large" or encompassing cultural domains deemed important in a study. **Moving horizontally** means considering the relationship among domains, factors, subfactors, and variables that are at the same level of abstraction, and related to one another.

Cross Reference: See Book 5, chapter 4, "Recursivity, Induction, and Deduction: Moving between Levels of Abstraction" for further discussion of these processes

Definition: By conceptual level, we refer to "large" or encompassing cultural domains deemed important in a study

Definition: Moving horizontally means considering the relationship among domains, factors, subfactors, and variables that are at the same level of abstraction, and related to one another

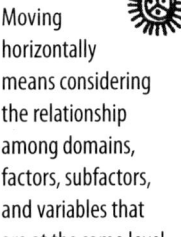

EXAMPLE 5.1

DEFINING DOMAINS HORIZONTALLY: RELATED DOMAINS AT THE SAME CONCEPTUAL LEVEL

In a study of women admitted to the hospital with complications due to abortion in Mauritius, the dependent domain was TYPE OF SERVICE SOUGHT FOR ABORTION (self-induced, "back street," and private medical practitioner). Researchers believed that domains at the same level of complexity or abstraction, such as FAMILY COMPOSITION and CONTRACEPTIVE HISTORY, also influenced the choice of abortion service (Schensul, Schensul, Oodit et al., 1994).

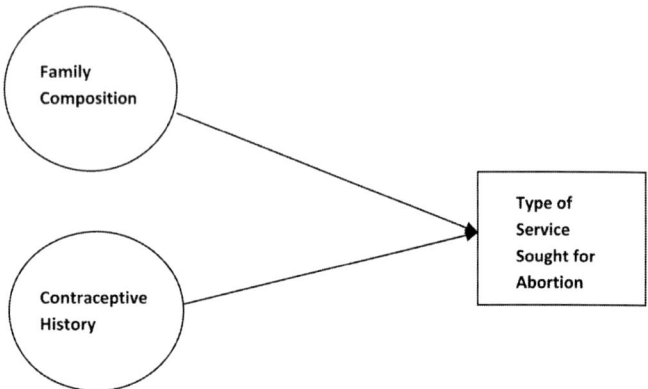

FIGURE 5.1 Defining Domains at the Same Horizontal Conceptual Level

This set of ideas is presented diagrammatically in Figure 5.1.

> **Definition:** Moving vertically means to organize phenomena cognitively from lower- to higher-order concepts, or from the most abstract to the most concrete, and vice versa

Moving Vertically

Moving vertically means to organize phenomena cognitively from lower- to higher-order concepts, or from the most abstract to the most concrete, and vice versa. Example 5.2 addresses the process of moving from very concrete to more abstract phenomena, or from the bottom up.

EXAMPLE 5.2

AN EXAMPLE OF MODELING FROM THE BOTTOM UP

> **Cross Reference:** See also Book 5, chapter 5, on "Ways to Begin Analysis" and Book 5, chapter 6, "Specific Coding And Initial Quatification"

Stephen Schensul consulted on a study conducted by Professor Tilak Hettiarachchy at the University of Colombo, Sri Lanka, on sexual risk among young women working in the free trade zone factories in that city. A major question in this study related to the ways in which women were exposed to risk. The factories were isolated behind high security walls and barbed wire fences. Women workers lived in protected dormitories housing up to ten women in each room. The young women workers, estimated at close to sixty thousand and primarily from rural areas, moved from work to the dormitories in large groups to avoid the "dangers" lurking between the "safety zones" of the dormitory and the work site. These dangers included groups of young and older men who attempted to interact with the young women and to gain access to their earnings, and jewelry and dress shops seeking to relieve them of disposable and nondisposable income.

The research team observed women moving quickly through the "danger zone," weaving their way with varying degrees of success among the groups of men, shops, restaurants, and other stands that filled the zone. As a result of these observations, the researchers created a domain they named EXPOSURE, meaning exposure to opportunities to meet men during the course of the workday and evening. Further observation of the "exposure" process suggested that there were subsets of exposure, which they called *factors*. One factor involved relationships formed with people who could engage them in potentially risky activities, including sex. The researchers called this factor "relationships." A second subset involved events where they could meet people and engage in intimate behaviors. This factor was called "activities." The team also observed that some young women rushed through the "danger zone," while others took their time, talking to people and shopping. They labeled this domain TIME SPENT OUTSIDE THE FACTORIES AND THE RESIDENCES (i.e., in "unprotected zones"). More ethnographic exploration produced information about each of these factors. They were further divided into subsets or variables (things that varied—either by presence-absence or in degree from high to low). "Relationship" variables included "having a boyfriend or not" (yes/no), and "having friends involved in risky behaviors" (yes/no or number of such friends). A variable situated under activities was "going to musical evenings" (yes/no)—events in the evening that were outside in quasi-public places where young men and women could meet and sit together. A variable within the factor "time spent outside safety zones" was "the amount of time taken in the walk between work and home." These variables were identified through observations and interviews as part of the formative model. They were later quantified for use in a survey to test the model on a larger sample of respondents. Using these and other variables measured in the survey under the domain EXPOSURE, the study was able to demonstrate quantitatively what the formative model suggested qualitatively—that is, the EXPOSURE domain was a strong predictor of sexual risk (Hettiarachchy and Schensul 2001).

Moving Up and Down Vertically in Recursive or an Iterative Way

 **Cross Reference:** See Book 5, chapter 4, on recursivity

Shifting from higher or more abstract concepts to lower-order concepts and back again involves moving from the domain to the variable level, and then returning to revise the domain level. Example 5.3 illustrates such recursivity.

EXAMPLE 5.3

AN EXAMPLE OF RECURSIVITY IN VERTICAL MODELING

Motivated by the global HIV/AIDS pandemic, the notion of "sexual risk" has been a driving force in the research of Schensul and Schensul. They began their study of HIV risk in Mauritius with a domain referring to the consequences of premarital sex (sexual risk), and within that domain a factor called "risk of HIV/AIDS or other sexually transmitted infection." In discussions with the staff of the Mauritius Family Planning Association and project staff, they were able to learn more about the consequences of sexual risk. They found that HIV and sexually transmitted infections (STI) were last on the list of concerns and fears among Mauritian youth. Young women who were interviewed in-depth added other consequences or negative outcomes of premarital sex that they felt were more important than HIV. These included pregnancy, loss of boyfriend, loss of virginity, loss of reputation, emotional and psychological problems, physical pain, reduced marriageability, negative feelings about men, abortion, STIs, and alienation from the family.

In this study the Schensuls began with the domain CONSEQUENCES OF PREMARITAL SEX and one factor, "sex risk," which included the variables "risk of HIV/AIDs" and "risk of STIs." They diagrammed this initially as in Figure 5.2.

Schensul and Schensul then reorganized their model at the factor level, creating a list of factors. They located each of the specific risk categories identified by the women as follows: *medical risks* (e.g., pregnancy/loss of virginity/abortion/STI; physical pain); *social risks* (reduced marriageability, loss of boyfriend, alienation from family, loss of reputation); and *psychological risks* (negative feelings about men, emotional and psychological problems) (Figure 5.3).

CONSTRUCTING FORMATIVE MODELS

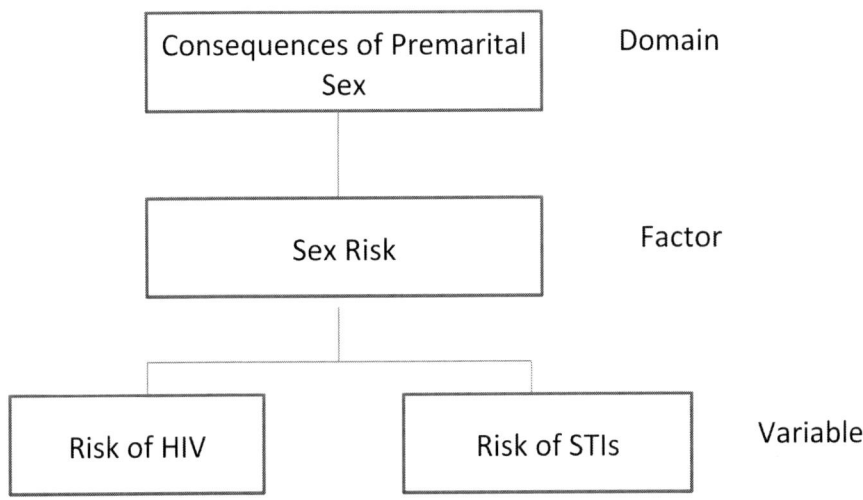

FIGURE 5.2 An Initial Draft of a Model

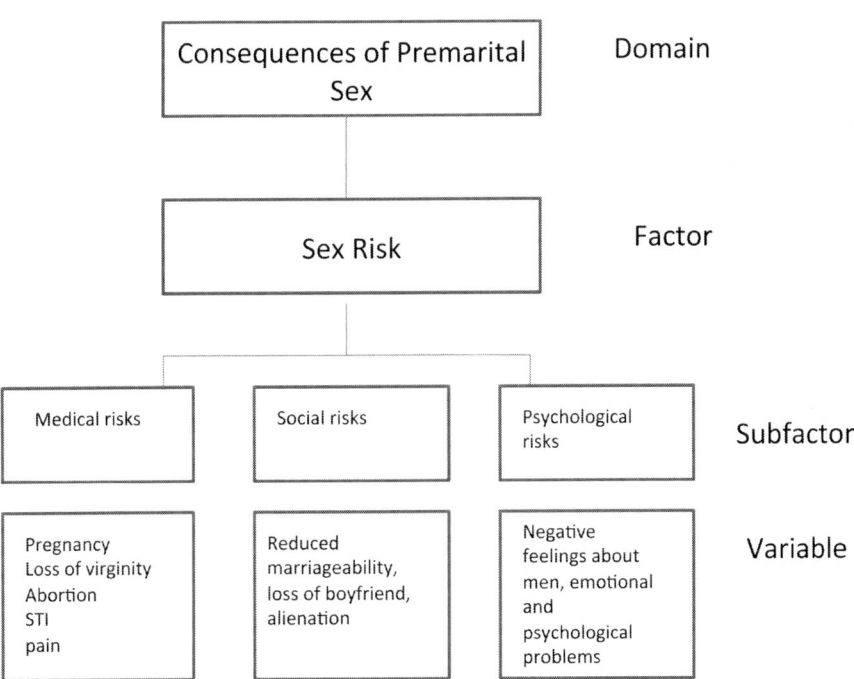

FIGURE 5.3 A Revised Version of a Vertical Model

DEPENDENT AND INDEPENDENT DOMAINS

The process of model construction at the DOMAIN level is the most abstract level of conceptualization. A model at this level will consist of three types of domains: (1) the dependent domain; (2) the independent domains; and (3) mediating domains. The **dependent domain** is the issue or problem to be studied. The **independent domains** are the domains that are believed to be associated with or even to predict the direction of the dependent domain. The **mediating domains** are the domains that "mediate" or stand in between the independent and the dependent domains and are influenced by the independent domain(s) and in turn, influence the dependent domains. The term *dependent domain* refers to a domain that changes in response to prior variations in other domains. Sometimes this is termed an *outcome problem* or particular situation that needs to be explained. Another way of describing the meaning of "dependence" in the dependent domain is to suggest that a change in the dependent domain is "caused" or influenced by changes in the independent domains. For example, tutoring programs (independent domain) are believed to improve student school performance (dependent domain); however, the obverse is not likely to be true.

Independent domains precede dependent domains in terms of linear "causality" and/or timing. Changes in independent domains are not affected by changes in the dependent domain. An independent domain logically precedes a dependent domain, and change in the dependent domain is in response to changes in the independent domain. For example, exposure to media through television and movies (the independent domain) is believed to have a negative influence on adolescent drinking behavior (the dependent domain) because it portrays positive images associated with the use of alcohol (hypothesis). Changes in exposure to the media, however, are not likely to occur because of changes in adolescent drinking. Instead, other factors such as parental control over the use of television or an increase in the cost of videos and movies are likely to change adolescent media exposure. In cross-sectional research (research that takes place at one point in time), it is difficult to know which is the independent and dependent variable since no time factor (one event preced-

Definition: The dependent domain is the issue or problem to be studied. The independent domains are the domains that are believed to be associated with or even to predict the direction of the dependent domain. The mediating domains are the domains that "mediate" or stand in between the independent and the dependent domains and are influenced by the independent domain(s) and in turn, influence the dependent domains

Definition: A dependent domain is one that changes in response to changes in other domains

Definition: An independent domain logically precedes a dependent domain, and change in the independent domain is not in response to charges in the dependent domain

ing the other) is involved, and the directionality of the effect could go either way. Thus logic and qualitative data, rather than time, determine the directionality of such an effect.

Mediating domains stand in between, or intervene in, the "normal" or direct relationship between independent and dependent domains. That is to say, they are affected by the independent domain(s) and in turn affect the dependent domain. So the independent domains no longer have a *direct* effect on the dependent domain. Instead, it is a "mediated" effect. For example, a mother's health status prior to pregnancy (the independent domain) affects the health of the infant in the first year (dependent variable). Pre-pregnancy health status may be defined in terms of many variables, including height for weight, age, and blood pressure. Health of the infant in the first year may be defined by such variables as birth weight, sickness, and weight for age. Researchers can theorize—with good evidence from experience and prior studies, and from observation from the field—that the better the mother's pre-pregnancy health status, the better will be the child's health in the first year of life. Prenatal care may be available for at least some mothers, and it may improve the health of these mothers and the fetus during pregnancy. Researchers can hypothesize that effective prenatal care will result in better infant health regardless of the pre-pregnancy health status of the mother. In this case, *prenatal care* is a mediating domain, intervening in or changing the relationship between the mother's pre-pregnancy health status and the health of the child in the first year. This relationship could be diagrammed as shown in Figure 5.4.

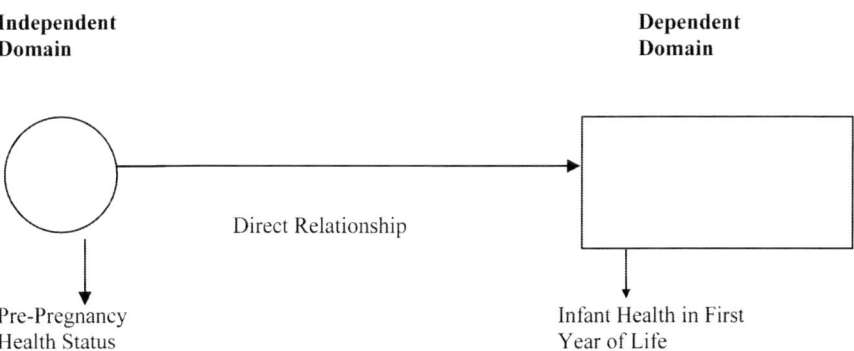

FIGURE 5.4 A Direct Relationship between Independent and Dependent Domains: Pre-pregnancy Health Status and Infant Health

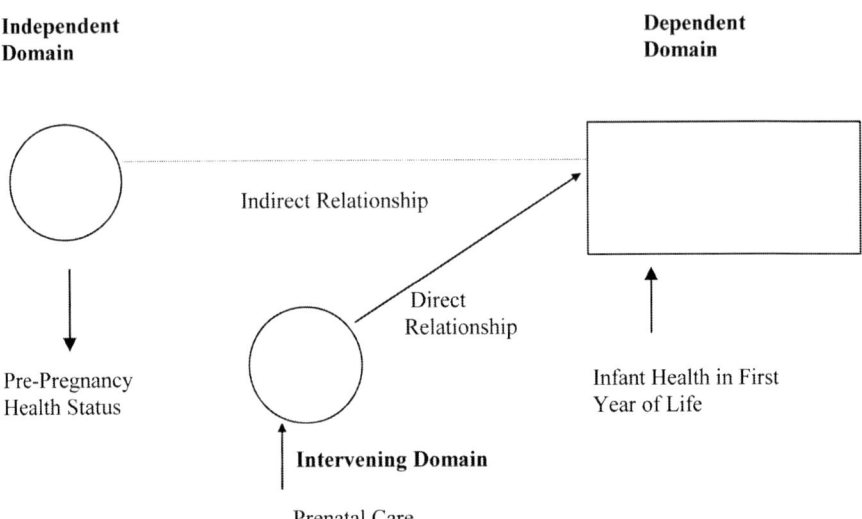

FIGURE 5.5 Prenatal Care: Intervening Domain Affecting Infant Health Status

Figure 5.4 depicts a direct relationship between the independent and the dependent domains; as the mother's pre-pregnancy health declines, infant health declines. This relationship is described as *direct*. When we add the mediating domain PRENATAL CARE, which becomes available *after* the mother becomes pregnant (e.g., after her pre-pregnancy health status is evaluated), we represent the relationships as in Figure 5.5.

In the diagram in Figure 5.5, the domain PRENATAL CARE stands between or mediates the direct relationship between the independent and dependent domains. It may reduce, eliminate, or even add to the effect of the mother's pre-pregnancy health status on the health of the child. The assertion as modified in Figure 5.5 now states that the more the mother is involved in prenatal care, the better the health of the infant. The assertion could also state that the addition of prenatal care to pre-pregnancy health status regardless of the health of the mother will improve the health of the infant.

Constructing the Dependent Domain

The construction of a research model at the domain level usually starts with delineation of the dependent domain—the phenomenon that researchers want to study. The study's research topic is reflected in the selection of the dependent domain. For example, researchers may be interested in sexual-risk behavior among adolescents (a population defined by age and developmental stage) in urban communities (particular type of location or place) in the United States. They begin by looking for a domain that corresponds to societal concerns, delimits the phenomena to be studied, and includes multiple indicators or manifestations that can be described and measured. Thus, they define sexual risk behavior as any intimate contact between two people that could lead to or result in the transmission of sexually transmitted disease and/or pregnancy. Kissing may be an indicator of sexual risk behavior, depending on the context. For example, in Sri Lanka if an unmarried woman engages in kissing, a very intimate behavior, it is a signal that she is willing to engage in intercourse. Sneezing without covering the mouth, on the other hand, would be an indicator of "flu risk behavior" defined as communication between two or more people that leads to the transmission of the flu virus, but not a sexually transmitted disease. Clearly bounding what is or is not within the dependent domain is crucial to the description of a problem, the theory development about the problem, and the measurement of its correlates or impact. Dependent domain selection should be congruent with the interests of the researcher, with the concerns of the population under study, and with the mission of funders or potential funders of the study. The problem or phenomenon that constitutes the dependent domain also should be one that shows variability. School achievement, use of tobacco products, fibromyalgia severity, exposure to environmental toxins, or dropping out of school are all examples of potential dependent domains that show variability, from low to high levels or amounts. Presence or absence may also define variability. The following examples illustrate dependent domains that show variability.

EXAMPLE 5.4

IDENTIFYING VARIABILITY IN THE DEPENDENT DOMAIN

Researchers Schensul, Schensul, and Zegarra were interested in factors associated with evolution of household construction in evolving shantytowns in the northwest quadrant of the city of Lima, Peru. They observed that in very new developments, there was no variation in the type of household construction, since when a newly migrated group seized public land and settled on it illegally, they constructed identical temporary residences, each consisting of four straw-matted walls, roofed with a straw mat supported by bamboo poles. However, over time, the city of Lima and the urban municipality in which the settlement was located granted the residents title to the land, and individual households gained possession of their homesteads. At that point, families gained residential stability, and more sturdy household construction flourished. What emerged over time both within and across legitimized settlements was a wide variety of household construction types, as measured by the presence or absence or degree of presence of electricity, piped-in water, latrines, glass windows, and durable (concrete and brick) construction of walls and roof.

Figure 5.6 illustrates the first step in developing the diagram for a study model. The dependent domain is located on the right side of the page.

Sometimes there are two dependent domains. For example, in a study of depression in older adults, the first dependent domain identified was "access to mental health care." A second dependent domain became "mental health status." The study team was fortunate to be able to create a study that could simultaneously examine predictors of mental health status and predictors of access to mental

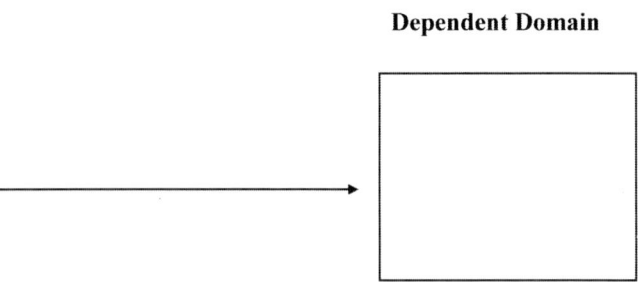

FIGURE 5.6 A Diagram Illustrating the Placement of the Dependent Domain in a Formative Research Model

CONSTRUCTING FORMATIVE MODELS

health care. In some instances these were linked, because some of the same predictors of poor mental health status (depression/anxiety) were linked to limited access to mental health care (Diefenbach et al. 2009).

The next task at this point is to identify independent domains that are associated with, believed to bring about, or to predict the dependent domain. The first step in identifying these independent domains is to construct a series of **hypotheses**. Hypotheses are statements that propose a relationship between two concepts such that by knowing the value of one of the variables, the value of the other is predicted. This predictive link is referred to as a bivariate relationship, or a relationship between two variables. Another way of explaining hypotheses is that they are if/then statements. For example, "If grass is watered it will grow"; "If dogs are leashed, streets will be cleaner"; "Women who work have more influence in their families"; "A better sense of personal well-being is associated with larger friendship networks." Hypotheses can start as observations of what has occurred, or as "hunches" or best guesses about what has occurred or will occur, given a specific situation or set of factors. They can evolve from or can be derived from theoretical models developed *a priori* or in advance, and they can be generated from the field situation itself. The formative conceptual model developed in the preparatory phase can be translated into a series of hypotheses at various levels (explanations for why and how domains are connected, or how factors and variables within and across domains are linked and why).

In a study of human reproductive health, one hypothesis might be the following:

> The higher the education level (the independent variable) of women in the community, the smaller the family size (the dependent variable).

This association can be stated in the reverse.

> The lower the education level (independent variable) of women in the community, the larger the family size (dependent variable).

Definition: Hypotheses are statements that propose a relationship between two variables such that by knowing the value of one of the variables, the value of the other is predicted

Cross Reference: See Book 5, chapter 9, Table 9.1

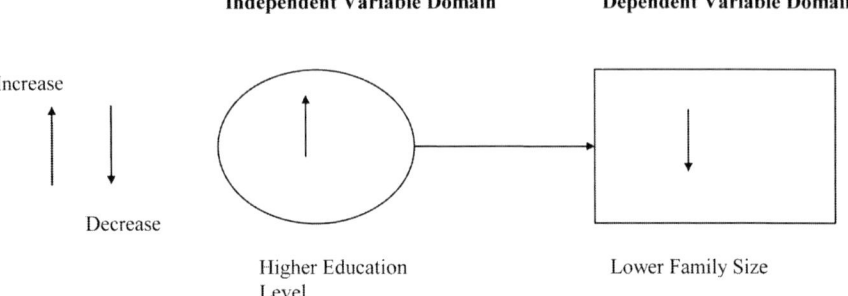

FIGURE 5.7 An Inverse Relationship between an Independent and a Dependent Variable Domain

In both cases, the association is inverse (high leads to low in the first association), or low leads to high (in the second expression of association). Figure 5.7 illustrates this inverse relationship between the independent and dependent variable domains.

It is clear, however, that complex societal issues are the product of multiple forces rather than single factors. Keeping in mind this complexity, the hypothesis might be reframed by adding another independent variable, "woman's income," as an additional predictor of family size. We would then state the argument as:

> The higher the woman's income, and the higher the education level of the woman, the smaller the family size.

This can be diagrammed as shown in Figure 5.8.

Social researchers have conceptualized the links among variable domains as a web of interrelationships in which independent domains are connected to both the dependent variable and to other independent variables. Thus the following hypothesis showing a *direct* relationship between education and income, both of which are *inversely* associated with fertility, might be posited:

> The higher a woman's education, the higher her income, and the higher are both, the smaller the family size.

The diagram that would result from the hypothesized interrelationships among these variables would look like that in Figure 5.9.

CONSTRUCTING FORMATIVE MODELS

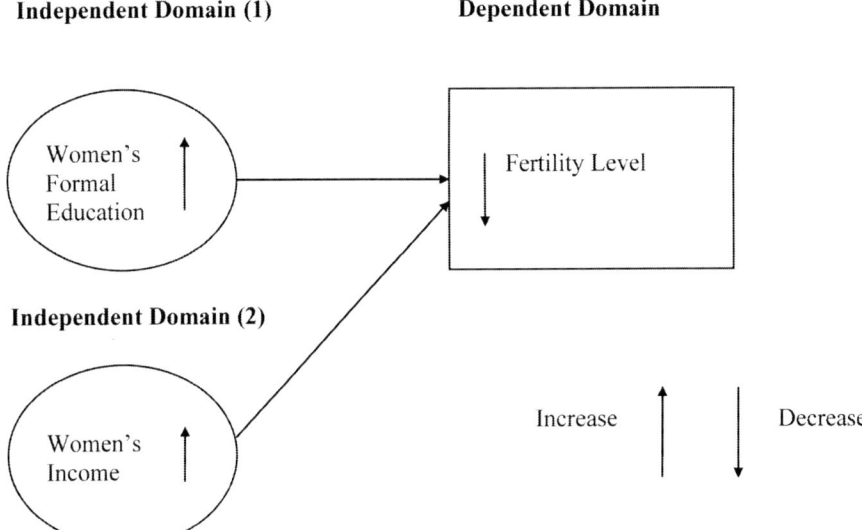

FIGURE 5.8 Another Inverse Relationship Introducing a Second Independent Variable Domain

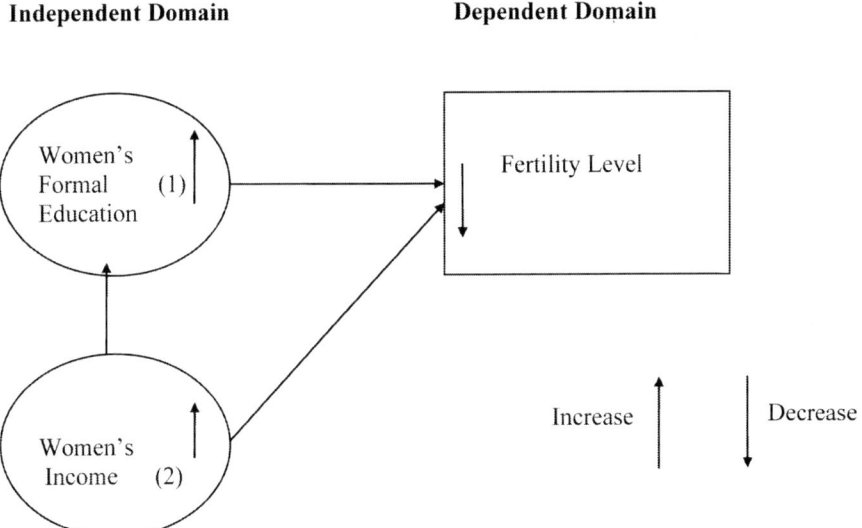

FIGURE 5.9 Relationships among Independent Variable Domains

These processes illustrate how researchers create the beginnings of a research model. It is important to keep in mind that cultural domains are "packed" with or include many variables, and the direction of the relationships among domains will not be known at first. Thus it is possible simply to hypothesize that associations, or relationships, exist without predicting their direction. In a more elaborate design, with a larger number of independent variable domains based on more field experience, a careful literature review and multiple discussions with key informants and research partners, the associations might resemble Figure 5.10, which illustrates the formative research model with which researchers Schensul, Silva, Schensul, and de Silva began their work on AIDS risk in Sri Lanka. The model included three independent (startup) domains—FAMILY, PEER, and SCHOOL—and one dependent domain—SEXUAL BEHAVIOR.

In the Sri Lanka formative research model represented in Figure 5.10, the single lines indicate predicted significant relationships among domains; the dotted lines indicate anticipated weak or nonexistent relationships among domains. The hypothetical associations were numbered.

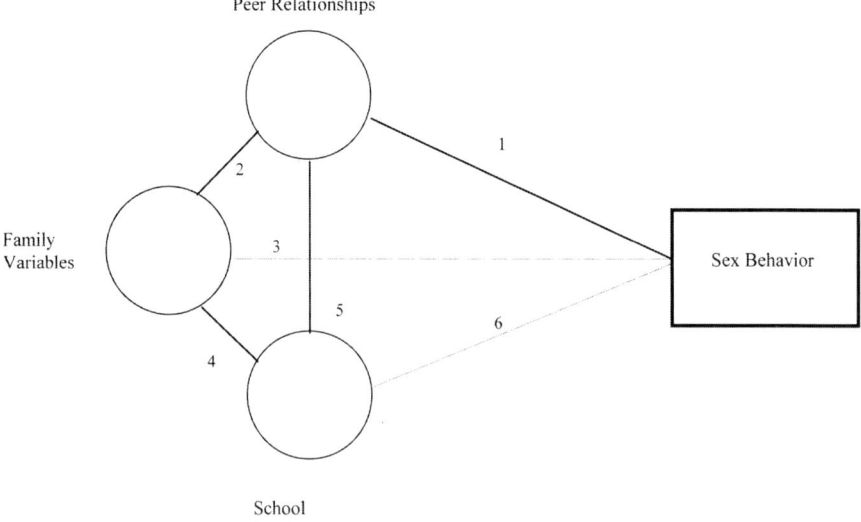

FIGURE 5.10 A Formative Research Model Showing Hypothesized Strong and Weak Relationships among Independent and Dependent Variable Domains

CONSTRUCTING FORMATIVE MODELS

1. Peer relationships have a *significant* effect on adolescent participation in sexually risky behavior.
2. Family variables have a *significant* effect on an adolescent peer relationships.
3. Family variables have *little relationship* to adolescent sexual behavior.
4. Family variables have an *important effect* on adolescent performance in school.
5. School performance is *significantly related* to peer relationships.
6. School performance has *little or no relationship* to participation in sexually risky behavior.

The diagram and the set of six hypothesized relationships describe a more complex model involving the three main domains that constitute the world of an adolescent: FAMILY, SCHOOL, and PEER RELATIONSHIPS. Families have an effect on the degree to which adolescents participate in school and who their friends are. School performance is associated to some degree with peer relationships (for example, the more time spent studying, the less time for friendships and leisure-time activities). However, the model shows that researchers anticipated that the strongest association in the model would be between peer relationships and risky sex behavior. They believed that the other domains would be indirectly related to risky sex or not related at all. The hypotheses, the diagram, and the narrative are three important components of the conceptual framework for any research. They can, however, be generated in any order that is comfortable and that responds to the complexities of the research process. In other words, domains, factors, and variables and the hypotheses that link them can be added at any time. The narrative can be expanded; domains can be constructed with reference to data collected from the field site and relevant literature, and a rationale added for each additional domain. For example, the researcher may have an opportunity beforehand to conduct focus groups or in-depth interviews with a number of adolescents, leading to a narrative description of the situation. Later on, this description can be transformed into a series of hypotheses that then can be incorporated into a model such as the one portrayed above.

Cross Reference: See chapter 1 of this book and Book 5, chapters 8 and 9

Cross Reference: See Book 3, chapter 8, for more information on focused group interviews

Cross Reference: See Book 3, chapters 6 and 7, for ways of conducting different types of in-depth interviews

Searching for Independent Domains

One of the strengths of ethnographic research lies in the ability of ethnographers to identify independent domains that have not been previously recognized as associated with the dependent domain. These domains can be identified through the following:

- In the initial phases of unstructured observation and key informant interviewing
- Through a review of other research related to the choice of dependent domain
- By using ecological, critical or other guidelines to help researchers identify and examine contextual factors and "sectors" likely to be overlooked in other fields

The process of searching for independent domains and diagramming a theory-informed model has several main components:

- Consideration of the existing conditions in the study community, for example, the nature of the residential community, characteristics of school and school system, the health care delivery system, the workplaces and transportation systems, or governmental policies that might influence daily life
- Characteristics of families and households, including household socioeconomic status, employment situation, family values, family dynamics, child rearing, and socialization practices
- Knowledge, attitudes, and behaviors related to the dependent variable (for example, in the case of family planning or HIV, knowledge of contraception, attitudes toward premarital sexuality, condom use behavior)

The ability to search for and find new and relevant independent domains is a major strength of the ethnographic approach. The following example illustrates how new independent domains can be located.

CONSTRUCTING FORMATIVE MODELS

EXAMPLE 5.5

LOCATING NEW INDEPENDENT DOMAINS

Dr. M. W. Amarasiri de Silva of the Department of Sociology of the University of Peradeniya, Sri Lanka, was evaluating the **impact of mosquito repellent-impregnated bed nets** (the independent variable) in an endemic malarial area in southern Sri Lanka. The project recorded little reduction in the **incidence of malaria** (the dependent variable). Unstructured observation and interviewing led him to examination of sleeping patterns in this area. Most of the houses consisted of one room, with a mother sleeping with young children and a father sleeping on his own. In order to have some privacy, the couple was required to leave their bed nets and go outside, into the garden, frequently at a time when the mosquitoes were at their most active. In this case, observation revealed that household "crowding," which forced people to seek privacy in malaria-infested outside locations, was a more important factor in exposing people to malaria than not using bed nets inside the house.

Casting a "broad net" is a real advantage in finding important independent domains.

The following example, drawn from Margaret LeCompte's study of an arts program in a middle school, shows how various sectors of the school community offered theoretical propositions that helped to guide the formulation of the research design for an evaluation study.

EXAMPLE 5.6

HOW STUDY PARTICIPANTS CAN HELP TO IDENTIFY THEORETICAL PROPOSITIONS

LeCompte and her associates began meeting with the principal of Centerline Middle School, and its teachers and parents in the community in April 2005, to identify research questions and problems in which the various constituencies involved in the program were interested and to see if they had developed any theories about why the program upon which they were embarking would be effective.

Parents had ideas about the relationship between student achievement and student attitudes toward school; they supported the Arts program because they thought it would increase their children's enthusiasm for school and consequently, their achievement.

Domain: ARTS PROGRAM → children's **enthusiasm for school** → children's **achievement**

The **teachers** firmly believed that the arts provided a kind of discipline in both thought and practice that would help the students do better in their regular schoolwork.

Domain: ARTS DISCIPLINE → improved **schoolwork performance**

Factor: cognitive discipline; behavioral discipline

Both the **principal** and the **parent group** supported the program because they hoped it would increase enrollment at the school and fend off efforts by the school district to close it.

Domain: ARTS PROGRAM → increase **student enrollment** → **school preservation**

The **principal** and **key non-arts teachers** also wanted to make sure that the arts program would enhance the climate of the school as a whole and that it would not interfere with what they perceived to be an already effective academic program.

Domain: ARTS PROGRAM → improve school climate → retain **effective academic program**

LeCompte and her research team used these ideas to develop an evaluation design that considered the effect of the Arts Focus program on Centerline Middle School as a whole, and a set of research questions that focused both on the characteristics of the instruction offered by the arts teachers and the links between specific arts instructional practices and attitudes the students had about school, themselves, and how they engaged with intellectual ideas.

Considering Independent Domains in the Target Populations' Context or Environment

Many ethnographers and other social scientists focus only on independent domains that have to do with the target population or community, forgetting about broader social, structural, or policy issues that could be important in a study. Categorizing independent domains into two main components—organization and "population"—forces researchers to consider both components when developing a formative research model. This approach involves classifying all independent domains into two groups: (a) structural, institutional, or "organizational" factors: those domains related to institutions, organizations, or policies; and (b) population or individual/family domains. For example, domains in the institutional/organizational group may include:

Cross Reference: See chapter 8 for more information on how to construct a systems model

- Governmental laws
- Regulations
- Services
- Nongovernmental organizations at any level
- Local health or educational service system

Thus, when considering research on health care access, it is useful to focus not only on institutions providing services (e.g., hospitals, community health centers, health maintenance organizations, group and private practices) but also other institutions that may affect how they deliver it (e.g., Social Security, Medicare/Medicaid, or other public-funding guidelines, insurance companies, and provider advocacy groups). Aspects of these institutions will constitute important components or domains in a study of health care accessibility.

Focusing on "populations" or "communities of people" suggests the following possibilities:

- Those who experience a specific educational or health problem (and their families)
- Those at greater risk of acquiring the problem (and their families)
- All those with a common health or education problem
- The above cohorts or groups defined by demographic characteristics such as age and ethnicity
- Occupational groups (for example, union organizers, tanners, teachers, plumbers, and construction workers)
- Employees at a common worksite (urban industrial workers in Port Louis, Mauritius)
- Individuals and families that reside in the same sociogeographic area

Cross Reference: See Book 1, chapter 5, especially Table 5.1, for a discussion of ways to identify populations

Readers will find a broader discussion of ways of identifying study populations in Book 1.

Domains of relevance to populations could include any number of arenas of knowledge, attitudes, behaviors, social relationships, psychological states, sports or other types of activities, dietary patterns, food preparation, and material style of life, among others.

EXAMPLE 5.7

CONSIDERING ORGANIZATIONAL AND POPULATION DOMAINS IN A STUDY OF ADOLESCENT HEALTH AND SEXUAL RISK

In the Sri Lanka study conducted by researchers Stephen and Jean Schensul, K. Tudor Silva, M. W. A. de Silva, and others, independent organizational domains with the potential for contributing to sexual risk in adolescents included:

- Access to adolescent-oriented **health services**
- Level of service **provider training** on adolescent needs and approaches
- **National policies** on sex education and fertility control influencing the distribution of contraceptives and sex education in schools
- **School attitudes** toward sex education

If they had not considered the "organizational" sector, researchers might have ignored these important domains in considering what might affect youth sexual risk attitudes and behavior. Within the *youth population*—the target population for the study—domains believed to be relevant to influencing risky sexual behavior and exposure to AIDS included the following:

- Knowledge **of protective behavior; sexuality**
- Youth **attitudes and values toward sexuality**
- **Boyfriend/girlfriend relationships**
- **Peer types** among youth
- **Youth activities** with their peers

Cross Reference: See Book 3, chapters 3, 4, and 5, on exploratory data collection

The selection of the independent and the dependent domains underpin the study's formative theory and guide the process of exploratory data collection discussed in chapters 3, 4, and 5 of Book 3.

At the same time, the results of unstructured interviewing and observation allow ethnographers to identify new domains, eliminate domains originally included in the formative research model, and identify and refine the variables that are included in the domains. Through these means, the ethnographer discovers and examines realms that others are not likely to consider.

By now it should be obvious that the development of formative theory is an interactive process that identifies the most valid and locally appropriate domains while using methods that extend the opportunity to do so.

DIAGRAMMING AND MODELING THE FORMATIVE RESEARCH MODEL

Once the relevant domains have been identified, the next step is to organize them into a formative research model that expresses relationships as a function of closeness of association. Guidelines for locating independent and mediating domains in relation to one another in a diagram are the following:

- Independent domains with closer and more direct relationships to the dependent domain as indicated by time or logical linkage should be located closer to it
- Independent domains with closer associations with one another should be clustered together
- Only some independent domains should be directly related to the dependent domain; others should be indirectly related or not at all
- Only some independent domains should be directly related to each other

The variables can be located in a two-dimensional grid in which the dependent domain is placed in the far-right column(s); the far-left column then includes background and antecedent domains; and the middle columns include independent domains that are direct precursors to the dependent variable. Clusters of domains can crosscut these columns. The template for the organization of the initial

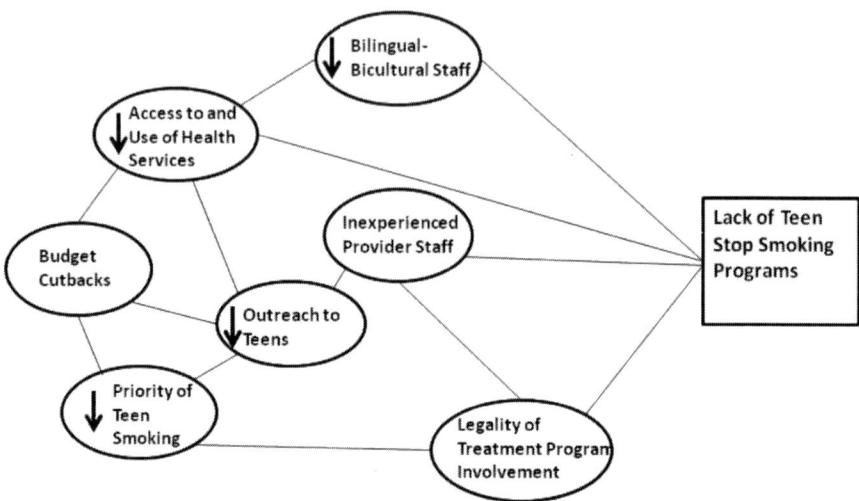

FIGURE 5.11 Constructing a Model using Organizational Domains Believed to Be Associated with the Dependent Domain: Lack of Teen Stop-Smoking Programs

model on a two-dimensional surface could be represented in the diagram in Figure 5.11, which includes the primary organizational domains associated with the absence of smoking cessation programs for teenagers.

The objective of this first stage of modeling is to identify as many independent domains as the researcher can hypothesize to be directly or indirectly related to the dependent domain. Some researchers refer to this as a *conceptual model,* in contrast to an *operational model,* which includes only the domains and variables to be studied, rather than all of the domains that can be thought of as relevant. Researchers should conduct the same exercise with respect to community or population level domains. One such result is portrayed in Figure 5.12.

The next step in the generation of the research model is to consider the system and population models and identify the most important dependent variable that will be the focus of the investigation. It might be either of the two identified in the figures above—"stop smoking programs" or "adolescent smoking"—or a composite domain. Subsequently, a process of prioritization and inclusion/exclusion will produce the **best set of independent domains** possible early on in the study, thus creating its formative or initial operational model. As a general rule, researchers should

CONSTRUCTING FORMATIVE MODELS 127

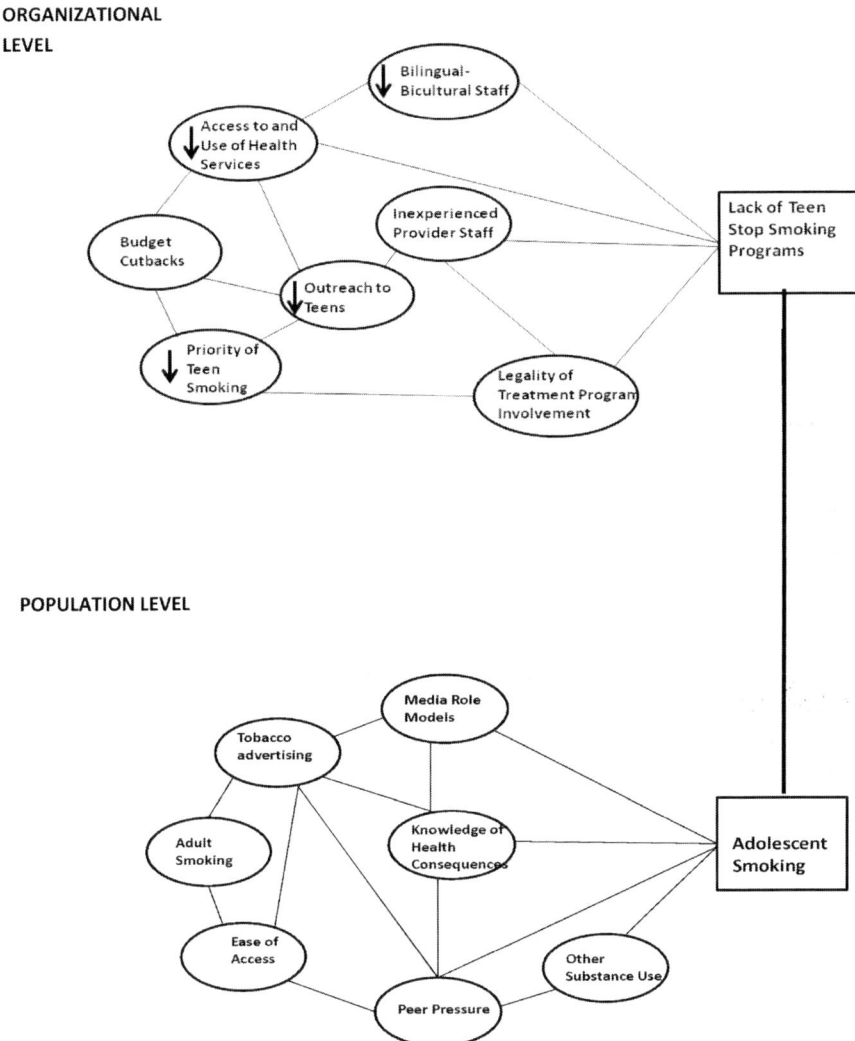

FIGURE 5.12 Constructing a Model Using Community or Population Level Domains Believed to Be Associated with the Dependent Domain: Adolescent Smoking

limit the number of independent domains in a study to between two and five.

External factors that also should be taken into consideration in selecting the most relevant independent domains include:

- Domains identified in previous studies
- Domains listed by key **informants**
- Domains identified through researchers' firsthand experience
- Domains that are compatible with the researcher's disciplinary background and resources

Cross Reference:
See chapter 4 in this Book; see also Book 1

Internal factors to be considered when prioritizing the selection of independent domains include:

- A selection of different domains that vary in proximity to the dependent variable
- The centrality of an independent domain; that is, to what extent it is viewed as directly related to several other independent domains as well as the dependent domain
- A balanced selection that includes independent domains identified from both organization and population analyses

The result of this process is a formative research model that represents:

- An initial theoretical paradigm for how things work to be tested and modified based on primary data collection
- The criteria for comparing between the expected (or what the researcher hypothesizes will occur) and the observed (or what the researcher actually verifies)
- A map or research design that guides all stages of data collection
- A set of criteria for establishing valid and reliable research and measurement instruments

Cross Reference:
See Book 1, chapter 4, for a discussion of research designs in ethnographic research

CONSTRUCTING FORMATIVE MODELS

A NOTE ON GENERATING HYPOTHESES

Hypotheses or propositions can be defined as causal or predictive statements that, when validated and linked with other hypotheses, help to build a comprehensive and complex picture (theory) of a topical area in a study population. Hypothesis generation, however, is not a process limited just to esoteric research and scholarly investigation. People create hypotheses or make cultural predictions in many ways every day. An individual in the United States reaches out his or her hand, expecting that a reciprocal gesture, a handshake, will be carried out by the person being greeted. Such an hypothesis is based on locally specific behavior; there is no guarantee that an outstretched hand in a different country will be met with a hand to be taken in return. People stop their cars at a red light, predicting that other cars will stop behind them, and that if they continued to move forward, they would most likely be hit by a car crossing the intersection in front of them. In many parts of the United States, people avoid picking up food with their fingers; this is appropriate behavior while dining. However, if the meal is served in an Indian household in Mumbai, India, or at a barbecue in Memphis, Tennessee, in the United States, or if it involves eating hot dogs in New York or Chicago on the street, *not* eating with one's fingers will look peculiar; the lack of expected response on both sides can produce a sense of disorientation and the desire to know why the predicted response did not occur. Such hypotheses are tested every day. Thus human beings generate hypotheses in their effort to make sense of reality today and to try to predict what will happen in the future. The ability to predict future actions and events based on current knowledge is essential to survival, to science in general, and to ethnography.

Hypotheses are associative or predictive statements about the relationships or connections between a set of domains, factors, or variables. They provide the rationale or explanation for these relationships or connections. Domains, factors, and variables in a model are always connected to each other (though not all domains may be connected to every other domain), and explanations for the relationships must exist or the model will not make sense. In other words, every time a domain (or factor or variable) is connected with another by an arrow in a diagram, there must be a logical explanation for the existence of the arrow.

Researchers generate and modify their hypotheses at higher or lower levels of abstraction during their entire time in the field. What appears to be an association or predictive statement one day may be contradicted by another observation the next. Observing children during recess period in a playground one day may produce an hypothesis stating that children cluster by ethnic/racial group. However, on the next day the children may appear to cluster by gender. On the third day, the researcher may notice that the activities on the playground during recess vary from day to day, which in turn may have something to do with how children cluster. In this way, with repeated modifications and redefinitions, the overall study hypothesis and subhypotheses are refined, relationships are clarified, and the formative model emerges and develops.

SUMMARY

The process of conceptualization in research, including the development of paradigms, theories, and models, has always seemed shrouded in an aura of mystery. For some investigators, the process involves sitting in an armchair, staring for hours at a blank wall; for others, every observed act and overheard phrase leads to queries that stimulate the discovery of theory. Conceptualizing is a serendipitous process, and it is made more mysterious by the fact that although students take classes and seminars where they learn *about* theories, they rarely take a class where they learn how to construct theories themselves. They thus are led to believe that "theory" is difficult, challenging, abstract, and something that could well be beyond their capabilities.

In this chapter we have tried to demystify the process of conceptualization and theory building, though at the same time we recognize that we have oversimplified by presenting it as a linear process. In fact, what really occurs in the process of generating models is simultaneously vertical and horizontal, usually dynamic, to some degree, idiosyncratic, and always inspired by intuitive, tangential, and "out of the box" thinking. Nevertheless, this chapter has attempted to outline a set of guidelines that can be applied to most situations and that will successfully generate useful local formative theories and research models. The key elements in these guidelines are:

- Establishing the focus of the study—the dependent domain
- Identifying independent and modifying domains that are believed to influence the dependent domain
- Diagramming the model on a two-dimensional surface to clarify conceptual thinking and making the conceptualization process accessible to others
- Explaining the reasons behind the hypothetical relationships among the independent and dependent domains in the model
- Eliminating domains based on their importance and perceived centrality in the study, and the time and human resources available for conducting the study
- Finalizing the model as a proposal for research funding and the conceptual start point for the study
- Altering the model as data are collected and throughout the data collection and analysis process

This formative process has been presented as both a top-down and a bottom-up operation. This means that researchers start with a review of the literature, their own personal hunches, a small number of key informant interviews with whomever is available in the area, accounts of field experiences by other investigators, and perhaps a little bit of very preliminary fieldwork. They then proceed to integrate this more or less deductive material with induction, stemming from bottom-up observations in the field. The result is that they work recursively, both "up" and "down" the conceptual ladder of abstraction.

Theory and model-building skills do not come automatically; they need to be developed over time. The more they are practiced, the easier they become. We hope that this approach stimulates ethnographers to view themselves as theoreticians and to improve on existing descriptions of ways in which local and middle-range theories can be generated.

6

OPERATIONALIZATION AND MEASUREMENT

- Operationalization
- Using the Research Model to Frame Research Goals, Objectives, and Hypotheses
- Linking Stages in Research Design with Stages in Data Collection
- Summary

OPERATIONALIZATION

The function of social science research is to "explain social phenomena." The term **social phenomena** refers to social or cultural patterns of thought, social organization, and cultural practices. As stated in the previous chapter, a researcher's first step in an ethnographic project is to define which social phenomena are to be studied. This begins the process referred to as *operationalization*, or describing phenomena in such a way that other researchers and nonresearchers will recognize the phenomenon when they see, hear, or otherwise sense it, even if what they are identifying is an abstract concept, like "love" or "self-esteem" that, because it cannot be seen directly, must be rendered visible by measuring its manifestations. Defining the phenomena to be studied requires:

- *Bounding:* establishing boundaries or canons for inclusion and exclusion to distinguish the particular phenomenon to be studied from others and to communicate that distinction to other researchers
- *Measurement:* finding ways to describe or measure the phenomenon quantitatively
- *Establishing validity:* assessing the adequacy of the observations/measurements used in representing the phenomenon

Definition: Social phenomena are patterns of thought, social organization, and cultural practices

- *Establishing reliability:* ensuring consistency in the observation/measurement process over time and among the researchers carrying out the measurement activities

Pelto and Pelto define operationalization as "striving for . . . better and better research operations in order to generate *more accurate observations*, hence more effective theory building and testing. Specification of operations enhances control of extraneous variables, increases the precision of basic measurements . . . and provides the framework for information that permits the researcher to trace his or her steps mentally in order to understand both predicted and unpredicted results" (1978, 39). Through operationalization, primary elements (terms) of researcher descriptions and theoretical propositions are structured or phrased in language that makes it possible for research teams and research participants to understand each other.

Conceptual versus Operational Definitions

Cross Reference: See Book 1 and Book 5, chapters 4 through 7, for additional descriptions of how to operationalize

Bernard (1995) makes a distinction between *conceptual* definitions and *operational* definitions. "Conceptual definitions are abstractions, articulated in words, which facilitate understanding. [They are] the sort of definitions we see in dictionaries . . . Operational definitions consist *of a set of instructions on how to measure a variable* that has been conceptually defined" (1995, 6, italics ours).

Operationalization renders visible even phenomena that are not readily observable directly, and it calls for processes of logic and observation. As we have seen in the development of formative theory, the process of operationalization can start from the:

- Top down (deductive, from *a priori* taxonomies or definitions)
- Ground up (inductive, from the data)
- Middle (at midrange levels of abstraction, working recursively and interactively from both top down and bottom up)

OPERATIONALIZATION AND MEASUREMENT   135

"Top down" processes (see Table 6.1) mean disaggregating, unpacking, or breaking down an abstract domain into its component factors, its factors into subfactors (if appropriate), and its subfactors into variables. The final step in top-down processing is to isolate the concrete items or units from which the domain is built. This process moves from the most abstract to the most concrete components in a model or a database.

"Bottom" or "ground up" processes mean first identifying phenomena at the variable or even at the item or "thing" level and then aggregating them within the proper subfactors, factors, and domains, in that order.

Beginning in the "midpoint" means identifying factors or subfactors—that is, components that are in the mid-range between abstract and concrete—sorting them into domains, or "conceptual bins," as we term them in Book 5, and at the same time identifying and measuring the variables associated with them. Table 6.1 depicts what we mean by this transformation process.

Cross Reference: See Book 5, chapters 4 and 5, for a discussion of top-down and bottom-up approaches to defining units or variables; and chapter 6 for how to organize units or variables into patterns (factors) and structures (domains or higher-order abstractions) during analysis

TABLE 6.1 Operationalizing—Transforming Information from One Level of Abstraction into Another

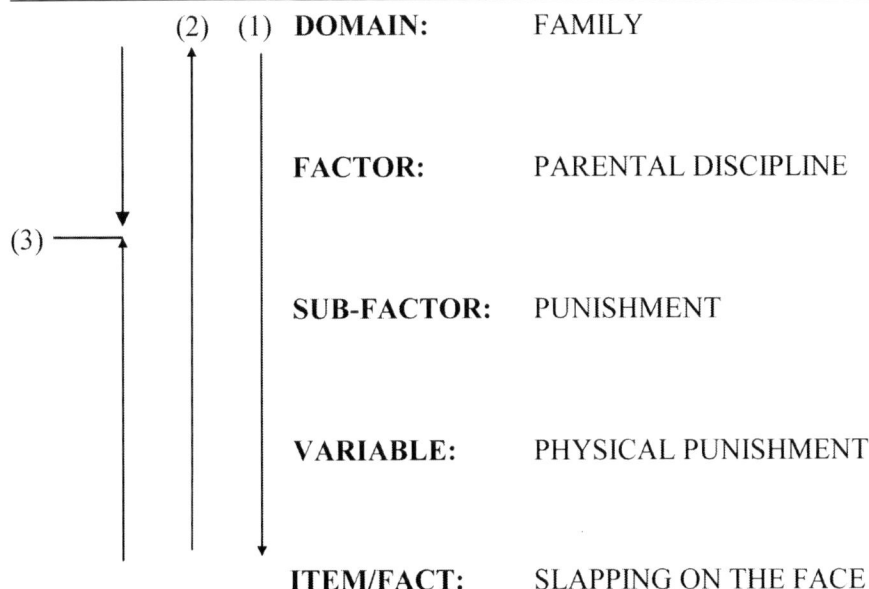

When initially planning their investigations, researchers must decide whether, for example, they wish to study the factors contributing to high levels of infant mortality (death), or high levels of infant morbidity (disease), or whether to combine them (morbidity leading to mortality versus morbidity leading to survival). Or if they are studying the effectiveness of educational innovations, they must decide how to distinguish between the impact of teachers' instructional techniques and that of children's behaviors in cooperative learning settings, or see if there is a relationship between the two.

Next, they must decide how to "measure the phenomenon," or how to identify it consistently in the social setting. Measurement appears simple when the topic is something like individual mortality: the observable quality is death of an individual. However, even so apparent a phenomenon as the "absence of life" or death can be complex in an era when some aspects of "life" can be prolonged by mechanical and medical means. Further, measurement can become even more complex when the information sought is not for individuals, but groups—the actual number of deaths and the households in which death occurs—and when this information is not readily available. In some places deaths are not recorded. In others, certain types of deaths, such as suicides or the deaths of children less than a year old, may neither be reported nor recorded. Many homes do not have addresses, so even if there were a record of all deaths, the location of those deaths might not be available. Measuring cause of death is always a problem, since death may have multiple causes, records may be absent or inaccurate, and, if there are no records, the study must depend on people's ability to remember the patient's symptoms. In such cases, data may be as faulty as the fallibility of recall. Assessing the effectiveness of instructional techniques used by teachers in cooperative learning programs is even more challenging. Researchers must observe teachers' behavior over time, determine which behaviors relate to cooperative learning, define these behaviors, and apply the definitions to observations of behavioral streams in the classroom. They then must find ways to determine whether or not students show gains in learning that can be attributed to the teachers' efforts. Recognizing and attending to such measurement problems is a central component in the conduct of ethnographic research on social phenomena. *It is important for researchers to realize that measurement as we discuss it here does not require mechanical devices and that many measurements are not expressed in terms of scores or numbers. Measurement simply permits the researchers to recognize the presence of a variable, describe it, and assess its variation.*

Key point

One approach to making these transformations is to locate items or observations at an appropriate level of abstraction, based on the researcher's judgment. Researcher judgment about where to place an item conceptually comes from a variety of different sources:

- Prior personal experience
- General knowledge of the phenomenon obtained through field observations
- Instruments developed by other researchers that measure the phenomenon
- Logic
- Feedback from others

Operationalization from the Bottom Up

A second approach to transformation is based upon "insider perspectives" or the hierarchical classification systems and sets of meanings that the study participants themselves have learned from their culture or environment, and use to categorize and classify their world. Elsewhere we have referred to this approach as an *emic* perspective. These systems can be derived by using elicitation techniques that have been variously described as "componential analysis" (Goodenough 1956), "folk taxonomy" (Frake 1964), and free listing and other systematic data collection methods (Weller and Romney 1988; Werner and Schoepfle 1987). Using these inductive or "bottom up" approaches to the development of taxonomies, informants can be asked where concepts or behaviors identified at the variable level fit (e.g., where does "a father slaps a child" fit in a taxonomy in which the domain is FAMILY, as in Table 6.1 or Table

Cross Reference:
See Book 1, Book 5, and Pelto and Pelto 1978

Cross Reference:
See Book 3, chapter 2, by Borgatti and Halgin on free listing, pilesorting, and consensus analysis

Cross Reference:
See Book 5, chapters 2–7, for a detailed discussion of the ways researchers elicit classificatory systems from text data

Cross Reference:
See Book 3, chapter 9, on the construction of ethnographic surveys, and Book 5, chapter 8, for a discussion of how to analyze data from ethnographic surveys and to construct indices and scales for quantitative data analysis

6.3), or respondents can be asked to sort a series of items (e.g., yell, slap rear end, slap face, punch, stop speaking, send to room, add chores) into groups (pilesorting) relating to parental responses to child misbehavior. They can then interpret each classified action, and name and classify the groupings as domains (big cultural categories) or factors (subcategories of a domain). Informants can be asked to list items; for example, "List all types of ways parents discipline a child" or "List all the things parents do when a child misbehaves." This is referred to as free listing. These classificatory systems also emerge through careful scrutinizing of qualitative field notes and interviews as well as through specific structured approaches to interviewing.

The next challenge is to place the item, "thing," or observation in an appropriate position on the continuum of abstraction, a task that is easier to do than to describe. It is easiest to situate items properly at the variable level. To do so, researchers ask: "Is the procedure for accurate identification reliable (i.e., can it be replicated?)" "Would two observers watching a parent's hand meeting a child's cheek agree that this behavior is 'slapping the child' (an item) and that it is a component of the variable 'physical punishment'?" At the factor level, researchers must ask whether the concept has enough breadth to place it at a higher (i.e., more inclusive) level of abstraction than a variable. To situate a concept at the domain or most abstract level, researchers should be able to generate a full taxonomic structure, including factors, subfactors, and variables.

Ethnographers use operationalization for organizing, understanding, and analyzing qualitative data; for improving the precision of their data collection; and as a means of organizing hierarchical coding systems for their qualitative data. This approach also facilitates the organization of items (at the most concrete, observable, measureable level) into variables that can be quantified into indices and scales for use in the construction of an ethnographic survey.

Operationalization from the Top Down

The next section describes operationalization from the top down. This parallels the process described in Book

5, chapters 4, 5, and 6. The formative research theoretical model provides the first step in operationalization by directing the researcher's attention to the domains of interest and their potential interrelationships. The next task is to move down the levels of abstraction in each of the domains in the research model (vertical modeling) to define factors, subfactors (if necessary), and variables that are valid indicators or measures of those domains. It is important to recognize that, even in this process, ethnographers use both deductive and inductive processes to weave a rich fabric of description and analysis. To accomplish this task, it is most useful to use the technique of **tree diagramming** (cf. Weller and Romney 1988). A tree diagram must have two or more levels. This method of categorization is represented in Figure 6.1.

Definition: Tree diagramming involves organizing information into hierarchical taxonomies in which items are subsumed under broader categories

Using tree diagrams requires several steps. First, researchers return to the research model to select the domain to be unpacked (see chapter 2). Second, they "unpack" the domain by disaggregating it into constituent components or parts at each level in the hierarchy of abstraction: factor, subfactor, and variable. In effect, they are identifying or defining the elements or components

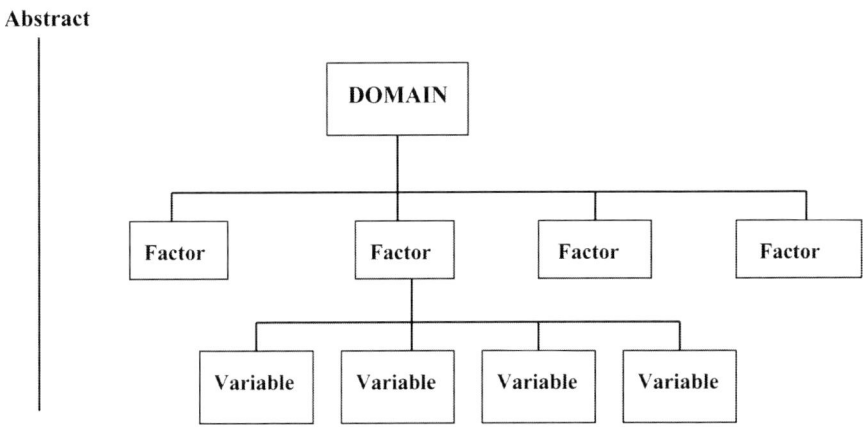

FIGURE 6.1 Operationalizing—Organizing Information into Hierarchical Taxonomies by Degree of "Abstraction" or Inclusion of the Concept

within a factor (or a subfactor), the items within a variable. This process represents a transformation from more abstract (factor and subfactor) to more concrete (variable and item) levels. The end product of the transformation is a set of operationalized or measurable variables. Difficulties encountered at any stage in the operationalization process are an indication that further transformations need to be made. This is especially the case at the variable level. Figure 6.1 suggests that transformations from the domain to the variable level can be made in three steps, but it may require as many as four or five levels for many concepts to become fully operationalized. Regardless of the number of steps, making transformations from the domain to the variable level is based on many considerations, such as:

- Intuition (personal experience)
- Prior research studies
- Data gathered from each stage of the ethnographic research process
- Logical reasoning

To illustrate, if the domain FAMILY arises in the course of a discussion with a key informant, an ethnographer can follow logically with the question: "Can you tell me more about families in this community?" Answers to this question and observation of families in the course of fieldwork will lead to identification of the constituent components of the domain FAMILY from the point of view of the population under study. These might be "family membership," "family interaction," "family activities," "family socialization practices," and others. Generally, ethnographers try to induce informants to provide information that can be situated at the "factor" level, because the informants may or may not think and speak in terms of the logical taxonomies that are required to fully understand the content of a domain. Usually it is the researcher's task to reorganize the information provided by study participants into factors, subfactors, and variables and to identify the items that form the elements of scales and indices (which are also variables).

Cross Reference:
See Book 5, chapters 4 and 5, for graphic portrayals of how these levels of abstraction line up with actual data

Semistructured interviews and observations are useful for further identifying and operationalizing factors. For

OPERATIONALIZATION AND MEASUREMENT

example, the factor "discipline" may emerge as important in the FAMILY domain. A semistructured interview that asks respondents to describe experiences with parental discipline is likely to identify initial subfactors and/or variables that clarify and refine what "discipline" means and what types exist. These will be important as the researcher goes about measuring and collecting data on the factor of discipline. Respondents may describe different ways that parents discipline their children, including verbal discipline (telling children what to do, when and where, or criticizing children's actions), physical discipline (hitting, beating, or slapping children); modeling behavior (demonstrating how children should behave or recounting stories or fables that illustrate what proper behavior should be); emotional discipline (cajoling, embarrassing, persuading, etc.) and social discipline (encouraging feedback from others). These become factors within the domain PARENTAL DISCIPLINE.

The identification of variables and their respective options may be concrete enough to permit their transformation into closed-ended items on a survey instrument. If researchers learn that one subfactor associated with the factor "discipline" is physical discipline or corporal punishment and one variable within corporal punishment is beating with a cane, they may want to ask a structured or closed-ended question such as, "Have you ever been beaten with a cane?" the answer to which is "yes" or "no." The next question might be, "Are there other ways that you have been punished, for example . . . slapped, hit, beaten with hand, kicked, etc.?" These responses are all items within the subfactor "physical punishment." Each level of abstraction in the operationalization process produces useful and valid information on the phenomena being studied, and at the same time, it also provides the basis for further operationalization down the ladder of abstraction toward more concrete items.

This approach to operationalization also permits movement from the concrete back to the abstract. For example, "caning" (an item) may be discovered first. It can be recorded as such. Then, on the basis of additional ethnographic data collection, it may be classified under the more inclusive cat-

Cross Reference:
See Book 3, chapter 7, for detailed information on how to conduct semistructured data collection

egory or subfactor labeled "corporal punishment." Once the subfactor "corporal punishment" is identified as valid and important in the study, "caning" (either yes/no or amount/harshness) can become one item in a scale measuring the broader concept, "corporal punishment."

Further investigation using semistructured or even key informant interviews would lead researchers to identify other behaviors comparable to "caning" that are indicators of the subfactor or concept "corporal punishment." Depending on the ethnographic context, "corporal punishment," a subfactor, may be situated within "family discipline," a factor, or it may equally well be situated within another factor termed "family relationships." Situating this subfactor within family relationships would require extensive ethnographic investigation and the development of a rationale for including it in that specific factor. Working "up the ladder" of abstraction, the factor location for the subfactor "corporal punishment" will depend on the questions raised in the original study, and the ways in which behaviors are conceptualized and categorized in the local setting. Thus, in this approach each data item can have a conceptual home, allowing the researcher to avoid "orphaned" facts and isolated information.

Of course, there may be occasions when "facts" and information or "items" do *not* fit. Discovering that something does not fit into an existing taxonomy or classification system is important, because it signals either that the phenomenon observed and recorded is not known or well understood, or that the taxonomies and domains are inadequate, and the new observation requires more inquiry. This approach to operationalization also establishes categories for the coding of textual data.

EXAMPLE 6.1

OPERATIONALIZING THE FAMILY DOMAIN AMONG YOUNG MAURITIAN WOMEN IN THE WORKFORCE

The Schensuls and their Mauritius research partners knew that the family played a crucial role in the lives of the young women they studied in a project examining AIDS-related risk behaviors among unmarried young women working in the industrial zone in Mauritius. Having identified the domain FAMILY as important, the research team began to delineate its constituent factors. Their objective in this

OPERATIONALIZATION AND MEASUREMENT   143

task was not to identify every possible factor associated with the domain FAMILY. Instead, it was to locate and focus on those components hypothesized to be related to the dependent domain: AIDS-RELATED RISK BEHAVIORS. The team's first attempt at identifying family factors associated with AIDS-related risk behaviors is illustrated in Figure 6.2.

Their next task was to further operationalize each of the factors identified as components of the domain FAMILY. Figure 6.3 shows how the factor "family economics" (meaning "household economic characteristics") was disaggregated into a number of variables, one of which was material goods. "Material goods" refers to material items or possessions owned by the household.

Some of these variables already were sufficiently concrete or operationalized. For example, the Schensuls could ask young women in the industrial zone to respond to the question: "What percentage of your monthly income do you contribute to the household?" and expect that the

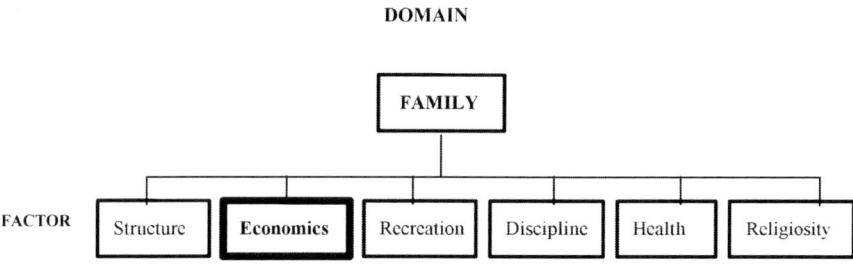

FIGURE 6.2 Identifying Factors Associated with the Domain FAMILY

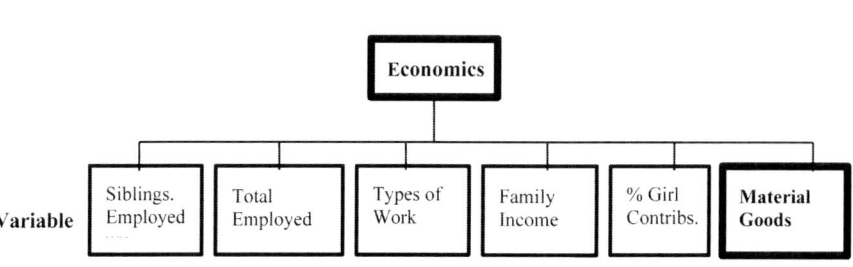

FIGURE 6.3 Operationalizing the Factor "Economics"

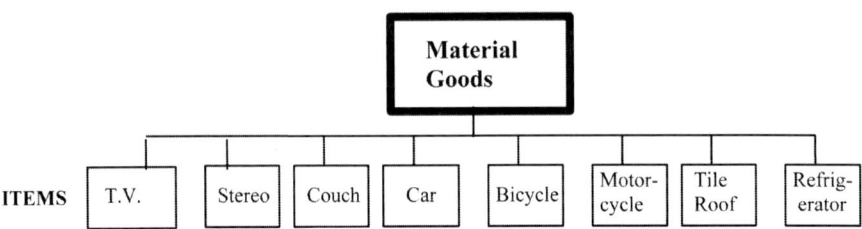

FIGURE 6.4 Operationalizing the Variable "Material Goods"

Cross Reference: See this book, chapter 5, for more information on observation of material style of life indicators and Book 5, chapter 8, for a discussion of scales and indices and an example of a material style of life scale

type of answer required would readily be understood. Others required further operationalization, such as description and enumeration of the material goods owned by the household. Figure 6.4 shows how they operationalized this variable. The figure illustrates a series of items that could be further defined by their presence or absence in a household. In the analysis stage, it was possible to combine these items into a "material style of life (MSL)" scale by summing the number of items present in each household to create a household score.

The research model discussed in the previous chapter, which was based only on domains, can be defined as a "horizontal" model. The process of creating this formative research model is termed *horizontal modeling* because it proposes relationships at *only* one level—the level of the domain. By contrast, the "tree diagram" described in Figures 6.2 to 6.4 is described as a "vertical model" because it uses logic, empirical observation, and inquiry to generate linkages or relationships from the most abstract level (domain) down to the most concrete level (variables and items or attributes).

Cross Reference: See Book 1, chapter 7, and Book 5, chapters 10 and 11, for a further elaboration on identifying items and units and constructing patterns and structures

The delineation of taxonomies (or "tree diagrams") in the formation and conduct of an ethnographic study gives researchers tools to begin to construct units, patterns, and structures. Figure 6.5 illustrates the relationships between domains that can be explored at the variable, subfactor, and factor level through statistical analysis of quantitative data. It also demonstrates how relationships among subfactors and factors can be explored by linking appropriately coded blocks of qualitative or text data.

OPERATIONALIZATION AND MEASUREMENT 145

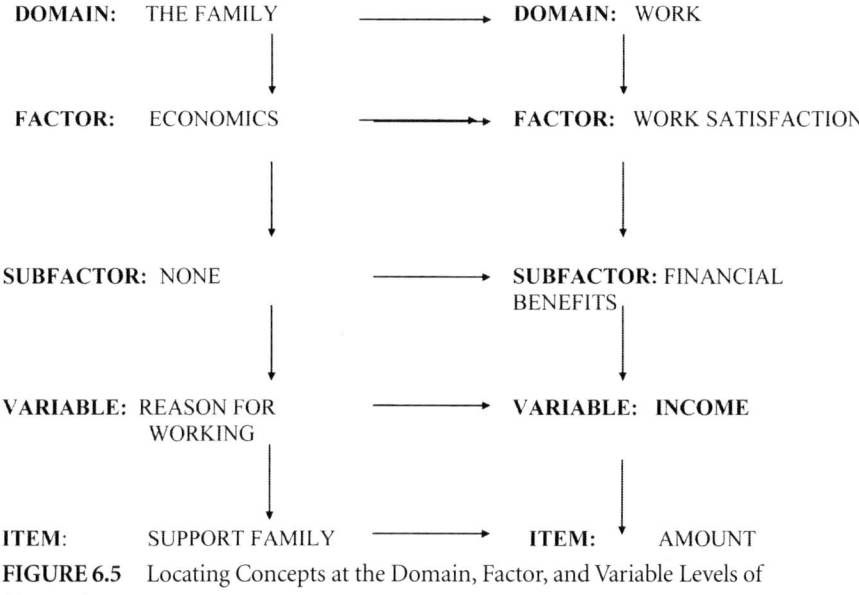

FIGURE 6.5 Locating Concepts at the Domain, Factor, and Variable Levels of Abstraction

The conceptual work completed to this point provides the basis for creating a clear formative research model. The model acts as the basis for developing a research design and writing a research proposal or prospectus that can be reviewed by colleagues, supervisors, review committees, and potential funders.

Cross Reference: See Book 2, chapters 2 and 3, for how to write such proposals in preparing for the field

USING THE RESEARCH MODEL TO FRAME RESEARCH GOALS, OBJECTIVES, AND HYPOTHESES

As has been stated, the first step in developing a research design built on a research model is to generate a statement of research purpose. This statement should be based on the dependent domain or the research "problem." Table 6.2 illustrates some examples of problem statements focusing on the dependent variable alone, or on relationships between independent and dependent variables.

The next step is to develop a series of research objectives related to the purpose of the research and directed toward explicating the relationship between the independent and dependent domains, as illustrated in Table 6.2.

TABLE 6.2 Purpose Statements Based on a Theoretical Research Model

Purpose	Dependent Domain	Independent Domains
The **purpose** of this research is to understand how older Latina women interpret, report, and manage **symptoms of diabetes**.	Symptoms of diabetes	
The **purpose** of this research is to identify factors associated with variations in **children's performance in math**-related activities.	Children's performance in math-related activities	
The **purpose** of this research is to describe **the diffusion of an agricultural innovation (dependent variable)** among farmers in rural Iowa.	Diffusion of an agricultural innovation	
The **purpose** of this research is to identify **peer, community, and family factors** influencing **conflict-resolution skills** in young adults.	Conflict-resolution skills	Peer Community Family
The **purpose** of this research is to examine the association **of self-esteem, social influences, and the media** on **running away from home** among adolescents.	Running away from home	Self-esteem Social Influences Media

Then a specific set of research questions or hypotheses should be generated that can be explored or tested by considering the relationships among factors and variables, as illustrated in Table 6.3, an example drawn from research conducted in Mauritius. Note that when ethnographers speak of "testing" a relationship, they are not speaking of the kinds of statistical or probabilistic relationships obtainable in a controlled experiment, but rather, are searching for (or exploring) the existence of hypothesized associations and conjoint variation between and among domains, factors, and variables.

Figure 6.6 draws from the conceptual taxonomy of domains, factors, and variables illustrated in Table 6.4, which includes two domains, FAMILY and SEXUALITY. It selects two critical domains in the study, FAMILY and SEXUALITY, two factors drawn from the family domain, "parental role" and "respondent's relationship to the family," and one factor from the sexuality domain, "sex behavior."

After reviewing the variables included in each of the factors, researchers selected one from each of the two family factors, and one from the sex behavior factor (see

OPERATIONALIZATION AND MEASUREMENT 147

TABLE 6.3 Constructing a Research Design Using the "Domain, Factor, and Variable" Framework: An Example from Mauritius

Title:	Young Women, Work, and AIDS-Related Risk Behavior in Mauritius
Purpose:	To identify factors associated with sexual attitudes, behavior, and risk (pregnancy, abortion, STDs, and AIDS) in young women working in the Mauritius Economic Production Zone (EPZ).
Objective:	To describe and understand the relationship between social/contextual domains (family, peer, and work) and factors, sexual risk, and sexual attitudes of young women aged fifteen to twenty-five in the EPZ.

variable column in Table 6.4). Variables are located in the circles in Figure 6.6.

Having chosen the variables, researchers then speculated as to what the relationships among them might be. The directional hypotheses as stated in the study are as follows:

Hypothesis 1: The loss of the father as a wage earner will mean that young women are forced (rather than freely choose) to enter the EPZ to support their families.

Hypothesis 2: The loss of the father will be associated with greater levels of sexual behavior for young women.

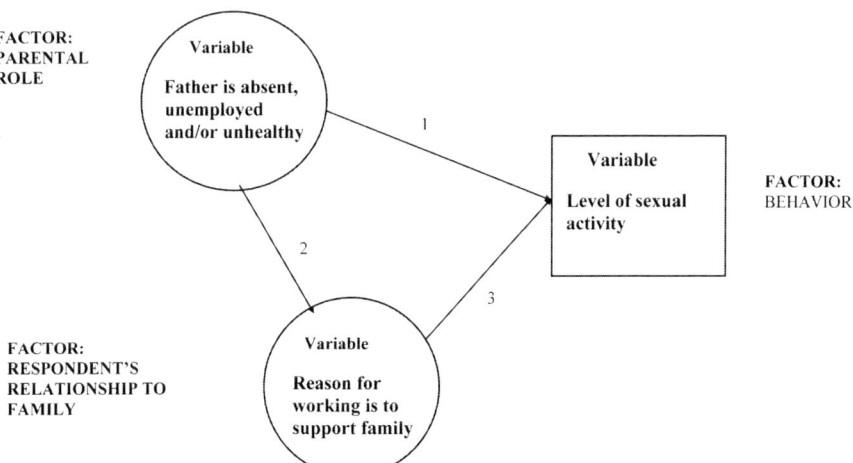

FIGURE 6.6 Generating Hypotheses about Relationships among Variables within Factors and Domains: Mauritius Study, FAMILY Domain

TABLE 6.4 Conceptual Taxonomy (Tree Diagram) for FAMILY Domain and SEXUALITY Domain: Mauritius Study

Domain	Factor	Variable
FAMILY	Parental role	Father's presence, health, employment
		Mother's presence, health, employment
	Siblings	Number
		Employment
		Birth order
	Family environment	Scale of traditionality
		Family approval of work
		Scale of family violence
		Family problems
		Family activities
	Respondent's relationship to the family	Approval of work
		Hours of housework
		Working to support family
SEXUALITY	Behavior	Participation in behaviors ranging from holding hands to oral sex
		Condom use
	Values	Premartial sex
		Virginity
		Men
	Knowledge	AIDS transmission
		Condoms
	Risk perception	Loss of virginity
		Becoming pregnant
		Acquiring STD
		Acquiring AIDS

OPERATIONALIZATION AND MEASUREMENT

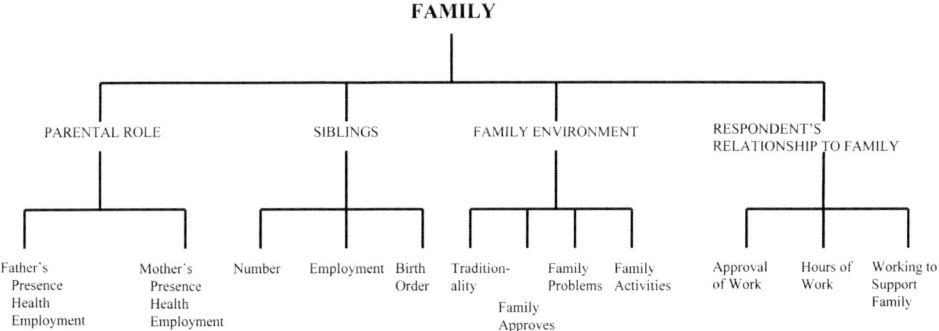

FIGURE 6.7 A Tree Diagram: Conceptual Taxonomy for the Domain FAMILY

Hypothesis 3: Women who are forced by household poverty (rather than choosing) to work in the EPZ will show higher levels of sexual activity.

Table 6.5 summarizes the links between elements of research design and their conceptual source or inspiration using the modeling process that we have described.

TABLE 6.5 Links between Components of Research Design and Conceptual Source Using Tree Diagrams

Research	Conceptual Source
Purpose	The Dependent Domain
Objectives	The Relationship between the Independent and Dependent Domains
Research Concepts	Tree Diagrams
Hypotheses	Relationships among Factors and Variables

LINKING STAGES IN RESEARCH DESIGN WITH STAGES IN DATA COLLECTION

Two of the greatest challenges facing ethnographic researchers are how to mesh qualitative (text) data with quantitative (numerical data) and how to know when in the sequencing of a study to choose one approach to data collection over another. The approach we have outlined in this chapter provides the basis for both by linking stages in conceptual development and modeling with specific research methods. Table 6.6 summarizes these stages.

TABLE 6.6 Stages in Research Design, Selection of Research Methods, and Study Objectives

Conceptual Component	Research Method (Books 1, 2, 3, and 4) and Sampling Approach (Book 3, chapter 10)	Research Objectives
Stage 1: Building Research Questions and Research Model	Reviewing Secondary Data (Book 4, chapter 2) —secondary databases —prior experience in study site —researcher experience	—Development of initial domains —Selection of domains —Construction of hypotheses
Stage 2: Domain	Exploratory Data Collection (Book 3, chapters 4, 5, 6) —key informant interviews —unstructured observation —participant observation Sampling: Unique Cases; Extreme Cases	—Discovery of new domains —Testing of domain selection —Beginning operationalization at all levels
Stage 3: Factor	Semistructured Data Collection (Book 3, chapter 6, 7; Book 4, chapter 2) —semistructured interviews —semistructured observation —focus groups —elicitation (free listing and pilesorts) Sampling: Quota Sampling	—Operationalization of factors and variables —Identifying language and terminology for study —Identifying cultural consensus
Stage 4: Variable	Structured Data Collection (Book 3, chapter 8) —structured interviewing —questionnaires, surveys —structured observation Sampling: Probability or Systematic	—Operationalization of variables —Obtaining representative sample of responses —Testing hypotheses

Cross Reference: See Book 4, chapter 2, on using secondary and archival data

The objective of Stage 1 is to develop the formative research model by using personal/professional experience, prior research, and a review of secondary and archival data. This involves identifying a set of independent and dependent domains and constructing hypotheses that link them. Researchers should remember that the formative research model is just that, and it is subject to modification, refinement, and improvement at any point throughout the life of the study. Johnson describes the useful distinction between exploratory and explanatory approaches to research. He notes that "Exploratory approaches (our stages 1–3) are used to develop hypotheses and more generally to make

OPERATIONALIZATION AND MEASUREMENT   151

probes for circumscription (exploration), description and interpretation of less well understood topics . . . Exploratory research can be the primary focus of a given design or just one of many components" (Johnson 1998, 139).

Having formulated their initial model (Stage 1), researchers should begin their work with methods of data collection that emphasize "discovery" (Stage 2). Discovery is useful in:

- Determining the utility, appropriateness, importance, and definition of the **DEPENDENT DOMAIN**
- Discovering and selecting the **INDEPENDENT DOMAINS**
- Beginning to **OPERATIONALIZE DOMAINS** (deconstructing or unpacking them into their respective factors and variables)

Stage 2 focuses on the development and elaboration of the domains in the formative research model, as we have explained in chapters 4 through 6 of this book. Exploratory data collection techniques are most useful in elaborating on the definition and "unpacking" of domains. During Stage 2, new domains are discovered as researchers find that units do not logically fall into initially identified domains. During this stage, the first steps in operationalization also take place. As items emerge, they are identified as factors, subfactors, or variables, in a developing conceptual taxonomy.

Stage 3 focuses primarily on exploration at the factor level through semistructured data collection techniques. The **factor** is the first-level subset of a domain. If a domain consists of HIV risk behavior, a factor within that domain might be "unprotected sexual encounters"; a second factor might be "injection drug use," and so on. Semistructured interviews help to identify factors and can also provide information on the variables within each factor, such as the frequency of sex without a male or female condom or the frequency of partial penetration. Semistructured interviews and observations provide information that helps to confirm the existence of factors and identify variables. Questions asked in these forms of data collection allow us to explore the range of possible responses or options that could be

Definition:
The factor is the first-level subset of a domain

Cross Reference:
See Book 3, chapters 7 and 8, on semistructured interviewing and focused group interviews

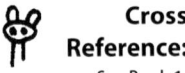 **Cross Reference:** See Book 1, chapters 5 and 7, and Book 5, chapters 5 and 6, for the definitions of variables and their attributes

included as variables or as attributes of a variable. At the same time, semistructured data collection allows ethnographers to learn much more about the broader meaning of variables, factors, and domains than quantitative measurement alone could reveal. These data prove useful in interpreting survey results at the end of the study.

Researchers create a list of open-ended questions about a factor and ask the same questions to a number of people, seeking for variations in the responses. The variations are at the variable or unit level. For example, a researcher might ask fifteen or twenty people their opinions about public versus private schools. Altogether, they might provide a list of ten different opinions, such as "public schools have limited resources," "students can get a quality education in both schools," and "private schools restrict entry." Or they might interview between forty and fifty respondents to find out about their reasons for quitting substance use, or their history of use of smokeless tobacco during pregnancy, or their efforts to obtain care for a child with asthma. The list provides the alternative responses for closed-ended survey questions and ideas for additional interviewing.

In Stage 4, researchers explore the range of variation in a representative sample of the target population usually through quantitative investigation (surveys or other means of measuring variation in a large population). Analysis explores and tests hypotheses based on the original conceptual framework as well as emerging ideas. Johnson refers to Stage 4 as explanatory research, suggesting that "explanatory approaches generally involve testing elements of theory that may already have been proposed in the literature or that have been informed by exploratory research" (Johnson 1998, 139).

Many social science researchers now readily accept the idea that ethnography includes both qualitative and quantitative approaches to data collection. However, they have not fully embraced either the utility of different forms of data in making a good argument for the researchers' propositions or how to sequence and integrate qualitative and quantitative data at various points in the research process. The process we have described here makes it possible for researchers to shift back and forth between qualitative and quantitative data in straightforward steps that produce an integrated mixed-methods approach. The guidelines we offer permit the use of qualitative research to define quantitative measures, and explanations and interpretations of quantitative associations with the same qualitative data. Proceeding in this manner allows us to approach the analysis of qualitative (in-depth and semistructured text data) and quantitative (survey) data in much the same way: by describing variables and exploring the relationships among them. In chapter 7, we provide detailed examples of this process.

Cross Reference: See Book 5, chapters 9–11, for a detailed discussion of the analysis and integration of qualitative and quantitative data

SUMMARY

In this chapter, we have reviewed the basic steps in the operationalization of a formative research model. Most researchers begin with a question that is elaborated as they move through the stages of research outlined in Table 6.5. The initial research question rapidly becomes transformed into a "dependent variable domain" or a problem or topic for research. However, the domains and factors associated with it may not fully emerge until later in Stage 3 of the research process. Many researchers may be satisfied to collect and analyze in-depth and semistructured interviews and other forms of exploratory data to test their research model and answer their research questions. Others will choose to test their model quantitatively with a larger and more representative sample. Researchers may choose either strategy, knowing that both the qualitative and the quantitative data they have so painstakingly collected will apply directly to the dimensions they have identified in their theoretical model.

7

MIXED METHODS MODELS, MEASURES, AND CASE EXAMPLES

> Introduction
>
> Definitions of Mixed Methods Research
>
> When Should Qualitative and Quantitative Methods Be Used?
>
> Integrating Qualitative and Quantitative Methods
>
> Relating or Sequencing of Multiple Methodologies: Models, Methods, Measures, and Case Examples
>
> The Role of Secondary Data in Mixed Methods Ethnography
>
> Summary

INTRODUCTION

> Mixed methods research is, generally speaking, an approach to knowledge (theory and practice) that attempts to consider multiple viewpoints, perspectives, positions, and standpoints (always including the standpoints of qualitative and quantitative research).
> —JOHNSON ET AL. 2007, 113

Mixed methods research can be defined as the serial or joint use of qualitative, quantitative survey, and quantified qualitative data collection methods to achieve a systematic understanding of both the magnitude and frequency of the phenomena (quantitative) under study and the context, meaning, and motivation of those phenomena (qualitative). Some refer to mixed methods research as the third paradigm in the domain of research methods (cf. Johnson and Onwuegbuzie 2004). However, the use of a number of different data collection traditions has a long history in the social sciences, particularly in anthropology, where in the 1970s, a small group of anthropological methodologists began to explore the utility of survey research and the use of qualitative approaches to formulate better survey instruments (Pelto and Pelto 1978). *The Journal of Quantitative*

Anthropology, whose articles address various dimensions of cultural measurement, was first published in 1989 and continued until 1996. The interdisciplinary mixed methods journal, *Field Methods*, first published in May 1989, was developed specifically to highlight multiple methods of data collection and analysis used by ethnographers and other community-based researchers in the field. These resources make it clear that the use of mixed methods; that is, the integration of qualitative, quantitative survey, epidemiological, and numerical data collection increasingly has become a mainstream practice for ethnography and the social sciences.

This chapter shows how formative models intersect with stages and steps in mixed methods research design and data collection. Using brief examples and several longer case studies, the chapter illustrates how a mixture of quantitative and qualitative data, personal experience, and scientific hunches guides data collection to enhance and calibrate a formative model. Systematically collected qualitative data contribute to the creation of measures for concepts and constructs that test the formative model using surveys and other quantitative approaches. Conversely, quantitative methods can offer insights that are addressed through qualitative work in many different design options.

DEFINITIONS OF MIXED METHODS RESEARCH

There are many definitions of mixed methods research. Most of them emphasize a) planning for collection of multiple forms of data from the beginning of the study; b) conducting the data collection so qualitative and quantitative data are complementary in content; c) increasing understanding of phenomena in the field by using more than one way of "knowing"; and d) validating or verifying results through various forms of triangulation. Johnson's and Turner's fundamental principle of mixed research (2003) suggests that "researchers should collect multiple forms of data using different strategies, approaches, and methods in such a way that the resulting mixture or combination is likely to result in complementary strengths and non-overlapping weaknesses" (Johnson and Onwuegbuzie 2004,

MIXED METHODS MODELS   157

18). Recently Thomas Weisner, a mixed methods researcher, argued in the *Anthropology Newsletter* that good ethnography "will always benefit from the widest variety of data" (Weisner 2012, 3). The U.S. National Institutes of Health (NIH), hitherto a bastion of quantitative research, even has commissioned panels through its Office of Behavioral and Social Sciences Research (OBSSR) to provide guidelines both for qualitative research (2001) and mixed methods research to be used in NIH grants, and for fellowships, as well as training and center proposals.

Many methodologists have identified the primary differences between qualitative and quantitative methods (Creswell 2009; Greene and Caracelli 1997; Johnson et al. 2007; Schensul and LeCompte 1999; Tashakkori and Teddlie 2003). Chapter 4 in Book 1 of the *Ethnographer's Toolkit* (2010) also discusses these issues. Table 7.1 displays some of the main differences.

Cross Reference: See Book 1, chapter 1, for further discussion of these issues

During the 1970s and 1980s, a variety of methodologists categorized the primary strengths and advantages of mixed methods research. In a useful summary that reviewed published research articles, Greene, Caracelli, and Graham (Greene and Caracelli 1997; Greene et al. 1989) identified five main reasons for using mixed methods in

TABLE 7.1 Principal Differences between Qualitative and Quantitative Research

Qualitative Research	Quantitative Research
Focused on discovery of the unknown	Focused on the representation of the known
Describes the meaning, rationale, and interpretation of the focal phenomena	Measures the frequency and correlation of the focal phenomena
Primarily inductive, building theory from the ground up	Primarily deductive; testing *a priori* theory
Able to describe context, structure, culture, and institutions (macro)	Focused on individual, family, small group phenomena (micro)
Emphasizes validity	Emphasizes reliability
Uses purposive and selective sampling with the view that members of a group are not independent units	Uses random sampling to maximize representatives and generalizability
Uses case study	Uses cross-sectional and longitudinal designs
The focus is local, using face-to-face techniques	The focus of the study can be on both large and small populations

studies and provided rationales to accompany them. The reasons included:

- Increased capacity for careful triangulation (i.e., seeking convergence and corroboration of results from different methods studying the same phenomenon)
- Complementarity (i.e., seeking elaboration, enhancement, illustration, clarification of the results from one method with results from the other method)
- Development (i.e., using the results from one method to help inform the other method)
- Initiation (i.e., discovering paradoxes and contradictions that lead to a reframing of the research question)
- Expansion (i.e., seeking to expand the breadth and range of inquiry by using different methods for different inquiry components)

Purposes/reasons and rationales as suggested by Greene et al. (Greene et al. 1989, 259) are summarized in Table 7.2.

TABLE 7.2   Purposes and Rationales for Different Approaches to Mixed Methods Research

Purpose	Rationale
TRIANGULATION seeks agreement of results obtained from different methods.	To increase the validity of constructs and inquiry results by counteracting various sources of bias and extraneous interference
COMPLEMENTARITY enhances the results obtained from one method with results obtained from others.	To increase interpretability, meaningfulness, and validity of constructs and inquiry results by capitalizing on method strengths and counteracting biases in methods and other sources
DEVELOPMENT uses the results of one method to help to develop or inform another (including sampling and measurement).	To increase the validity of constructs and inquiry results by capitalizing on inherent method strengths
INITIATION interrogates or recasts results from one method with another.	To increase breadth and depth of inquiry results and interpretations by analyzing them from perspectives of different methods and paradigms
EXPANSION extends breadth and range of inquiry by using different methods for different inquiry components.	To increase scope of inquiry by selecting the methods most appropriate for multiple inquiry components

WHEN SHOULD QUALITATIVE AND QUANTITATIVE METHODS BE USED?

The rubrics produced by Greene et al. are helpful in considering why qualitative and quantitative methods *should* intersect, but they do not address how a researcher should determine *when* to use qualitative versus quantitative methods, which specific data collection approaches to use, and at what point in their studies they should use one or the other form of data collection. As we described in Book 1, ethnographers should consider qualitative methods when addressing the following:

Cross Reference: See Book 1, chapter 2, for an elaborated discussion of when to use ethnography

- *When the problem and its origin are unclear or poorly understood.*
- *When the phenomena have been established and are described in others' work or in theoretical arguments, but need to be understood from the perspective of the population under study* (Rhodes et al. 2005).
- *If the target population is still not fully discovered or very well defined,* such as when it requires finding hidden populations (Singer 2012; Sosulski and Lawrence 2008; Watters and Biernacki 1989). Or, the characteristics of the study population may be complex and subdivisions within it must be understood. Since most communities or other settings include a diversity of social groups that have different characteristics with potential implications for a study and its outcomes, researchers must use qualitative research in order to know which groups to include or exclude, and for what reasons.
- *If the phenomena under study involves an examination of structural, institutional, and community dynamics issues that require defining the boundaries and context of the community.* Only qualitative research, including in-depth interviews and observation, can identify exactly how to define the "community" or "bound the system" (Foster-Fishman and Droege 2010; Schensul, Saggurti et al. 2009). It also is required to identify which contextual factors are salient in relation to the study problem (Earp and

Ennett 1991; Guarnaccia et al. 1990; Lopez et al. 2012; Sunderland et al. 2012).

- *When new population or other trends have emerged that have changed study population dynamics*, for example, in- or out-migration as a result of changes and restrictions in housing policies, or declines in birth rates when least expected.
- *If measurement of key variables, factors, and domains (operationalization) is not clear.* For example, concepts such as "motivation to quit smoking," or "oral health self-management fears," may emerge as important in the study, but as yet there may be no existing measures that capture these concepts.
- *If independent domains are incomplete, or not fully defined.* In an early formative model, the independent domains are usually very broad (e.g. PEER, FAMILY, BELIEFS ABOUT RICE PRODUCTIVITY, ATTITUDES TOWARD SMOKING, ECONOMIC OPPORTUNITIES). These domains will require "unpacking" to identify their constituent factors and variables. Further, some initially identified domains may not turn out to be the most salient for the study. Qualitative inquiry is required to discover and define the most relevant independent domains.

Quantitative data are required when researchers want to:

- *Discover the distribution of a variable in a study population.* Only properly applied representative sampling strategies and quantitative measures can show the distribution of a variable in any study population. Qualitative inquiry can define the variable, and even can contribute items that operationalize it so it can be measured, but qualitative samples are not representative of a study population.
- *Test correlational or predictive hypotheses.* Many researchers want to explore the associations among variables, or to do more complex analyses that identify pathways to outcomes (dependent variables) in a population. Associational analyses can be conducted

with qualitative data, but the results are not representative of the study population.
- *Evaluate outcomes of an intervention.* Qualitative data are critical in understanding the processes through which interventions take place or are conducted, and even what happens to individuals and institutions in the course of the intervention. Displaying believable effects or impacts, however, usually requires quantitative research, measuring the outcomes, and showing how they differ across programs or settings with varying degrees of exposure to the intervention.

INTEGRATING QUALITATIVE AND QUANTITATIVE METHODS

Integrating qualitative and quantitative data to build a coherent description of the phenomena under study has proved to be a complex process. Creswell et al. (2010) call both for "merging" or integrating multiple forms of data and "connecting" data, in which researchers analyze one data set so as to inform the subsequent mode of data collection, in the "discussion section" of a study. While describing linkages between results from qualitative data analysis and those from quantitative data analysis certainly are key operations required in mixed methods studies, they still treat the two sets of data almost as constituting separate studies with different designs. A better approach is one in which mixed methods approaches are defined, as above, as constituting a "third methodological paradigm" that bases its analysis on the notion that qualitative and quantitative research *are based on the same research model.* Such an approach addresses the different kinds of data with careful and rigorous triangulation, regardless of the purpose or sequencing (cf. Table 7.3).

Chapter 4 of this text developed the argument for basing analysis on the "same research model." It suggests generating a "horizontal model" at the domain level; in other words, the model consists of a main dependent variable domain such as AIDS RISK BEHAVIOR or UNPRODUCTIVE FARMS, and a number of independent variable domains. Those domains were broad, but not so broad that the "modelers" (researchers and community partners) could not understand their implications. Equally broad independent variable domains can be identified as the "predictors" or "correlates" of the dependent variable. For AIDS RISK BEHAVIOR, these might be INCOME, HOUSEHOLD PRESSURES, and/or EMPLOYMENT OUTSIDE THE HOME. For UNPRODUCTIVE FARMS, independent variable domains might be QUALITY OF FARMING EQUIPMENT, ACCESS TO FERTILIZER, and FAMILY SIZE. It is difficult to separate the creation of a horizontal model from its operationalization or unpacking, because identification of the primary variable domains always requires some definitions. However, creation of the "horizontal domain model" here has been separated from the unpacking process for heuristic purposes.

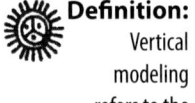

Definition: Vertical modeling refers to the operationalization of abstract conceptual domains into more concrete factors and variables

Definition: Operationalization means defining the factors in such a way that they can be observed and counted by others

Chapter 5 in this book defined and discussed "vertical modeling" and provided illustrations of how to carry it out. **Vertical modeling** refers to the operationalization of abstract conceptual domains into more concrete factors and variables. **Operationalization**, in other words, means defining the factors in such a way that they can be observed and counted by others. Formative research begins with initial horizontal and vertical models that evolve as multiple iterations, changes, and modifications occur over the course of the research. This process proceeds as existing preliminary results are calibrated and recalibrated through interaction with new and incoming data of different types. As the domains, factors, and variables become increasingly differentiated, and as decisions are made about the addition, consolidation, and elimination of factors and variables—and even domains—from the model, the model itself will change. This recursive process is one of the key characteristics of mixed methods ethnographic research.

Qualitative data tend to focus on the domain and factor levels and serve to define and help to operationalize these levels. As a reminder to readers, domains, factors, and variables make up a conceptual and organizational taxonomy that is differentiated by level of abstraction and is useful in organizing data. Domains can be thought of as

MIXED METHODS MODELS

the larger "umbrella terms" that include factors; factors are the constituent components of domains. These factors, in turn, consist of smaller- and lower-level conceptual categories that vary in presence/absence or quality and quantity and are called variables. Most qualitative methodologists use language similar to this. Spradley, for example, uses the terms *cover terms* and *included terms* (Spradley 1979).

At the same time, the systematic analysis of qualitative data (mainly in the form of in-depth and semistructured interviews and observations, consensus analysis, and sometimes through the use of focus groups) facilitates identification of variables within factors, as well as items that can be situated within variables and quantified in order to measure variables and their associations across a larger sample.

Quantitative data collection focuses on measuring variables, usually by means of a survey administered to a representative sample from a population, and examining the relationships or associations between those variables. If the first phase of a study focuses on the formation and calibration of a formative qualitative model depicting hypothesized associations among domains, factors, and variables, quantitative data are used subsequently to *test* how well this model matches the reality in the field. **When comparability of domains, factors, and variables exists across qualitative and quantitative data sets, the two types of data "match," and associational, verification, and explanatory analyses can be carried out across the two data sets.** This is illustrated in Table 7.3.

Cross Reference:
See Book 3, chapter 1, and Book 5, chapters 4, 5, and 6, for further discussion and ways of thinking about these hierarchies. Table 5.4 in Book 5 also displays how the language different researchers use to explain these processes can be equated

Key point

Linking Qualitative Data and Domains/Factors

Book 3 of the *Ethnographer's Toolkit* describes the utility and conduct of in-depth interviews with key informants or cultural experts. Interviews with key informants provide information at the community rather than at the personal level. Among other things, they tell researchers who the decision makers are in the setting, what rituals may be important, what problems exist in the community, the causes and consequences of these problems, and what out-

Cross Reference:
See Book 3, chapter 6

TABLE 7.3 Linking Conceptual Levels and Types of Data Collection

Conceptual Level	Qualitative Data	Quantitative Data
DOMAIN	Historical, observational, in-depth interviews with a few key informants	Designated sections of survey
FACTOR	In-depth key-informant interviews	Subsections of survey
VARIABLE	Semistructured interviews with participants, semistructured observations, listings in consensus analysis	Survey data scales (and some single variables)
ITEM	Semistructured interviews	Items in scales and single items (variables such as age)

side influences make a difference in community life. These interviews are extremely useful in identifying the key study domains and the factors that make up those domains in the study model, and they can also confirm the existence of any domains (and factors) identified from the literature or prior research. For example, key informants in buildings where senior citizens live told Institute for Community Research investigators that "depression" (a dependent variable) was a problem among older residents, and they described some of the factors they thought contributed to it, such as "social isolation," "poor health," "negative building environment," and "lack of physical mobility." In another example, teenagers in one Institute for Community Research summer youth research program created an initial horizontal model of the reasons for dropping out of school (a dependent variable) based on their own experience. In their initial model, predictors of dropping out of school (dependent variable domain) included family finances and pregnancy (predictors or independent variable domains). In-depth interviews carried out with peers, however, revealed that emotional stress was a critical mediating factor in dropping out. They reformulated their model, hypothesizing that family finances and pregnancy resulted in dropping out of school only when teens experienced high levels of emotional stress. They then added the STRESS domain to their horizontal model.

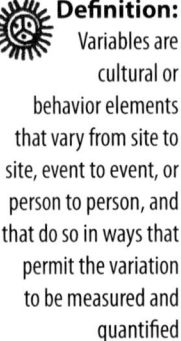
Definition: Variables are cultural or behavior elements that vary from site to site, event to event, or person to person, and that do so in ways that permit the variation to be measured and quantified

Semistructured interviewing is focused on unpacking both domains and factors, and as well, on generating variables that can be measured. **Variables** are cultural or behavior elements that vary from site to site, event to event, or person to person and that do so in ways that permit the variation to be measured and quantified. Variables constitute the basis for quantitative measurement; the variables and their composite measures (scales and indices) generate the questions that are included in an ethnographic survey instrument. Semistructured interviews can identify both the variables and the items that should be included as indicators of those variables. For example, a key variable relevant to a household's economic status might be "material style of life," meaning the material items that the household owns or commands. Items included under "material style of life" could be such things as "radio," "television," "car," "dishwasher," "recreational vehicle," and others. These items can be discovered easily by asking respondents to list the "things" that they own, and describe them, and then noting the presence/absence (categorical variables) of each item for each respondent. This information is useful in understanding the range of variability in material style of life (MSL) in the community, and at the same time, is critical in measuring material style of life in a survey.

A great deal of coding is done at the factor level. There are, however, many times when qualitative data also are analyzed (and even counted) at the variable level. This is, as noted throughout the *Toolkit*, an iterative process. In the example below we show ways that coding emerged and is quantified at the domain, factor, and variable levels.

 **EXAMPLE 7.1**

CODING AT THE DOMAIN, FACTOR, AND VARIABLE LEVELS

In a qualitative ethnographic study of use of the recreational drug Ecstasy (MDMA) among young adults, Singer and Schensul were able to define and examine qualitatively the risks and benefits associated with use of Ecstasy. RISKS and BENEFITS were considered as independent domains. Initially, the researchers proposed to look at the balance of risks and benefits in relation to ECSTASY USE, a dependent domain. In a review of the data, they observed that perception of control was also important and connected to risks, benefits, and use. So they added PERCEIVED CONTROL to the domains as a mediator of risks and benefits. The equation then read: The balance of risks and benefits led to perceived control, which in turn was associated with amount of Ecstasy used. Coding involved the identification of all statements representing perceived risks and perceived benefits of Ecstasy use. These "items" were classified into larger groupings (factors), and described qualitatively. Then these domains (perceived risk and perceived benefits) were treated as variables. The items were weighted and counted, and based on this quantification individuals were scored as higher or lower in perceived risk and perceived benefits. The same process was applied to perceived control and estimations of the amount of Ecstasy actually used. In their paper, the researchers were able to describe the "meanings" of these domains based on factors, illustrated by "items" (descriptive passages), and at the same time to show quantitatively the association between perceived control, amount of use, and perceived benefits (Singer and Schensul 2011). The emergent study model was descriptive and formative, because the sample was not representative of the general population of hidden Ecstasy users, the measures were quantified through estimate, and neither the sampling approach (non-representative) nor the sample size (too small) enabled inferential or confirmatory statistical techniques to be used.

Such techniques summarize trends and patterns in the data (pattern recognition) and characterize patterns numerically; they are based on forms of data crunching typical of qualitative data. **Data crunching** means organizing, classifying, and reducing or collapsing a large amount of concrete data bits into larger and more conceptual codes or groupings.

An ethnographic survey consists of questions that elicit responses about many different variables. Its results can be used just as they are received, but they also can be recoded and classified into larger or just different variables. For example, AGE measured as exact age can be recoded into three categories: zero to ten years of age, eleven to fifteen years of age, and sixteen to twenty years of age; or a variable called MATERIAL STYLE OF LIFE can be computed by adding up all of the items that households have purchased with disposable income and now own. More specific techniques of "data reduction," including principal components analysis (PCA) and scale development (using Cronbach's alpha), statistically examine the associations among items included in a variable or variables in a factor, and in this way, seek to improve and strengthen the measures. The goal in a good mixed methods approach is to use the

> **Definition:** Data crunching means organizing, classifying, and reducing or collapsing a large amount of concrete data bits into larger and more conceptual codes or groupings

> **Cross Reference:** Book 3, chapter 8, and Book 5, chapters 7 and 8, show how quantitative data can be collected, crunched, and analyzed

same model to look at the patterns that emerge from the data. The ideal mixed methods approach allows researchers to use the same model to examine similar patterns and associations in both qualitative and quantitative data. In the qualitative data, patterns and associations may be found at the factor or even at the variable level. In the quantitative data, they will be found through the quantification and correlation of numerical variables. This process is referred to as triangulation, which is discussed in greater detail in Book 5. If triangulation of the qualitative and quantitative data sets produces results that are conceptually and structurally similar, researchers can be more confident of results, and can explain them better. This process is described in more detail in Example 7.2.

EXAMPLE 7.2

OPERATIONALIZING THE FACTOR "SPOUSAL VIOLENCE"

A research model exploring factors contributing to HIV exposure in a low-income community in Mumbai included the domain WIFE-HUSBAND RELATIONSHIP. One of the factors subsumed within that domain was spousal violence. In the qualitative data, spousal violence was coded whenever behaviors such as the following appeared: yelling, slapping, punching, kicking, beating with a weapon, and forced sex. A complete review of the qualitative data produced an exhaustive list of behaviors that could be included as a part of spousal violence. These behaviors were listed and used to operationalize the construct "spousal violence" in the ethnographic survey created to measure outcomes of an intervention to reduce exposure to HIV risk. Based on the way violent behavior was expressed in the interviews, these items were formatted into a Likert scale with three points: regularly, sometimes, and never. The items formed a scale of "spousal violence." The qualitative data that were coded for spousal violence included narratives by women and men who had described their experiences with spousal violence and its role in their lives. These descriptions clarified the nature of spousal violence, and at the same time, permitted the construct to be examined in relation to other factors that were both quantitatively and qualitatively operationalized.

The qualitative descriptions of factor (and domain) codes can help to explain the frequency and variation of responses to quantitative variables, and the associations among qualitative variables can help to explain those same associations generated through quantitative analysis. The "story" or interpretation then represents an integration or triangulation of both approaches to the data, describing, verifying or confirming, and explaining the study results.

EXAMPLE 7.3

A MIXED METHODS APPROACH USING QUALITATIVE AND QUANTITATIVE DATA TO ASSESS SUCCESS IN THE LEARNING CIRCLE PROGRAM

The Learning Circle is an afterschool program in Phoenix, Arizona, dedicated to the development of listening, speaking, reading, and writing skills in English among urban Native American children from multiple tribal backgrounds. Its developer, Sandra Wilks, and the program director, Beth Fordemwalt, were committed to center the program on the cultural heritage of the children, even though doing so was difficult, given that they came from many tribal and mixed Anglo, Latino, and Indian backgrounds. They spent months developing a curriculum web that involved developing reading, writing, listening, and speaking activities that required children to elicit information from members of their family or group and present it to their classmates. They had to find out, for example, how their own ethnic group explained natural phenomena like lightning and wind, what stories were told in winter and summer and why, and what their clan and ancestry names and structures were. To get this information, the children had to do research and contact those relatives who still retained such information; the stories they amassed on these topics, of course, differed greatly.

The key dependent variable in the Learning Circle study was STUDENT ACHIEVEMENT, measured by the school district's standardized tests, the classroom teachers' rating scales of reading fluency, student grades, and attendance. These all were quantitative measures, derived from the school's own records, and used to answer one of the key questions in the study: "Does the Learning Circle have a positive impact on the language achievement of Native American students?" These data were referred to as the "quantitative data." However, the independent variables were not known, and they were needed to answer the other key research question: "To what can the success—if any—of the Learning Circle be attributed?" Qualitative investigation was required to identify what the independent variables might be; it included observations in all classrooms and program activities including teacher and staff meetings, interviews with teachers in the Learning Circle and the regular program, the administrators, parents, and children. The qualitative data collection began with initial unstructured observation and interviewing and moved to semistructured interviewing.

Independent variable domains identified in this initial phase included TEACHER BEHAVIOR, TEACHER ATTITUDES, CURRICULUM CONTENT, INSTRUCTIONAL ACTIVITIES, PARENT ACTIVITIES, DISTRICT SUPPORT, and PARENTAL PARTICIPATION.

A theme that ran through all of the qualitative data was how completely the Learning Circle differed, by design and in its commitments and activities, in its treatment of Native American culture and Native American people from "regular" school. Parents indicated that the Learning Circle was the only experience with public schooling they ever had where they were treated with respect. They especially appreciated that teachers, rather than truant officers, visited their homes and that when a Learning Circle meeting was held at the school, parents were invited and a meal was served. Teachers worked hard to make sure that the multiple heritages of all students were celebrated. The curriculum was designed so that each child could focus on aspects of the background of each of their ancestors and family members, no matter how different. A typical parental comment was, "It's the first time my daughter has ever told people she was an Indian, rather than lie and say she's Mexican. She's finally proud of who she is!"

The semistructured data gathering permitted the identification of a number of themes, including PRIVILEGING INDIAN WAYS OF KNOWING, FOLLOWING INDIAN CUSTOMS FOR SOCIAL ACTIVITIES, LEARNING ABOUT ONE'S NATAL CULTURES, and USING REAL TEACHERS FOR COMMUNICATION WITH PARENTS. Taken together, the researchers felt that these themes constituted a new domain that they named RESPECT FOR INDIAN CULTURE, which they believed contributed to student achievement, and added it to the study's conceptual model Additionally, the semistructured data collection identified another key domain, which the researchers felt had to do with DEVELOPING PRIDE IN ONE'S CULTURAL HERITAGE. Based on research by other investigators, the researchers with the Learning Circle felt that this domain was also connected with the major outcome variable, STUDENT ACHIEVEMENT. The addition of these two domains completed the study's formative model.

The next step involved developing a structured ethnographic survey and administering it to parents and teachers. Questions in this survey focused on the six factors listed above, including quantified participant opinions regarding to what degree they believed these were important characteristics of the program and what impact they had on the children. Analysis of the quantitative data provided mixed results, but they were clarified by results from the survey. Children did not show gains in language achievement on standardized tests, the school district's gold standard. However, they did show considerable improvement in school attendance, and, according to the teachers' rating scales and grade cards, they also had increases in oral language fluency and self-confidence in speaking before groups.

A summary of results from the ethnographic surveys indicated that teachers had indeed focused on behaviors that established parity of esteem between teachers and parents. Parents indicated that their children no longer wished to miss school because they did not want to lose out on Learning Circle activities. Parents also noted their children's increased interest in school and their zeal in following up on Learning Circle activities by eliciting stories and cultural information from family members and relatives; these assignments had been described by teachers as designed specifically to bring families together. Because children rehearsed their daily presentations with parents, their daily progress, as well as the teachers' interest in their culture, became increasingly apparent to the parents. Similarly, teachers reported on the surveys that parents were increasingly active attendees at school activities; the parent responses to the survey indicated that, for the first time, they felt welcome at school activities put on by the Learning Circle, and they confirmed that improved attendance was a consequence of their children's enthusiasm for the program, its activities, and the content of what they were studying.

The researchers reasoned that the disappointing standardized test results could be explained; examination of the tests demonstrated that the skills upon which the program focused were not those assessed by the tests. However, the researchers believed that increased attendance and self-confidence on oral tasks eventually would translate into improved test scores. More important in explaining the outcome variables were the survey results. The researchers found that the new dependent variable, DEVELOPING PRIDE IN ONE'S CULTURAL HERITAGE, was linked to all of the activities that the Learning Circle organized and that were measured in the survey. These, in turn, fostered the children's pride in their accomplishments, the parents' increasing comfort level with school activities and in interaction with teachers, and the children's improved enthusiasm for school attendance. All of these provided the foundation for engaging children in their schoolwork on a consistent basis, and thereby, improving their overall academic achievement. Looking at results from either the qualitative or quantitative data alone would not have created the overall portrayal of what happened in the program, nor explained why a focus on culture, and not just on language studies and grammar, produced the results it did (LeCompte, Aguilera, Wiertelak, et al. 1998 [2000]).

RELATING OR SEQUENCING OF MULTIPLE METHODOLOGIES: MODELS, METHODS, MEASURES, AND CASE EXAMPLES

There are many different ways to show the relationships between or to determine where to place mixed methods data collection sequentially in mixed methods research. In their 2004 article on mixed methods research designs, Johnson and Onwuegbuzie provide a framework for considering the weight and sequencing of the relationships between qualitative and quantitative research. They suggest thinking of studies as mixing qualitative and quantitative methods *concurrently, sequentially, weighting them equally, or placing them in ranked order* (Johnson and Onwuegbuzie 2004, 22). Johnson and Onwuegbuzie's description is used here as a starting point, keeping in mind that these authors do not consider the ongoing interplay between qualitative and quantitative work *over time*. Here, in the *Ethnographer's Toolkit*, such interplay is described as *multiphase research*.

Sequential Designs

Ideally, an ethnographic study starts with qualitative data collection based on an initial formative model that emphasizes discovery, elicitation of peoples' perceptions, and collection of descriptive narratives. This provides a broad picture of the study phenomena. As time goes on, the researcher narrows the research lens and shifts to a more focused set of qualitative data collection that could include both semistructured observation and interviewing. The more focused qualitative data collection will yield variables that, once transformed and formatted into survey questions, will be represented on a survey instrument or a structured observation protocol. This quantitative phase can be followed by a further step in which quantitative results are explained and elaborated by qualitative data, as in Example 7.2 above. **When the same conceptual model drives both the qualitative and quantitative work, and the survey is built on the conceptual model and concepts and constructs derived from the culture of the study population and the related study model, the qualitative data used to explain the quantitative results are derived from the same study.**

Key point

This ethnographically rooted approach to mixed methods research is arguably the most logical and systematic of the variety of mixed methods designs in the literature.

There are times, however, when qualitative work may follow quantitative research; for example, when the first phase of a study is based on quantitative secondary data or the survey phase of a study adds domains and measures that are not reflected in the qualitative data. And additional qualitative research may at times be needed if the explanations for ethnographic survey results are not apparent from the earlier qualitative research because insufficient data on the topic were not collected during that phase. Creswell et al. (2011) terms the latter a *sequential design* in which one type of data builds on another. Morse, in 1991, referred to this same process as *sequential triangulation*, noting that "sequential triangulation is utilized when the results of one approach are necessary for planning [for] the next [data collection] method" (Morse 1991, 120). Most methodologists do not seem to view this last step as an inherent part of a mixed methods design, but in ethnography it is *essential*, both for member checking and for sharing data with the study community. Example 7.4 illustrates a mixed methods approach used in research on HIV in Mumbai. Following the Johnson and Onwuegbuzie matrix, this design is sequential and gives equivalent weight to qualitative and quantitative phases of the study.

EXAMPLE 7.4

A SEQUENTIAL MIXED METHODS DESIGN WITH QUALITATIVE/QUANTITATIVE EQUIVALENCY

Cross Reference: See chapter 8 in this book for more information on how cultural concepts can guide and steer research and intervention

In a collaborative six-year intervention study (2001–2007) to reduce the risk of HIV/STI transmission among men in low-income communities in Mumbai, Schensul and Verma first conducted qualitative research to search for a culturally embedded concept that could serve as an anchor for the study. A cultural "hook" or anchor is a concept that is well understood and has significant meaning to members of the study population, and is related, or potentially related, to the problem. Through key informant interviews, they identified the culturally based concept of *gupt rog* (literally "secret illness"). *Gupt rog* refers to a wide range of men's sexual problems, including performance quality, semen inadequacy, and disease (Schensul et al. 2004).

Semistructured interviewing, including free listing and pilesorting, identified a taxonomy under the domain *GUPT ROG*, consisting of the factors *kamjori* (sexual weakness), *dhat* (semen problems), and *garmi* (heat-related problems with a disease dimension). Each of these factors included a series of symptoms (items) which could be measured as present/absent or in terms of degree of seriousness or severity. These symptoms together constituted a single *gupt rog* scale.

Cross Reference: Book 3, chapter 7, on semistructured interviewing, and Book 4, chapter 3, on free listing, pilesorting, and consensus analysis

The scale consisted of three subscales, one for each type of problem under the umbrella of the domain *GUPT ROG*. The initial qualitative work showed that men with symptoms of *gupt rog* were concerned about their sexuality, and that some of these men were seeking sexual partners outside of marriage. Details on their sexual behavior obtained in the qualitative phase of the study provided the basis for measuring another set of variables within the domain SEXUAL RISK. The indicators for sexual risk included sex with nonmarital partners and unprotected sex. The overall scale was used to evaluate the hypothesized relationship between *gupt rog* (loosely translated as men's sexual dysfunction) and sexual risk behavior. A survey instrument was administered to a random sample of 2,408 men in three study sites. The results showed that the overall prevalence of *gupt rog* was 53 percent. Further analysis showed that sexually risky behavior (including extramarital sex and risky behavior with friends) was significantly associated with *gupt rog* symptoms. These results produced additional qualitative investigation into the factors associated with *gupt rog*, which included alcohol use, marital conflicts, financial problems, and poor communication with spouse which were, in turn, quantified and used in additional quantitative analyses.

Simultaneous and Multiphase Designs

Creswell et al. (2011) describe three additional mixed methods designs: *convergent*, in which both qualitative and quantitative methods are used concurrently; *embedded*, in which a basically qualitative study has a quantitative component or a quantitative study has a qualitative component; and a *multiphase* design in which separate but related studies are sequenced over time. To some degree, these correspond to the classifications of Johnson and Onwuegbuzie, Morse, and others, although the former weights the relative significance of qualitative and quantitative components. Below each of these is reviewed with examples from the authors' work.

Convergent designs. In convergent designs, both methods, qualitative and quantitative, are used at the same time. The emphasis on one method versus the other will depend on the study design and the preferences of the research team. One form of convergence involves qualitative research that parallels the quantitative research by attempting to ask the same questions of both types of data. Here, the convergence is on answering questions in parallel fashion using the same domains as guidance, but without shifting downward to the factor or variable level. For example, a quantitative component of a study on food control behaviors in older adults might quantify and examine the correlates of food control behaviors. A qualitative or narrative component might obtain stories and critical events that illustrate food control and the settings in which it occurs. Triangulation would look for parallels and illustrative data that explain results of the quantitative analysis.

A second form of convergence mentioned earlier occurs when the same domains are unpacked to the factor or even the variable level, variables situated within study domains are quantified, and correlations or associational analysis conducted on the quantitative data are paralleled with the qualitative data and the results are used to explain the quantitative correlations or the variance. Convergence is illustrated in Example 7.2 and in the following example.

EXAMPLE 7.5

CONVERGENCE OF QUALITATIVE AND QUANTITATIVE METHODS IN THE EVALUATION OF CHANGES IN GENDER-EQUITABLE NORMS IN A STUDY POPULATION IN MUMBAI

In a second study in a low-income area of Mumbai (2007–2013) on women's exposure to sexual risk and HIV, the Schensuls and their collaborators identified *safed pani* (white discharge) as an indicator of marital problems and other negative life situations. These included poor communication between husband and wife, husbands' lack of concern with wives' health, inadequate economic resources, *tenshun* (tension) stemming from marital violence, and stressful living circumstances, including problems with in-laws and housing. Researchers converted these issues into a multilevel intervention focused on counseling for women and couples on improving marital relationships, and the promotion of gender-equitable norms at

MIXED METHODS MODELS

the community level. The promotion of gender-equitable norms at the community level was an especially important component of the intervention because without it, women would have found it difficult to assert their desires for improved communication; men who wished to behave in more supportive ways with their wives would have been criticized by their peers as not sufficiently masculine, and mosques, traditionally perceived as endorsing masculine-dominant norms and behaviors, could undermine intervention efforts.

Because the institution with the greatest capacity to reach large numbers of men was the mosque, the project staff began to work with the imams (clergy) in the study community to develop gender-equitable messages about marital relationships. Working together, project staff, imams, and NGO staff created messages that supported positive marital relationships, reduction of violence, increasing the priority of women's health, and sexual risk reduction. To ensure consistency with Koranic scriptures, they sought the advice and counsel of an Islamic scholar. Imams then embedded the messages in their weekly sermons at Friday *takrir* (sermon). NGOs then also used the messages in communitywide campaigns, emphasizing gender equity and women's rights.

To evaluate the degree to which messages were delivered and the extent to which they changed perceptions and beliefs, the study *simultaneously* made use of both qualitative and quantitative methods. First, a gender equity scale (GES) based on items related to male/female relationships was developed. These items were derived from in-depth interviews previously conducted with both women and men. The scale was tested in the community with married men and women, and reduced to twenty-nine items. The GES scale was administered three times over a three-year period, from 2009 to 2011, each time to a random sample of approximately 950 married women and men in the community (Kostick et al. 2010). The purpose was to determine whether there was a trend toward more equitable gender norms over time as a result of the intervention by the NGO staffs, and especially by the mosques. The scale was also administered to participating imams and NGO staff. At the second time point, results showed improvements in beliefs about gender equity and equitable relationships among men and women.

At the same time a series of qualitative methods were used to evaluate community impact in terms of gender equity. These involved observations at *takrir*, and in-depth interviews with community leaders, NGO staff, and imams. The results currently are being triangulated to explain how and why gender norms are changing at different rates and in different ways across the study populations.

Embedded designs. In their 2004 article on mixed methods research designs, Johnson and Onwuegbuzie consider the weight and sequencing of the relationships between qualitative and quantitative research. They suggest thinking of studies as mixing qualitative and quantitative methods concurrently or sequentially, and as weighted equally or in ranked order (Johnson and Onwuegbuzie 2004, 22). In embedded mixed methods designs, either qualitative or quantitative approaches may be dominant, ranked or stacked, or used equally. And in both instances they may be concurrent, or sequenced in either order (Johnson et al. 2007). Research on HIV prevention in India provides a good example of embedded mixed methods design.

EXAMPLE 7.6

AN EMBEDDED DESIGN WHERE QUALITATIVE DATA SUPPLEMENT THE RESULTS OF QUANTITATIVE EVALUATION DATA

The earlier-mentioned intervention study involving preventing HIV infection among women through improving couples' relationships and fostering gender equitable norms includes two counseling interventions, one for women alone, and the second for couples attending group sessions. This part of the project is a typical factorial randomized, controlled trial (RCT) carried out in collaboration with a public health clinic serving women in one very large slum area in eastern Mumbai. The counseling interventions are a partnership between the researchers' institutions, the Tata Institute of Social Sciences (TISS), Mumbai, a local hospital and medical school, and the associated community health center where physicians from the hospital are the main service providers.

Women who come to the health center for reproductive health problems are recruited into the project and randomly assigned to individual counseling (IC), couples' intervention (CI), a combination of the two (IC + CI) or a control group. The design tests which component of the intervention is more effective. The outcomes of the counseling intervention are measured with a quantitative instrument; the Women's Structured Survey (WSS). The WSS is administered to each woman at baseline (prior to the intervention), six months (after the intervention), and one year. Variables in the WSS include relationship variables, indicators of tension, violence, conflict, income-related factors, and indicators of sexual health. Supplemental to the surveys, the research team conducts qualitative in-depth semistructured interviews with a sample of women who have completed individual counseling (IC) to assess their perceptions of the intervention and its impact on their lives. These interviews are coded and analyzed thematically for effects, including those measured by the WSS. In addition, the same trained qualitative researchers conduct observations on every fourth group attending the counseling intervention (CI). This intervention consists of six sessions per group. Each group is composed of spousal pairs. Observations are focused on intervention fidelity, as well as indications that pairs, or individual participants, are gaining communication skills and insights in handling conflict, reducing or eliminating violence, and negotiating health and other needs more effectively. A subsample of husbands and wives are also interviewed separately about their perceptions of the sessions and the usefulness of the sessions in improving their own relationships. The results obtained from the qualitative work are thematic, reflecting dominant trends and patterns in the data and providing narratives of experience and resulting effects to complement the results of the quantitative outcomes.

Some researchers who conduct primarily qualitative studies add numerical data that are intended to show demographic patterns, to obtain important quantified information central to the study, and to help to organize the qualitative data into groups of cases for comparative analysis. LeCompte, for example, shows how she collected some quantitative data on Native American students' attitudes toward school in Tables 7.1 and 7.3 of Book 5 of the *Ethnographer's Toolkit*. Researcher Geoffrey Hunt conducts primarily qualitative research on youth and young adult drug and alcohol use and gang involvement in the San Francisco area (Hunt et al. 2005; Laidler and Hunt 2001). To accompany the in-depth interviews that are his methodological trademark, Hunt generally adds a brief survey in which he collects demographic data (ethnic/national group, age, education, residential situation, income, etc.), a matrix that collects systematic and accurate information about types of drugs used, how frequently and how much, and another form to collect family characteristics and other data that are used to describe overall patterns and to develop subsets that consisted of up to three hundred in-depth interviews taken from the overall data set. These subsets could be analyzed comparatively by drug use pattern, ethnic/cultural background, and other important differences.

Jean Schensul's qualitative study of the use of MDMA (a recreational drug popularly called Ecstasy) among 123 young adults in the Hartford, Connecticut, area also was accompanied by a brief survey instrument. The instrument included a history of MDMA and other drug use, locations where respondents used MDMA or knew that MDMA was used, and specific sexual behaviors commonly associated with Ecstasy use. While the in-depth interviews were allowed to vary to some degree, researchers needed to collect consistent information in these domains from all respondents (Singer and Schensul 2011).

Multiphase designs. Multiphase designs are defined as designs that address a single topic but are separate and distinct, and follow each other in time. Margarete Sandelowski and others might refer to this pattern as a "research program" (Sandelowski in Johnson and Onwuegbuzie 2004, 121), but research programs can be differentiated from multiphase designs. One type of multiphase design is a funded sequence that includes a capacity building/infrastructure phase, a research or intervention research phase, and a dissemination/scale up or translational phase. A good example of this type of design is a funded program of the National Institute for Dental and Cranial Research that supported a two-year pilot effort to be followed by a five-year intervention. The National Institute for Research on Health Disparities recently announced an eleven-year funding program that included a three-year capacity building effort to create research infrastructure and assess intervention potential, a five-year intervention study, and a three-year translation/dissemination phase.

A much more common type of multiphase design tends to evolve from a long-term relationship with study communities. An increasing number of such ventures are described in the research literature; they are the result of efforts during the 2000s to build university community research engagement programs and community-based participatory research alliances as described in Examples 7.7 to 7.10.

EXAMPLE 7.7

LONG-TERM URBAN RESEARCH IN DETROIT

A long-term partnership between agencies in Detroit and the University of Michigan School of Public Health was begun in 1995 with funding from the CDC. Similar efforts began in New York and Seattle. In the initial phases, partnerships were formed in each of the cities using the auspices of the Urban Research Center. These partnerships provided the basis for drawing in other sources of funding to address significant public health problems such as asthma and cardiovascular disease. In 2003, though funding for these centers ended, the centers themselves continued. Continuity rested on commitment to community-based participatory research efforts, obtaining funding for new projects, cost sharing, and long-term commitment (Israel et al. 2006).

EXAMPLE 7.8

THE NUTRITIONAL HEALTH RESEARCH, EDUCATION, AND ADVOCACY PROGRAM OF THE HISPANIC HEALTH COUNCIL

The Hispanic Health Council, an independent community service, education, and advocacy research center, has worked in the Hartford area to improve the health of Latinos and other groups experiencing disparities in health compared to mainstream populations for the past thirty years. In the late 1990s, an ongoing alliance with the University of Connecticut's Department of Nutritional Sciences resulted in the development of an NIH-funded center to address health disparities among Latinos. Among the nutrition-related issues affecting the Hispanic community in Hartford, Connecticut, Type 2 diabetes is probably the most significant. The Center for Excellence in Health Disparities and Latinos's (CEHDL) first programs consisted of NIH-funded clinical trials to improve diabetes management. Since that time, a number of other nutrition and food-justice programs have been mounted in the community. Each phase of development is preceded by conversations in the community to determine what issues are central to community welfare. In this way, a multiphased program of research in the area of diet, nutrition, and the management of related health problems has evolved over time (Fitzgerald et al. 2008; Pérez-Escamilla 2009; Tanasescu et al. 2000).

The following example highlights a long-term program of AIDS research in Hartford, Connecticut, based on alliances among a number of community organizations concerned with the impact of the HIV/AIDS epidemic on men and women injecting drugs and involved in risky sexual exchanges.

EXAMPLE 7.9

A LONG-TERM PROGRAM OF AIDS-RELATED RESEARCH IN HARTFORD, CONNECTICUT

Long-term alliances with bases in community settings can mount multistage research projects that emerge from their ongoing interaction with the world of research on the one hand, and community needs on the other. In 1986, a Hartford-based coalition of organizations including the Health Department, the Hispanic Health Council, and the Urban League of Greater Hartford recognized that HIV among drug users was becoming a serious problem in Hartford. In 1987, the Institute for Community Research was formed and joined the alliance, as did AIDS Project Hartford and its Latino arm, Latinos Contra SIDA. This consortium worked together on AIDS-related research for many years. The first AIDS study addressed knowledge, beliefs, and attitudes about AIDS in Hartford's neighborhoods. The infrastructure that was generated by these state-funded studies allowed the consortium to obtain federal research funding for culturally specific intervention to prevent HIV risk.

Next, with the growing recognition that HIV could be transmitted through unclean injection equipment, the same consortium backed the formation of a needle exchange program in the city and an evaluation of its reach and effectiveness. Subsequently, the consortium expanded to include prevention education, case management, a study of the role of violence in promoting susceptibility to HIV, and many studies of female-controlled protection options including microbicides and female condoms. Research also included studies of HIV exposure in older adults and in youth (Radda et al. 2003; Schensul et al. 2005; Schensul et al. 2003). In this way, a multiphased series of studies transformed over time into a long-term program of research that has been referred to as the Hartford Model of AIDS Practice/Research Collaboration (Singer and Weeks 2005).

EXAMPLE 7.10

MULTISTAGE RESEARCH ON HIV RISK PREVENTION AMONG MARRIED COUPLES IN MUMBAI COMMUNITIES

Another long-term example of a multistage project is S. Schensul, Verma, and colleagues' work since 1997 in a low-income community of five hundred thousand people. The first project (1995–2000) began with funding from the Ford Foundation to examine the issues of *gupt rog* and related sexual concerns and their treatment by nonallopathic providers. This project (see Verma and Schensul 2004) used a sequential design of qualitative interviews with men and providers followed by a survey instrument with both men and women. The results of this research led to an NIMH-funded project during 2001 to 2007 involving the prevention of HIV/STI among married men, again using a sequential design involving qualitative interviewing with fifty-two men, a baseline and postintervention cross-sectional survey with 2,408 men, and a one-year cross-sectional follow-up with 2,730 men. The research led to a supplement during 2002 to 2006 that focused on women and assessed their risks of HIV/STI transmission within marriage. This study involved in-depth interviewing with sixty-six women and a baseline survey instrument administered to 260 men. The cumulative data using both qualitative and quantitative methods in each discrete project led to the development and implementation of an NIMH-funded project during 2007 to 2013 that focused on sexual risk reduction for married women. Each of these projects used mixed methods sequentially and in a convergent and an embedded approach.

Many more such examples of multiphase programs of research that evolve based on research and needs in the local setting can be described. All use various approaches to mixed methods and make use of a variety of ways to integrate qualitative and quantitative methods. When research is conducted over a long period of time in a series of phases, the emphasis is on accumulating a body of knowledge that is a product of multiple methods. While the initial step may be qualitative or quantitative, the specific combination or sequence over time may be less important than the continued accumulation of results leading to evolving iterations in understanding the phenomena under study.

THE ROLE OF SECONDARY DATA IN MIXED METHOD ETHNOGRAPHY

Most countries, states and provinces, districts and municipalities collect quantitative data for the purposes of monitoring population, economic development, health, education employment, tobacco use, and other factors. ICF International, in combination with USAID, has conducted Demographic and Health Surveys (DHS) for two decades in over seventy countries at multiple time points. The U.S. Centers for Disease Control (CDC) has conducted many health surveys in multiple countries. In the United States, the National Health and Nutrition Examination Survey and the Longitudinal Study of Adolescent Health are just two of a vast number of surveys of interest to policy makers, researchers, and administrators. Many of these data sets are available electronically for both public and professional access. For an ethnographer, these data can be an excellent way to initiate local qualitative and quantitative research; they also provide data against which to compare ethnographic results generated from a localized setting.

> **Cross Reference:**
> See chapter 2 in Book 4 on "Sources and Uses of Secondary Data"

Mixed methods designs also can use **secondary data** in a number of ways. Secondary data can provide needed background for an ethnographic study before the researcher enters the field. The results of secondary data analysis, for example, can be used to create an initial formative model and a series of hypotheses. These data can also be used while the researcher is in the field to test localized results or qualitatively observed associations, on a larger, but similar national sample, to see if these associations are supported. Local results can be described with reference to similar patterns at the state or national or even the international level.

> **Definition:**
> Archival data consist of summary and analytic reports and analyses of data sets. Secondary data *sources* are actual raw data sets that can be manipulated to obtain new or desired results

Archival data, which differ from secondary data sources, also can be used in mixed methods research. **Archival data** consist of summary and analytic reports and analyses of data sets. Secondary data *sources* are actual raw data sets that can be manipulated to obtain new or desired results. Obtaining access to the data sets significantly increases the potential for their use as a part of an ethnographic study, since once obtained, the data can be manipulated in many ways to increase comparability. For example:

> **Cross Reference:**
> See Book 4, chapter 2

- The location of the sample can be arranged into subsets so that the data reflect only urban or rural populations or populations from the same state.
- The sample can be organized into subsets on the basis of demographic factors such as age, gender, marital status, household structure, and many other variables.
- Variables can be selected for an analysis that comes closest to the ethnographic focus, while those variables that are less relevant to the focus can be eliminated from the data set.

EXAMPLE 7.11

THE USE OF A NATIONAL DATA SET IN INDIA TO COMPARE CORRELATES OF ANEMIA IN SLUM COMMUNITIES IN MUMBAI WITH A LOCAL STUDY COMMUNITY

The National Family Health Survey (NFHS) of 2009 is India's version of a cross-national survey on family and reproductive health, known as the Demographic and Health Survey (DHS), which is administered in more than 100 countries on a regular basis. In preparation for a study of unmarried adolescent girls in a low-income community in Mumbai, medical student Dylan Graetz was able to use NFHS data as the basis for preparation of her mixed methods study. She first chose from the data set a sample of unmarried young women from fifteen to nineteen. Though her intention was to focus on unmarried girls between the ages of thirteen and eighteen, the minimum age of girls included in the NFHS data was fifteen. She then extracted the data set for Mumbai and further refined it to obtain the data for low-income communities in Mumbai, technically referred to as slum communities. Slum communities are differentiated, enumerated, and included as a separate coded category in most large national data sets. As a result of these exercises with the data, she was able to obtain a substantial sample of young women in similar communities throughout the city with which she could test a series of hypotheses about the antecedents of anemia. After obtaining the prevalence of anemia in a sample of girls in the study community, and collecting data on possible predictors, she matched the prevalence (and the predictors) with the NFHS data for slum communities, Mumbai overall, and then with slum communities in five other urban areas in India.

In addition to using large national and regional data sets, many new ethnographic researchers return to follow up on mixed methods research done earlier by other researchers, but in the study community where they plan to do their work. Although they may choose topics that are different from those addressed in the earlier studies, prior data can afford insights into the dynamics of the study community and can help to define some of the independent variables and variable domains for the new study. While much of the available secondary data is quantitative, there also may be a considerable amount of de-identified qualitative data that can prove crucial in the development of a study.

Cross Reference: See Book 4, chapter 2, for a detailed discussion of the availability and uses of various types of secondary and archival data

EXAMPLE 7.12

USING PREVIOUSLY COLLECTED QUALITATIVE AND QUANTITATIVE DATA TO SHED LIGHT ON A NEW TOPIC

While preparing for research in Mumbai, Marie Brault, an anthropology graduate student, read forty-three in-depth interviews that had been conducted with married women about their sexual and reproductive health in one study community in the eastern part of the city during 2009 to 2010. This data set included information on fertility control and sterilization. Marie's own interest was in fertility control, with particular emphasis on the antecedents and consequences of sterilization. She further explored these issues in a quantitative survey data set that had been collected in 2005 to 2006 in three communities, with 260 married women. These data formed the basis for her master's thesis on factors related to sterilization among married women in a low-income community in Mumbai (Brault 2012).

SUMMARY

Weisner states, "the future of . . . the social sciences is far more likely to be characterized by interdisciplinary methodological pluralism" (Weisner 2012). This chapter has described such methodological pluralism as the complementary and sequential nature of the mix between qualitative and quantitative methods and their roles in ethnography, with special emphasis on sequential and multistage approaches. While the ideal approach may be to start with the advantages of the discovery potential of qualitative methods, move to operationalize the results into an ethnographic survey, and return to qualitative methods to explain correlations and gaps, mixing methods can occur in any number of ways. The key to successful integration of mixed methods studies is to triangulate the data results and integrate the multiple approaches to create the most complete understanding possible of phenomena. Doing this requires using the most appropriate methodological choices and measures for each phase of the research. In the final chapter of this book, we describe how to use the procedures and models discussed herein for the construction of effective intervention models and strategies for inducing social change and solving problems.

8

MODELING ETHNOGRAPHIC INTERVENTION APPROACHES

> Introduction
> Definitions of Intervention
> Ethnographic Intervention Designs
> Guidelines for Modeling Interventions
> Steps in Designing Interventions: A Systems Analytic Approach to Using Modeling Techniques
> Linking Resources for Change to the Independent Variables: Systems Analysis as a "2 × 2 Table"
> Operationalizing the Intervention Model
> Summary

INTRODUCTION

This book has focused on establishing the basis for ethnographic fieldwork by discussing field preparation, pre-data collection research models, and the development of proposals that include models, methods, and measures and how to formulate them. In this chapter we encourage researchers to prepare in advance for the dissemination of their anticipated ethnographic research results by conceptualizing how their research could be used to inform and advise policy makers, and to design interventions. The standard basic science approach to ethnographic and social science research is to develop and formulate a theoretical model, collect data to evaluate the model, see how the data fit with and explain the model, and revise the model in line with the new understanding based on empirical data. Social scientists then publish books, book chapters, and/or peer-reviewed journal articles that describe research results with implications for policy and practice. There are several reasons why the research process should extend *beyond* this typical three-step approach.

> **Definition:**
> An associative model is one in which the variable domains are correlated but cannot be said to be predictive because the study takes place in one period, rather than over a longer period of time

> **Definition:**
> A cross-sectional design takes place at one point in time and usually can explain phenomena for a relatively short period, up to a year

> **Definition:**
> A longitudinal design follows people, communities, and situations over time

First, the end product of the research project itself is a final model that the ethnographic researcher feels best describes the focal problem, its antecedents, its consequence, and its context. Depending on whether the research design is cross-sectional or longitudinal, it will be a "causal" or predictive model or an "associative" model. An **associative model** is one in which the variable domains are correlated but cannot be said to be predictive because the study is cross-sectional; that is, it takes place in one period, rather than over a longer period of time. Such a **cross-sectional design** usually can explain phenomena that occur over a relatively short period of time, for example, up to a year, because insufficient time exists to determine whether one situation actually leads to or causes another that happens later. A **longitudinal design** follows people, communities, and situations over time. In such a design, it is possible to see how preceding events and factors/variables actually could "cause" an outcome, at least in the short run. But how accurate and valid might that final model be? In statistical terms, we would be extremely happy if a multivariate regression model predicted 50 percent of the variance of a dependent variable, leaving 50 percent of the variance unexplained. Thus, in most instances, our final models leave much still to be explained.

A further problem in social science research is that any research model describes the population and the phenomena under study only during a given time period, even if it is prospective and follows people and situations over time. Structural, group, and community dynamics and change do not cease when data collection is completed; new events and challenges continue to transform communities and other settings, which always means that the final research model will lag behind current realities (S. Schensul 1985). Continued research is always needed to adjust the model to emergent situations. In addition, social science research takes place within dynamic systems in which components change constantly in interaction with one another. Dynamic systems models try to take into consideration that multiple factors interact over time to produce unanticipated results and "emergent causality" (Kallis 2007; Nowotny 2005; Schneider and Somers 2006; Weidlich

2005; Winder 2007). Dynamic systems researchers refer to the process of fitting the model to new realities as *calibration* (Homer 2006; Oliva 2003).

A *second* approach to model verification over time is to design long-term, longitudinal, or multistage studies. Examples of long-term studies in field sites that have endured more than twenty or thirty years include the Vicos Project in Peru, where many social scientists worked at a former hacienda in which the land and governance were turned over to the workers (Greaves et al. 2010), Donna Deyhle's thirty-year study of Navajo and Ute families in the Four Corners area of Utah and Arizona, Shirley Heath's ten-year examination of child language acquisition and schooling in two communities in the American southeast (Heath 1970), or J. and S. Schensul's health and education related research in Hartford, Connecticut (Schensul and Schensul 1978; Schensul 2006; J. Schensul 2010; Schensul, Radda et al. 2009). Most ethnographers, however, do not track the same research issue over a long period of time in a single site. To test and retest a model, the research would have to focus on the same question and monitor changes over time rather than diversifying the research to address new questions in the same field locations. An exception is the work of Douglas White and colleagues who tracked changes in a Turkish population over a decade of field research (White and Johansen 2005). Several researchers working in the area of adolescent substance use also have tracked changes in their populations over three generations. Similarly, others have tracked changes in family composition and networks (Cochran et al. 1990) and children's welfare (Weisner 2005), and it is possible to do longitudinal studies with national data sets such as the National Health and Nutrition Examination Survey (NHANES) on health and nutrition, or the National Longitudinal Study of Adolescent Health (Add Health) on adolescent risk behavior and sexual health. With such data sets researchers can examine how independent variables measured the same way over time interact differently with the key dependent variables at different developmental time points.

A *third* approach is to disseminate results to policy makers and decision makers and then assess the role of

Cross Reference: Diversification in multiphase or multicomponent studies is described in chapter 7 of this book

these results in affecting subsequent change. This approach seeks to validate results in the "court of public opinion" as well as to increase the utility of the results in contributing to positive change. To implement this strategy, ethnographic researchers need to understand how to study decision makers and be familiar with the format of the reports different audiences will need, as well as the types of evidence that such audiences find acceptable.

Experimentation is a *fourth* approach to model verification. Experimentation is at the heart of the scientific method. A experiment can be defined as a scientific test carried out in order to discover whether a theory is correct or what the results of a particular course of action would be. Introducing systematically implemented scientific experimentation into the ethnographic research process is a way of reaching this goal. ***Experimentation means using the research model as the basis for guiding changes, the results of which would verify or validate the study's predictive model.*** This is done by transforming the independent variable domains that bring about negative outcomes in the dependent variable domain by introducing changes in them that could transform the outcome from negative to positive. If changes in the *independent* variable domains as a result of the intervention (experimentation) result in a significant positive impact on the *dependent* variable domain, additional support for the validity of the final research model can be claimed. This approach places experimentation (or intervention) at the heart of the research effort because it actually *tests* one or more components of the final formative research model through action, rather than solely by making inferences based on statistically significant results. Intervention strengthens the scientific validity and integrity of the research model. Of course, at the same time that they produce valid models, interventions also serve to bring about desired change. Thus, interventions are valuable and critically important in and of themselves.

 Key point

DEFINITIONS OF INTERVENTION

The term *intervention* has many meanings depending on disciplinary reference. In psychology, the concept of intervention often refers to strategies to introduce externally designed and implemented changes into the lives of individuals, families, and larger groups. Increasingly, psychologists have referenced culture as an important influence on the construction of planned change efforts, and some psychologists have moved toward collaboration with partners—teachers, students, and agency staffs—in the development of culturally specific intervention programs (Bernal and Sáez-Santiago 2006; Varjas et al. 2006; Varjas et al. 2005). Community psychologists also are recognizing that contextual factors play an important role in individual, group, or family behavior; they generate interventions to address these phenomena (Logan et al. 2002).

Educational interventions are common, generally aimed to improve the performance of students, teachers, or both. Educational social scientists have increasingly recognized that educational policies and whole-school or systemic changes are required in order to produce good educational outcomes. Schools also may be used as sites for other types of interventions, including establishing drug use prevention programs, testing children for eye and ear problems, introducing drivers' education to improve automobile safety among adolescents, creating breakfast and lunch programs to alleviate malnutrition among school children, and designing programs to prevent mental health problems and relational and social abuses such as bullying and teen dating violence.

Despite the reluctance of theoretical and empirical sociologists to shift toward a more applied focus (Burawoy 2005), sociology also has a long history of intervention research, mainly focused on the introduction, evaluation, and critique of social policies (Oakley 1998), including educational policies. Sociologists also may develop and evaluate large-scale social welfare interventions; for example, wraparound services in school settings that assist both students and their families (Bruns and Walker 2011), the development of new forms of housing and housing communities, and employment-to-work programs for impoverished people in low-income neighborhoods. Fals Borda, Paulo Freire, and other social science and educational researchers conducted interventions in which participants were intro-

> **Cross Reference:**
> Book 7 discusses various approaches to the use of ethnography in various forms of intervention research in education, participatory action research (PAR), policy-related fields, and administration

duced to sociological analyses of social and economic conditions leading to, or in the context of, ongoing strikes, acts of resistance, and social movements. Analysis of the impact of these interventions can be used to frame their subsequent social change strategies (Fals Borda and Rahman 1991; Freire 1970). Some might say that ethnography itself is an intervention because of the ways in which researchers interact with relevant people and in social settings. However, interaction with participants and ethnographic research activities by themselves do not involve intentional change, even though they could have some unintended consequences for the lives of people in the setting or for the ways that policies and practices are carried out once the research is completed. For example, in the course of his intervention research in rural Anole in Uganda, Stephen Schensul put his vehicle to frequent use as an ambulance to convey women with obstructed labor to the hospital in the nearest town. While this action presented intervention, it was neither planned nor systematic. Planned or intentional interventions refer to specific efforts to bring about change in individuals, groups, communities, institutions, and policies, and in sociocultural norms and practices, preferably with those directly affected by the situation.

By contrast, most anthropologists have tried to avoid the term *intervention* because of its association with acts engaged in by colonial government administrations and twentieth-century U.S. urban social engineering and psychological studies (Grillo 1985; Milgram 1974; Rylko-Bauer et al. 2006), none of which may have served the needs of local people, and many of which may indeed have been contrary to their interests, especially those of the most dominated and marginalized peoples. Social engineers and even many public health researchers may hold that the public should have little or no say in the interventions constructed for them, even though members of that public are participants in them. This approach to intervention research places scientists in positions of power over others whose behavioral changes they are determining, presumably for their own good, or some larger social good. Thus, despite their uneasiness with the term, many anthropologists have been interventionists for decades. Over the past

>  **Cross Reference:**
> See Book 1, chapter 10, and Book 6 for discussions of the ethical consequences of such interventions and as well, procedures set in place to alleviate harm to research participants

fifty years, many anthropologists have made active efforts to stand in solidarity with communities and marginalized groups, working with them to devise alternative strategies to improve their lives and strengthen their voices. Anthropological interventions have included community development efforts (Schensul and Schensul 1978; S. Schensul 1978; S. Schensul 1980; van Willigen 2002; van Willigen 2005), disaster relief efforts (Oliver-Smith 1996; Oliver-Smith and Goldman 1988), health intervention approaches at multiple levels (Dickson-Gomez et al. 2006; Fernández et al. 1998; Mosack et al. 2006; Weeks et al. 1995), educational change strategies (Eisenhart 1999; Fetterman and Pitman 1986; LeCompte 1996; LeCompte et al. 1998/2000; J. Schensul 2011; Schensul, Gonzalez Borrero, and Garcia 1985), fisheries management applications (Coburn et al. 2006; McGoodwin 1993), and the testing of new technologies to reduce disease, to improve efficiency of use of natural resources, and to reduce the effects of global climate change (Fiske 2009; Fiske 2006). Hahn and Inhorn in their second edition of *Anthropology and Public Health* include a section on health intervention research (Hahn and Inhorn 2009); and in the same year, Schensul and Trickett published a collection of articles on multilevel interventions, including four ethnographically driven case studies (Schensul and Trickett 2009; Weeks et al. 2009). An ethnographic approach to intervention involves people in the community of study. It is a participatory process in which members of communities or groups under study exert agency over the design and implementation of any intervention, along with involvement in the formative research that precedes it. In the sections below, we describe ways of using ethnographically embedded conceptual modeling to establish the frameworks for developing locally situated, culturally embedded participatory interventions.

There are several reasons to work *with* communities to make desired changes based on formative work. ***The first is the conviction that research should be useful in improving some aspect of the quality of life for the study population, and to be meaningful to the participants. The second is the scientific desire to test the validity and predictability of theories that constitute the summa-***

Key point

tion of the formative research. Research directs, shapes, and guides intervention. At the same time, by engaging in interventions, researchers can learn much about what "works" and what could constitute the next steps in both research and active efforts to bring about change. The pages that follow describe ways that the modeling and intervention process can become participatory by engaging gatekeepers, key informants, residents, and other important actors in the setting in intervention modeling, design, implementation, and even evaluation.

ETHNOGRAPHIC INTERVENTION DESIGNS

Ethnographers are in an excellent position to design, implement, and evaluate interventions that both contribute to the population involved in the study and extend and validate the results of the formative research process. Over time, dynamic systems changes may interact with the initial theoretical framework and the intervention, bringing about the importance of "continuous assessment" or "calibration of the model" (Flood 2010).

In Figure 8.1, we illustrate the interplay between research, observation, intervention, and the next steps in research. M_1 represents the predata collection model, O_1 represents mixed methods data collection, and M_2 is the postdata collection model revision. For most ethnographers, these three phases constitute a completed research

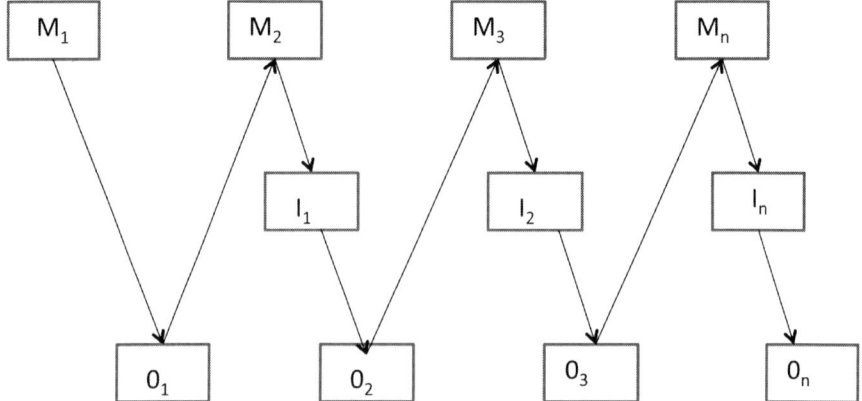

FIGURE 8.1 Iterations in the Research and Intervention Process

process. We suggest, however, taking some additional steps. M_2 can readily be transformed to yield an initial intervention I_1, using a procedure that is outlined later in this chapter. That intervention tests the validity and predictive capacity of M_2 through a new data collection stage, O_2. This process documents the intervention implementation, determines whether it changes the conditions that lead to the dependent variable, and assesses whether the dependent variable changes in response. In the process, the original model, M_2, is modified and refined in interaction with the intervention so that it more effectively describes the phenomena under study while, at the same time, the intervention translates ethnographic results into positive change strategies. Since interventions never work perfectly, and the research models never fully account for all the variance in the study population and the results desired, and since the flow of time always brings social, economic, and cultural changes, it is necessary to continue the iterations of $M_n \ldots I_n$ to "catch up" with the dynamic changes manifested in each new time period ($O_3 \ldots O_n$). This is a fundamental scientific process practiced in different ways by social, psychological, and environmental scientists, including biologists.

GUIDELINES FOR MODELING INTERVENTIONS

Interventions in Communities

Throughout this chapter, the term *intervention* will be used specifically to reference work in community-based settings. The principles that are outlined herein are best applied to local situations rather than to overall changes in policy, although they could also be applied to policy change. The key, however, to the development of ethnographic interventions is a local "model" that hypothesizes "how things are" rather than how they should or might be. Studying "how things are" involves the identification of a focal dependent variable domain and interrelated "independent variable" domains and "causal factors" or "predictors," as we have discussed in earlier chapters 4 through 6, and as was illustrated in the study of the Learning Circle, Example 7.3, or the many other examples of modeling in chapter 7. The development of an effective intervention requires systematic modification of key elements of the conceptual or research model that affect or influence the occurrence, prevalence, incidence, or pattern of the problem(s) or outcomes. In the first iteration (I_1), intervention changes the independent variables in order to improve the problem or change the outcome; it is an *hypothesis* about "how things *could* work."

In order to conduct a research-based intervention, it is important that the problem already be recognized. The term **problems** refers to situations that have been identified by the researcher, the literature, the community, and/or the general society as undesirable, dangerous, or otherwise negative. Often they are sufficiently serious that public agencies and private foundations make funds available to increase understanding of the dynamics of the problem, to prevent problem occurrence, to reduce the severity of the problem, and to provide more effective services to individuals affected by the problem. There also are times, as in the case of the early days of the AIDS epidemic, when a "problem" may not be widely recognized. Political action or educational campaigns may be required both to render them a priority for the public at large and to convince legislators to allocate funds so the problems can be better understood. At that point, it may be possible to determine how best to address them. These political and educational activities fall under the rubric of advocacy, and though they are very important, they are not research-driven interventions.

It also is important to establish the focus of the intervention. This can be done by "treatment" and through "prevention." "Treatment" involves trying to address the problem after it has been manifested by, for example, improving the way the problem is managed—for example, increasing the efficacy of services and treatment and changing or modifying individual behavior. "Prevention" involves trying to reduce the prevalence of the problem by focusing more on changing those independent variables that can be modified to prevent the occurrence of a problem in the first place. These terms are usually applied to health-related problems, but they can be generalized to any other social

Definition:
The term *problems* refers to situations that have been identified by the researcher, the literature, the community, and/or the general society as undesirable, dangerous, and negative

issue. Encouraging people to seek early and effective treatment for malaria is an example of the first, the use of bed nets to protect against malaria in a malaria-endemic setting is an example of the second. It is possible to begin with the first (for example, a health problem such as tuberculosis or asthma), and to shift to the second. If health problems form a cluster (if, for example, more than a third of a population suffers from tuberculosis and asthma, or if TB is more common among those with HIV, and if food insecurity is more common among both), then it is likely that the same set of independent variables is to blame. The causal factors associated with health problems are usually interactive or "syndemic" (Singer and Clair 2003; Singer, Erickson et al. 2006). If, for example, we consider the concentrations of malaria in cities in Mumbai, or HIV in cities in the United States or other parts of the world, or poor childhood academic performance in urban areas, it soon becomes obvious that they tend to occur in areas that are resource limited, unstable, and impermanent, and with populations that are impoverished, stigmatized, and otherwise marginalized. The reasons are similar—limited resources, inadequate employment and income, poor access to health care, toxic environments, standing wastewater, lack of government investments in services, or the inability to raise sufficient funds as a consequence of deteriorating urban infrastructure. Some approaches suggest that tackling these infrastructure or economic problems or disparities first may attenuate the social or health consequences of the problem. Others prefer to address the problem initially at the level of symptoms or infection.

Moving from "identifying" which factors contribute to increased risk and determining how to affect a "positive change" in these contributing factors is not an easy task. Perhaps the best approach to the development of innovative research and intervention projects is to view them as intrusions in "systems" that can contribute to prevention and early detection of problems. This systems approach is based on some central principles. These principles are the following:

- *Problems are "holistic."* They are products of a complex and interrelated or systemic (hence the term *systems analysis*) set of factors. They involve problems that need resolution through positive change and programs that must work with and have impact on multiple factors that contribute to the manifestation of the problem.

- *Problems should be defined using an ecological approach.* An ecological approach enables researchers to identify the "root" causes of a problem that exist beyond the individual case. Many research and intervention programs focus on the so-called shortcomings of individual members of the affected populations, holding them responsible for causing the problem and therefore seeking solutions in changing or improving their behavior. This can involve trying to modify their risky lifestyles, fill gaps in their knowledge base, and change the dynamics of their relationships. These approaches, however, often miss the mark because they do not address other causes of the problem that may be linked to legal, structural, and organizational barriers and shortcomings emerging from societal policy, health service organizations, and the knowledge, attitudes, and practices of the providers of services. Intervention models should include ways to affect positive change at multiple levels: in the population to be served, with those who structure and deliver services to address the problem, and the societal factors that influence interaction between providers of services and focal populations.

- *Intervention programs should be culturally situated.* Intervention programs should connect to the salient beliefs, interests, needs, and priorities of *both* populations and service personnel with regard to a societywide, community, and household issue. Ethnographers should be particularly adept at creating those cultural or other connections. As noted earlier, such features or connections have been termed **cultural hooks**. A cultural hook is a culturally embedded concept or ritual that is broad, has historical depth and meaning, and is understood by most people in a community. An example of a cultural hook

Definition: A cultural hook is a culturally embedded concept or ritual that is broad, has historical depth and meaning, and is understood by most people in a community

that most people still relate to in the Puerto Rican community is the concept of the *comadrona*, or traditional birth attendant. Another such concept is the *cuarentena*, the forty-day period after the birth of a child during which mother and child are protected and isolated to ensure the health of both.

- *Intervention programs need to link local concerns with intervention goals.* Intervention programs need to make connections among both the priorities or felt needs of individuals and their reference groups/communities, and the goals and methods of the research and intervention program.
- *Interventions depend on the identification of local resources.* An important component of intervention modeling is the identification of economic and other resources that can be brought to bear on the problem. The use of these resources also can increase the salience, acceptability, cultural fit, and sustainability of the intervention program.
- *Intervention development must be participatory.* The research and intervention process will be effective only when there is direct participation of the targeted groups in all stages of research and intervention design. Intervention programs need to maximize the participation of members of the study communities in assessing needs, locating resources, designing intervention models, and evaluating outcomes.
- *Intervention design and development depends on multiple sources of information.* The development of intervention models must be based on individual professional experience, systematic research, relevant literature, available "experts," and members of the focal population(s). However, even being based on a body of "best available knowledge" will not guarantee that a program can achieve more than 50 percent of its stated objectives. As we have pointed out earlier, even the best intervention programs will fail to achieve their desired results more than 50 percent of the time, under normal circumstances. Different modes of evaluation treat this expectation differently; however, using the lan-

guage of typical quantitative measures, significant differences will exist about half the time and even then, effect sizes are likely to be small. Conducting prior ethnography should improve the accuracy of such predictions, but even with its addition, success of an intervention never is 100 percent guaranteed. Nonetheless, using ethnography to determine what went wrong is a crucial step in more effective intervention design and development. Both process evaluation (i.e., knowing what was done) and outcome evaluation (i.e., knowing the impact of the intervention on the health problem) are essential parts of intervention development. They ensure that *future* iterations of the intervention model will yield increasingly higher percentages of success in the achievement of objectives.

STEPS IN DESIGNING INTERVENTIONS: A SYSTEMS ANALYTIC APPROACH USING MODELING TECHNIQUES

Definition: Culturally defined interventions can be described as identifying and building on a set of collectively held beliefs and behavioral guidelines, widely understood practices, and core values in a community

One of the strengths of the systems analytic approach, when it is based on ethnographic methods, is the development of culturally focused interventions that emerge from ethnographic research. **Culturally defined interventions** can be described as identifying and building on a set of collectively held beliefs and behavioral guidelines, widely understood practices, and core values in a community. These beliefs and guidelines have continuity from one generation to the next and provide a cultural link that makes the intervention salient and relevant to the population. Within this framework, ethnographers need to take into account not only causal factors already detailed in the final ethnographic model but also the resources needed to address those factors. Although the focus of a problem often resides in a population located in a community, ethnographers and interventionists also need to understand the macro and micro institutions that affect those communities. For the purposes of this analysis, we will distinguish between the *organization* and the *population* under study.

Organization is a cover term or concept that summarizes the social/structural context of a problem and the people affected by it. Organization includes media, government (governmental laws and regulations), private and public services, voluntary agencies, churches, advocacy groups, and other such institutions operating at the international, national, regional, and local levels. For example, in the health realm, the local health service system (e.g., hospitals, community health centers, HMOs, group and private practice) must survive in the context of national and state Medicare/Medicaid guidelines, insurance companies, competitive forces, and provider advocacy groups at all levels.

Population can be defined as those individuals and groups of individuals (clusters, communities of residents, communities of identity) who

1. Have a particular health or social or educational problem
2. Have a greater risk of acquiring the problem, and/or
3. Are directly or indirectly affected by the problem

Populations can include patients with a common health problem, groups defined by such demographic characteristics as age and ethnicity, occupational groups, employees at a common worksite, and individuals and families that share common residence in a geographically defined area.

The systems analytic approach requires developing a research model as a device to assist in explaining how a *system* is currently functioning to produce a particular problem and how it affects the individuals and groups that interact with it. The system includes the organizational context and the population. The organizational context (organization) includes a dependent variable that occurs because of the influence of independent variable domains at the "organizational level." This primary organizational variable also serves as an independent variable in relation to the population component; that is, it is a systemic connector to the dependent variable found in the population sector. Within the population, a dependent variable domain becomes the main focus of the intervention.

> **Definition:** Organization is a cover term or concept that summarizes the social/structural context of a problem and the people affected by it

> **Definition:** A population is defined as individuals or groups of individuals who are directly or indirectly affected by a health or social problem

For example, for *teenage pregnancy,* an obvious dependent variable is "teen's use of birth control methods." The "problem" is that teens do NOT use birth control regularly. A simple response would be to institute an educational program to encourage them to engage in behavioral change (reducing partners, using birth control pills, using condoms, etc.). However, the problem usually is not that simple. Asking what organizational factors contribute to teen pregnancy might produce a variable "access to services," which in this case might be stated as "lack of access of adolescents to family planning services." Influencing or improving lack of access to bring about better use of family planning services requires asking about the contributors to this problem. If "lack of access" were selected as the dependent variable at the organizational level, unpacking it would require examining which characteristics of the health care system serve to limit access (e.g., inappropriate hours of operation, staff unprepared to serve adolescents, lack of resources, poor publicity, lack of outreach, inaccessible service locations). This simple example makes it clear that if adolescents are not obtaining birth control methods, intervention programs focused only on adolescent behavioral change (e.g., using condoms, reducing partners) might be very effective in creating demand for birth control methods, but if no organizational-level service had been created simultaneously to meet the demand for such methods, the intervention would prove to be ineffective. Such an undesirable outcome can be termed an *iatrogenic effect.* ***An "iatrogenic" effect is the reverse of the expected effect, or some other related, unintended and unanticipated negative effect that takes place as a result of a medical, social, or other type of intervention.*** A further iatrogenic effect of the birth control intervention described above could be consequences such as turning teens against reproductive health programs altogether because they are seen to be unavailable, unfriendly, poorly supplied, or inaccessible. The net effect might be to increase pregnancies rather than reducing them. The "root" cause of the problem in this case lies with the "organization" and not the "person."

Key point

Building an exploratory and explanatory theoretical and operational model to guide project design is greatly facilitated by using the diagramming technique described in chapter 4. This technique represents the interrelation of independent and dependent variables on a two-dimensional surface. In Figure 8.2, the model is made more complex because it consists of both an organizational and a population component. Figure 8.2 portrays a project involving smoking reduction in teens. The population dependent variable might be *adolescent smoking*, and the organizational dependent variable might be *lack of adolescent stop-smoking programs*. The two components that make up this overall model at the organization and population levels have been described in chapter 5 (Figures 5.10 and 5.11). The process of modeling is illustrated in Figure 8.2.

The organizational independent variables should be selected from a variety of domains, including those representing ascription to laws and regulations (administrative or judicial level), political perspectives and promotions (policy level), media representations and advertising (media level), location, transportation, and service accessibility and availability (organizational level), and social norms (community level). Population (individual, household, family, peer networks) independent variable domains could include knowledge, attitudes, beliefs, and behaviors of adolescents, their peers, and their family members. Figure 8.3 adds to

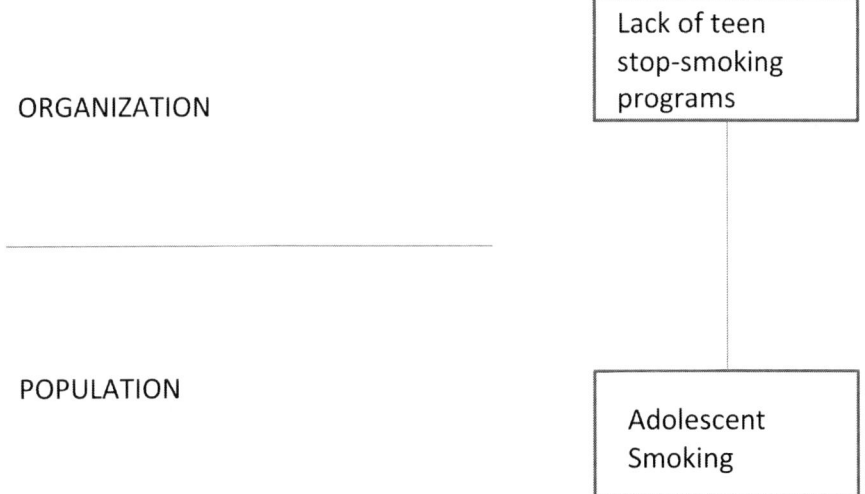

FIGURE 8.2   Modeling the Dependent Variables in a Systems Model

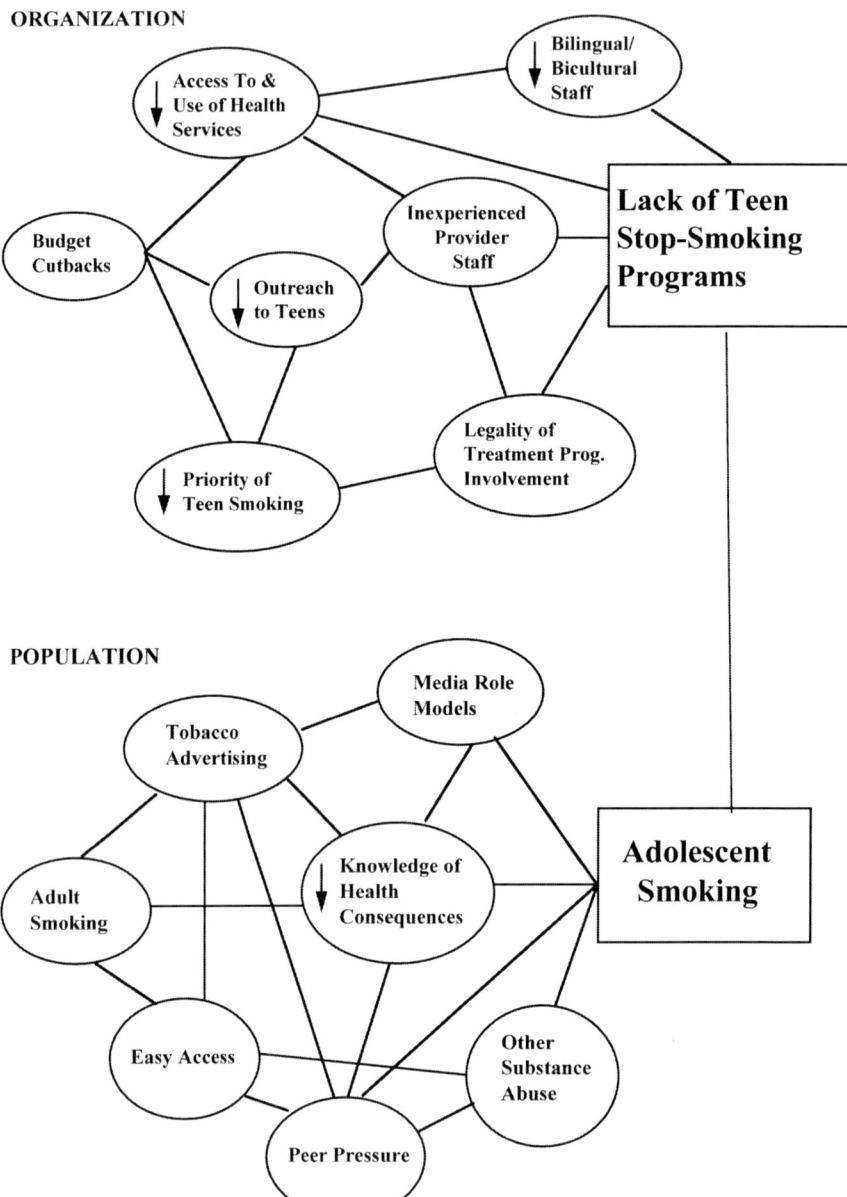

FIGURE 8.3 Independent Variables at the Organization and Population Levels

the diagram the independent variable domains that were identified from the "formative" or prior research model, but identification also could be achieved by encouraging a group modeling process with participants or stakeholders. Such a model would be based on what stakeholders, or in this case adolescents, actually say they know, do, and believe.

Selection of Independent Variables

Intervention projects especially should not include too many independent variable domains. Once the researchers and other stakeholders have identified those variables that are the most relevant, or have shown an empirical association (i.e., are statistically or otherwise related to the dependent variable outcome), they can then make choices about *which* independent variable domains will be the targets for the intervention. The selection process for key dependent variables is much the same as the delineation of *hypotheses* in a research study. As with other modeling exercises described in earlier chapters, the variables are drawn from "the literature," the "experts," clinical judgment, colleagues' views, people in the community, prior field experience, and results of prior research. Such variables are those that researchers and their partners believe to be most salient in predicting the dependent variables.

Selection of independent variables as the focus of intervention may be based on the following considerations:

- How important is it, or is it hypothesized to be, as a contributor to the health problem?
- How is it connected to other independent variables? Is it immediate, affecting the issue (dependent variable) directly, or does it work through other variables in the causal sequence?
- Is the variable within the project "scope" and "role"?
- Is changing the variable "do-able"?
- Are there resources available to make the changes required?
- Is there a balance among knowledge, attitudes, behaviors, and structural variables so that variables

are included that represent multiple sectors or ecological levels?

LINKING RESOURCES FOR CHANGE TO THE INDEPENDENT VARIABLES: SYSTEMS ANALYSIS AS THE "2 × 2 TABLE"

The final step in the modeling process is putting the organizational and population components into an overall "systems analysis." The organization and the population levels are deeply interwoven, and to be adequate, a theory must encompass an understanding of the *system* of interrelationships. The use of a 2 × 2 table is an approach to the examination of organization and population problems—it requires that both *organizational/systemic* and *population* resources be addressed in order to determine what efforts are required to make a difference in the dependent variables.

First, the selected organizational and population independent variables must be transferred to the table below. In the example of adolescent smoking, the following variables will be selected and transferred to the table to facilitate focusing on the intervention. These are noted in Figure 8.4.

Identification of Resources

Health service organizations, population groups, and communities may be a source of health issues and problems, but they also are a source for *resources* or various forms of capital that can assist in the intervention effort. Often these

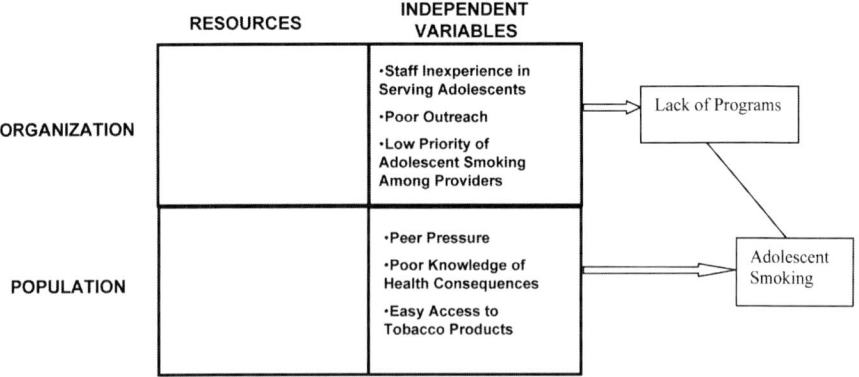

FIGURE 8.4 "2 × 2 table"

resources are not initially recognized, their potential in facilitating intervention may not be understood, they may not be used efficiently, or it may be that no one has yet thought to make the linkage. Engaging these resources requires understanding the degree to which the intervention agenda and the resource agendas overlap. Community resources can provide opportunities to reach out to people with specific problems, create partnerships among entities that have high salience for the focal group, and meet special needs for financial support, training, meeting places, and other important requisites for the intervention.

Organizational resources might include:

- Unions and discipline-based organizations
- Continuing education units
- Institutions from other sectors (e.g., schools, governmental departments)
- Organizational personnel with special linguistic, cultural, and community experience
- Churches and church groups and other community agencies with the capacity to provide services, meet needs, or otherwise act to remedy the problem
- Gangs, clubs, and organizations

Population resources might include:

- Local churches and church groups
- Local community and civic organizations
- Informal networks of peers or people working together such as block clubs, informal neighborhood and community leaders or other helping resources
- Immediate family members
- Extended kin groups
- Mentors, godparents, and other formal or informal supportive people

The next step in creating the 2 × 2 table is to identify those available resources with potential for addressing the selected independent variable domains. Social and cultural resources and assets also may exist that span both organization and population levels. Kretzmann and McKnight, for example, refer to community organizational and social assets and use an assets-mapping approach to identify these resources (Kretzman and McKnight 1993). Yosso uses a critical race approach to identify many different forms of cultural "capital" that can act as important resources in achieving positive resistance and solving intransigent psychosocial and structural problems (Yosso 2005). Jean Schensul and colleagues use ethnographically based participatory action research to support community voices in the conduct of community assessments (Schensul, Berg, and Nair 2012). Using the example of teen smoking portrayed in Figure 8.3, resources that might be used for intervention are illustrated in Figure 8.5.

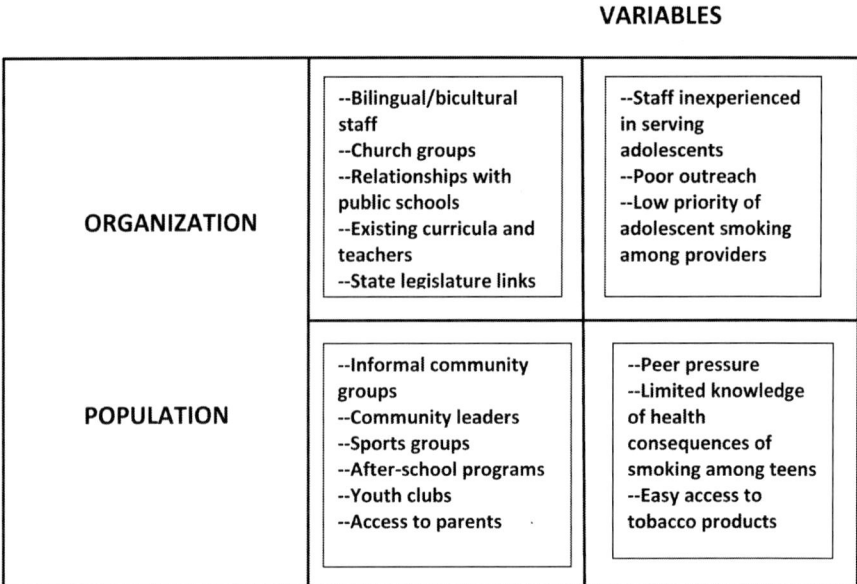

FIGURE 8.5 Resources at the Organizational and Population Level That Could Ameliorate the Problems Signified by the Independent Variables

Formulation of the Intervention

Once resources that can help resolve the dilemmas posed by the independent or "causal" variables are identified, it is then possible to formulate an approach to intervention. The steps are described below.

The completion of the 2 × 2 table allows us to make linkages between *resources* (R) and *independent variable domains* (IV). The resources are selected specifically to determine how best to ameliorate the *dependent variable* (DV) or health/mental health or other social problem. The integration of resources and independent variable domains represents an effort to affect the dependent variable domain, which can be represented as (R) × (IV) = DV. In this "formula," "×" means "in interaction with" or "are brought to bear upon a situation." Thus the statement (R) × (IV) is read as "resources (R) interact with or are brought to bear on (×) the independent variables (IV) to influence or change (=) the dependent variable (DV)." To identify and build these linkages between resources and the independent variables at the organization and population level, researchers can explore the following questions:

(a) How can *organizational* resources be brought to bear on or change independent variables at the *organizational level*? This can be stated as $R_o \times IV_o = DV$, which simply means that resources at the *organizational level* (R_o) are brought to bear on independent variables at the *organizational level* (IV_o) to bring about change (=) in the dependent variable domain (DV). In this case, the change might occur in the *dependent variable* (DV), either at the organizational level or the population level or both. Thus there is no (.) following the (DV). There always are problems at the organizational level that should be ameliorated in order to improve the status of the dependent variable or DV. For example, in a high school with no educational materials available to describe the dangers of binge drinking, a resource at the organizational level might be a social development teacher or counselor who was interested in introducing an alcohol curriculum into an already existing behavioral management program. Intervention programs generally should consider making changes at the organizational as well as at the population level, because the source of any given population problem almost never is at the individual level alone. Rather, population, organizational, or contextual-level factors combine to create a situation in which a complex intervention is required.

(b) How can *organization resources* meet *population needs*? ($R_o \times IV_p = DV$) This statement is read as, "Organizational level resources (for example, providing staff training in service organizations, rearranging systems of care, implementing new policies improving access to fertility control, additional strategies for eliminating garbage, more accessible tobacco cessation programs for teens) will change the factors at the population level (e.g., beliefs about tobacco, reluctance to enter reproductive health clinics, the habit of disposing of trash by dumping it in vacant lots) that are impeding the resolution of the problem within the population. One hypothetical example illustrating this transformation is establishing an antismoking program at a middle school that will improve knowledge about the negative consequences of smoking, which in turn will lead to quitting, or at least to reducing, the number of new tobacco initiators. Another is: Using bilingual/bicultural staff will improve the capacity for organizational outreach to Hispanic adolescents, which in turn will result in greater access to such tobacco cessation programs and higher levels of quitting.

(c) How can *population resources* meet *population problems*? ($R_p \times IV_p = DV$) Communities, population groups, and population sectors must be a part of the change equation since the job to be done always is beyond the capacity and capability of outside organizations and institutions alone. For example, informal advocacy groups in the community might identify business locations selling cigarettes illegally to underage youth in order to report them to authorities. Such actions might discourage sales to underage youth, and thus reduce the number of youth who initiate smoking.

(d) How can *population resources* meet *organization needs*? ($R_p \times IV_o = DV$) This approach is the most innovative because it links population resources to contextual change efforts, including changes in policies and the way health, education, and other forms of services are delivered. Efforts at the population level (for example, organizing informal organizations of youth against smoking) can make a significant impact on the marketing, promotion, and distribution of tobacco to minors.

MODELING INTERVENTION APPROACHES   209

The answers to the above questions, presented as equations above and represented diagrammatically in Figure 8.6, require using a systematic approach to making authentic community/contextually embedded connections among available community resources (at the population and organization level) and the independent variable domains at both levels. These linkages can then be evaluated for what they offer, assessed for feasibility and acceptability of inclusion, and integrated to form a coherent, well-argued, multilevel intervention design (see the center circle).

However, simply bringing resources together with those independent variables identified as causes or major contributors to a problem does not fully answer just how the linkages will be implemented or how the resources themselves will be operationalized in practice to make a difference. For that purpose, researchers and their intervention partners must turn again to other sources of information—community knowledge, the research literature, new ways of doing things identified on the Internet, attendance at conferences, and by talking with researchers and change activists in different parts of the country and the world.

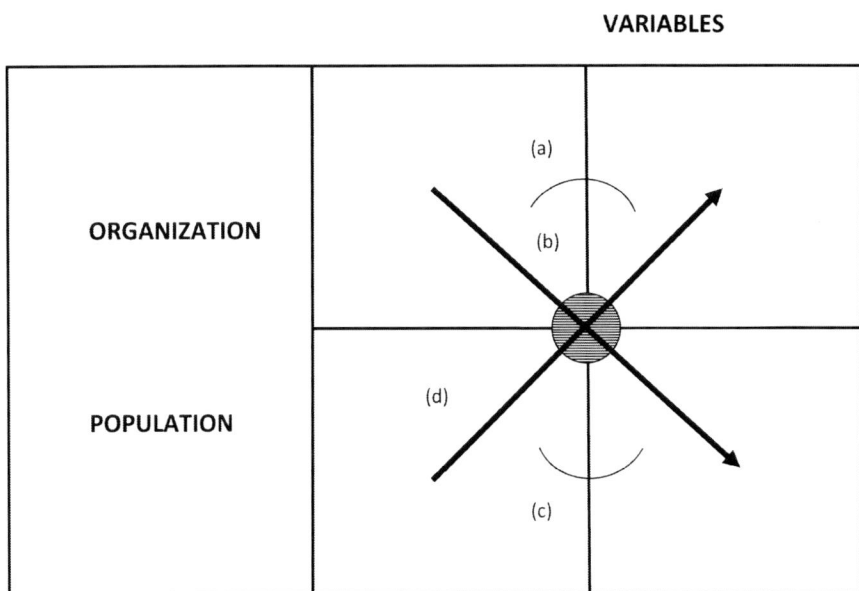

FIGURE 8.6   Linking Resources to Organization and Population Problems

OPERATIONALIZING THE INTERVENTION MODEL

The answers to the questions above are the starting point for the process of operationalizing the intervention model. **Operationalization** means transforming the identified resources into practices and programmatic elements that can bring about changes in the designated dependent variables. This is created by means of writing up a proposal for the intervention. As with any other "proposal," a proposal for an intervention is framed by its mission and purpose, goals, and objectives. These are enumerated below.

> **Definition:** Operationalization means transforming the identified resources into practices and programmatic elements that can bring about changes in the designated dependent variables

The Intervention Mission. The *mission* or the overall purpose of the intervention can be derived from the dependent variable on the *organizational* OR the *population level*. In this case, the mission focuses on the *population level* and is stated as: "To reduce the rate of current smokers among adolescents."

The Intervention Aims. The intervention **aims** or goals, which are higher-level or more general-directional statements about the actions to be taken, can be derived either from selected *population* or *organization,* independent variables, or both. The aims for a smoking reduction program are drawn from key resources at the organizational and population level that address and attempt to reverse or change the independent variable domains believed to contribute to adolescent smoking.

> **Definition:** The intervention aims or goals are higher-level or more general-directional statements about the actions to be taken. They can be derived from either selected *population* or *organization* independent variables or both

- Aim 1. Improve the skills of provider staff to work with adolescents (organizational level).
- Aim 2. Increase health service providers' understanding of the risks of adolescent smoking (organizational level).
- Aim 3. Decrease teens' access to tobacco products (organizational; population levels).
- Aim 4. Improve the capacity of the health service system to involve teens that smoke in stop-smoking programs (organizational level).
- Aim 5. Change adolescent smoking norms from prosmoking to antismoking (organizational level).

- Aim 6. Improve teens' knowledge of smoking risks (population level).
- Aim 7. Develop quit-smoking support groups (population level).

The Intervention Objectives. **Objectives** are the specific approaches or activities that are required to "operationalize" or transform or unpack into practice each of the intervention aims. Operationalizing the aims or goals involves assessing the content or qualities of the resources identified as (R), considering the literature related to each of these resources or assets and how they might have been used in other interventions, examining through discussions with partners their feasibility and potential for effectiveness in the local setting, and finally, stating them as specific actions. For example:

Definition: Objectives are the specific approaches or activities that are required to "operationalize" or transform or unpack into practice each of the intervention aims

- Objective 1. At the *population level*, smoking parents and teens who want to quit, or have already quit, are resources (R). They can be organized into "stop-smoking mutual support groups" (transformed IV) or dyads; and can act as community role models (transformed IV) to promote and endorse quitting smoking (DV). This addresses Aim 7 above.
- Objective 2. At the *organizational level*, enhance a school substance-abuse curriculum on smoking (R) to be implemented by trained peer educators (transformed IV) in a training program provided by the American Lung Association (R) to encourage (DV) smoking cessation. This would address Aim 6 above.
- Objective 3. Encourage the involvement of teens who smoke (IV) in an existing after-school exercise and nutrition program (R), which can lead to (DV) smoking cessation. This would address Aims 1, 6, and 7.

The example below shows how these steps were implemented.

EXAMPLE 8.1

USING THE 2 × 2 TABLE TO CREATE A MULTILEVEL INTERVENTION FOCUSED ON REDUCING SEXUAL RISK AMONG MARRIED MEN IN MUMBAI

Stephen Schensul and colleagues developed a multilevel intervention focused on the reduction of sexual risk among married men in a low-income community in Mumbai, India. Reduction of sexual risk in order to prevent sexually transmitted diseases, including HIV, was the purpose of the project. Extensive qualitative and quantitative ethnographic research identified factors at the organizational and individual levels that contributed to risk (the independent variables, or IVs). A key cultural concept fundamental to the intervention (the "hook"), was the idea of *gupt rog* or secret diseases of men, a problem of great concern to men, and, research showed, related to their involvement in sexual risk-taking behavior to alleviate their concerns about their masculinity and sexual performance (S. Schensul, Verma, Nastasi 2004; Verma and Schensul 2004). The key factors at the organizational level (IV) included (a) inadequate treatment of sexually transmitted infections (STIs) by nonallopathic (traditional or partially prepared) providers; (b) negative attitudes of allopathic providers toward culturally based concepts of men's health such as *gupt rog*; (c) gender inequitable norms leading to conflict and interpersonal violence against spouses; and (d) positive alcohol consumption norms for men. Key factors at the population level (independent variables, or IVs) included (a) poor marital communication; (b) men's extramarital sex; (c) married men's nonuse of condoms; and (d) men's drinking.

The development of the intervention involved both health care system and population resources. Resources at the population level included allopathic and nonallopathic providers, and community-based organizations (CBOs) that offered health education through local actors who conducted street plays on vaccination, HIV, violence against women, alcohol consumption, and other common behavioral health problems. Street dramas are a traditional form of communication of important social events and rituals in India (Limbu 2000; Mangai 1998; Pelto and Singh 2010; Sansthan 2006) in order to change social norms (R). The resulting intervention goals included improving knowledge, counseling and treatment capacity of local providers on sexual health, and changing behavioral norms. These goals called for intervention objectives at the *organizational level*.

Intervention objectives called for training of both allopathic and nonallopathic providers in two communities to address men's performance concerns by counseling around *gupt rog* and related marital and sexual behavior problems and to encourage syndromic management of STIs, and also by working with existing CBOs to support the development of street dramas and associated community meetings to illustrate through theater and to create small groups for discussion of ways to make clear the connection between male sexual health concerns and associated predictors and risk behaviors.

There is much more to be said about the development of ethnographically driven interventions using ethnographic modeling procedures. Objectives need to be broken down into specific action steps. Decisions must be made about the roles of staff and other collaborators, as well as allocation of time and specific tasks. Other decisions must be made with respect to evaluation, such as how to determine whether the intervention is effective because the outcome variable (DV) has changed in response to the changes in the independent variable domains, or because other factors intervened. Implementing interventions in the field with multiple components is a difficult and challenging enterprise, not the least of which is the inability to manage every aspect of the intervention. "Things" happen that are beyond the control of the intervention research team. Weather changes; wars and terror attacks occur; entire blocks of urban areas are razed for redevelopment; housing evictions are initiated; economic development programs are implemented; negative publicity, staff illness, and public service strikes interrupt normal programming; the government turns over through election or some other process; key staff members in institutions, such as supportive principals in schools, may take other jobs, institutions may be unable to meet intervention obligations; and donors may decide to cease funding for programs. All of these eventualities are possible in field interventions in the United States or any other part of the world. This chapter, however, is primarily concerned with how to design and model an intervention that has good potential for making a difference, one that is based on local resources and cultural relevance, and that is implemented in collaboration with local people and takes into consideration known local and national dynamics. Implementing and evaluating such an intervention in a fluid context is a topic that will be covered in Book 7. In sum, the chapter argues that ethnographic research is the most important foundation for interventions that actually can facilitate positive social change. Creating such an intervention requires:

- Initial division of the context into the realms of "organization" and "population"

- Identification of a dependent variable domain for both the organization and the population
- Delineation of the independent variables for both organization and population
- Selection of key independent variable domains as targets for intervention that will maximize the impact on the dependent variable domains
- Identification of organizational and population resources that can address the independent variable domains
- Exploration of linkages between resources and independent variable domains
- Development of a core concept for the intervention design based on the identified linkages
- Construction of a focus on culturally based interventions

SUMMARY

This chapter argues that preparation for the conduct of ethnographic research involves more than the simple development of a theoretical model and the creation of a plan for data collection. It also involves planning carefully the ways in which the research will contribute to the population under study. Research can contribute to this in a variety of ways, including dissemination of information, advocacy, promotion of policy change, and actual programmatic interventions. Interventions are emphasized since they have immediate effect with respect to contributing to further iterations of the research model and to improving the conditions of life among study populations. However, to ensure that ethnographic research delivers the hoped-for results, effective intervention requires:

- Collection of data on both the organization and the population levels
- Identification, not only of problems, but of resources needed to address them

MODELING INTERVENTION APPROACHES

- Opportunity to develop culturally based interventions that are linked to salient features of the study community
- Involvement of members of the group under study in both the research and the intervention

Further discussion of interventions of different types and at multiple levels can be found in Book 7 of the *Ethnographer's Toolkit*.

REFERENCES

Abrams, D. B., and R. S. Niaura. 1987. Social learning theory. In *Psychological theories of drinking and alcoholism*, ed. H. T. Blane and K. E. Leonard, x, 403. New York: Guilford Press.

Aguilera, D. A. 2003. Who defines success? An analysis of competing models of education for American Indian and Alaskan native students. Doctoral dissertation, School of Education, University of Colorado.

Albro, Robert. 2010. Anthropology and the military: AFRICOM, "culture" and future of Human Terrain Analysis (Respond to this article at http://www.therai.org.uk/at/debate). *Anthropology Today* 26(1): 22–24.

Amselle, Jean-Loup. 2002. Globalization and the future of anthropology. *African Affairs* 101: 213–29.

Appadurai, Arjun. 2001. Grassroots globalization and the research imagination. In *Globalization*, ed. A. Appadurai. Durham, NC: Duke University Press.

Arnault, Denise Saint, and Michael D. Fetters. 2011. RO1 funding for mixed methods research. *Journal of Mixed Methods Research* 5(4): 309–29.

Bakeman, R., and J. M. Gottman. 1986. *Observing interaction: An introduction to sequential analysis*. Cambridge, England: Cambridge University Press.

Bandura, A. 1977. *Social learning theory*. Englewood Cliffs, NJ: Prentice-Hall.

———. 1979. Self-efficacy: Toward a unifying theory of behavioral change. *Psychological Review* 84: 191–215.

———. 1986. *Social foundations of thought and action: A social cognitive theory*. Englewood Cliffs, NJ: Prentice-Hall.

Barbieri, Flavia Laura, Amandine Cournil, and Jacques Gardon. 2009. Mercury exposure in a high fish eating Bolivian Amazonian population with intense small-scale gold-mining activities. *International Journal of Environmental Health Research* 19(4): 267–77.

Barker, D. 2004. The scholarship of engagement: A taxonomy of five emerging practices. *Journal of Higher Education Outreach and Engagement* 9(2): 123–37.

Barro, Robert J., and Jong-Wha Lee. 2010. *A new data set of educational attainment in the world, 1950–2010*. Cambridge, MA: National Bureau of Economic Research.

Behera, D., R. Uppal, and S. Majumdar. 2003. Urinary levels of nicotine & cotinine in tobacco users. *Indian Journal of Medical Research* 118: 129–33.

Bernal, Guillermo, and Emily Sáez-Santiago. 2006. Culturally centered psychosocial interventions. *Journal of Community Psychology* 34(2): 121–32.

Bernard, H. R. 1995. *Research methods in anthropology: Qualitative and quantitative approaches*. Walnut Creek, CA: AltaMira Press.
Bhutta, Zulfiqar. 2003. Practising just medicine in an unjust world. *British Medical Journal* 327(7422): 1000–01.
Bingham, A. 1998. *The malaria ecosystem in southern Mexico*. Storrs, CT: University of Connecticut.
Boudon, R. 1991. What middle range theories are. *Contemporary Sociology* 2(4): 19–22.
Bourdieu, P. 1993. *The weight of the world: Social suffering in contemporary society*. Stanford, CA: Stanford University Press.
Brault, M. 2012. *The antecedents, process, and consequences of female sterilization for low-income women in Mumbai*. Master's thesis, Paper 235, Anthropology, University of Connecticut.
Brennan, S. J., and M. W. Schulze. 2004. Cultural immersion through ethnography: The lived experience and group process. *Journal of Nursing Education* 43(6): 285–88.
Bronfenbrenner, U. 1979. *The ecology of human development*. Cambridge, MA: Harvard University Press.
———. 1989. Ecological systems theory. In *Annals of child development*, ed. R. Vasta, 187–249. Greenwich, CT: JAI Press.
Bruns, Eric, and Janet Walker. 2011. Research on the wraparound process: Intervention components and implementation supports. *Journal of Child and Family Studies* 20(6): 709–12.
Burawoy, Michael. 2000. *Global ethnography: Forces, connections, and imaginations in a postmodern world*. Berkeley, CA: University of California Press.
———. 2005. For public sociology. *American Sociological Review* 70(1): 4–28.
Carley, K. 1991. Textual analysis using maps. Department of Social and Decision Sciences, Carnegie Mellon University.
Cefkin, M. 2009. *Corporate encounter: Reflections on research in and of corporations*. Brooklyn, NY: Berghahn Books.
Charron, D. F., ed. *Ecohealth research in practice: Innovative applications of an ecosystem approach to health* [Insight and innovation in international development]. New York: Springer, 109–18.
Coburn, L., S. Abbott-Jamieson, and P. M. Clay. 2006. Anthropological applications in the management of federally managed fisheries: Context, institutional history and prospectus. *Human Organization* 65(3): 231–38.
Cochran, M., Mary Larner, et al., eds. 1990. *Extending families: The social networks of parents and their children*. New York: Cambridge University Press.
Collins, Cyleste C., and William W. Dressler. 2008. Cultural consensus and cultural diversity. *Journal of Mixed Methods Research* 2(4): 362–87.
Corbin, Juliet, and Anselm Strauss. 2008. *Basics of qualitative research, 3rd edition*. Thousand Oaks, CA: Sage Publications.
Creswell, J. W. 2009. *Research design: Qualitative, quantitative and mixed methods approaches, 3rd edition*. Thousand Oaks, CA: Sage Publications.
Creswell, J. W., A. C. Klassen, V. L. Plano, and K. C. Smith. 2010. *Best practices for mixed methods research in the health sciences*. Bethesda, MD: OBSSR, NIH.

REFERENCES

DeLuca, Danielle. 2012. Human rights violations in Guatemala: Hearing indigenous voices. *Cultural Survival Quarterly* 36(2). http://www.culturalsurvival.org/publications/cultural-survival-quarterly/human-rights-violations-guatemala-hearing-indigenous-voices.

Dennis, Betty P., and Jane B. Neese. 2000. Recruitment and retention of African American elders into community-based research: Lessons learned. *Archives of Psychiatric Nursing* 14(1): 3–11.

Denscombe, Martyn. 2008. Communities of practice. *Journal of Mixed Methods Research* 2(3): 270–83.

Dickson-Gomez, Julia, et al. 2006. Times and places: Process evaluation of a peer-led HIV prevention intervention. *Substance Use & Misuse* 41(5): 669–90.

Diefenbach, G. J., et al. 2009. Anxious depression among Puerto Rican and African-American older adults. *Aging and Mental Health* 13: 118–26.

Din-Dzietham, R., et al. 2007. High blood pressure trends in children and adolescents in national surveys, 1963 to 2002. *Circulation* 116: 1488–96.

Dubet, F., and M. Wieviorka. 1997. Touraine and the method of sociological intervention. In *Alain Touraine*, ed. J. Clark and M. Diani, 55–76. Bristol, PA: Falmer Press.

Durrenberger, E. P., and K. Reichart. 2010. *The anthropology of labor unions*. Boulder: University Press of Colorado.

Earp, Jo Anne, and Susan T. Ennett. 1991. Conceptual models for health education research and practice. *Health Education Research* 6(2): 163–71.

Eisenhart, M. 1999. Reflections on educational intervention in light of postmodernism. *Anthropology & Education Quarterly* 30(4): 462–65.

Evans, Bronwynne C., David W. Coon, and Ebere Ume. 2011. Use of theoretical frameworks as a pragmatic guide for mixed methods studies. *Journal of Mixed Methods Research* 5(4): 276–92.

Fals Borda, O., and M. A. Rahman. 1991. *Action and knowledge: Breaking the monopoly with participatory action research*. New York: Apex.

Fernández, E. A., et al. 1998. Trial of a community-based intervention to decrease infestation of Aedes aegypti mosquitoes in cement washbasins in El Progreso, Honduras. *Acta Tropica* 70(2): 171–83.

Fetterman, D. M., and M. A. Pitman, eds. 1986. *Educational evaluation: Ethnography in theory, practice, and politics*. Beverly Hills, CA: Sage Publications.

Fielding, Nigel G. 2012. Triangulation and mixed methods designs. *Journal of Mixed Methods Research* 6(2): 124–36.

Fiske, Shirley J. 2006. Anthropology in pursuit of public policy and practical knowledge. *NAPA Bulletin* 26(1): 82–107.

———. 2009. Global change policymaking from inside the Beltway: Engaging anthropology. In *Anthropology and Climate Change: From encounters to actions*, ed. S. A. Crate and M. Nuttall, 277–91. Walnut Creek, CA: Left Coast Press.

Fitzgerald, Nurgül, et al. 2008. Nutrition knowledge, food label use, and food intake patterns among Latinas with and without type 2 diabetes. *Journal of the American Dietetic Association* 108(6): 960–67.

Flood, Robert. 2010. The relationship of "systems thinking" to action research. *Systemic Practice and Action Research* 23(4): 269–84.

Fosher, Kerry. 2010. Book review: Anthropologists in arms: The ethics of military anthropology by George R. Lucas. *Journal of Military Ethics* 9(2): 177–81.
Foster-Fishman, Pennie G., and Erin Droege. 2010. Locating the system in a system of care. *Evaluation and Program Planning* 33(1): 11–13.
Frake, C. O. 1964. How to ask for a drink in Subanum. *American Anthropologist* 66(2): 127–32.
Freire, Paulo. 1970. *Pedagogy of the oppressed.* New York: Herder and Herder.
Gagnon, Georgette. 2005. Targeting the Anuak: Human rights violations and crimes against humanity in Ethiopia's Gambella region. HumanRightsWatch.org. http://www.hrw.org/reports/2005/03/23/targeting-anuak.
Gagnon, J. H. 1991. The implicit and explicit use of scripts in sex research. In *The annual review of sex research,* ed. J. Bancroft, C. Davis, and D. Weinstein. Mt. Vernon, IA: Society for Scientific Study of Sex.
Gile, Krista J., and Mark S. Handcock. 2010. Respondent-driven sampling: An assessment of current methodology. *Sociological Methodology* 40(1): 285–327.
Gillan, Kevin, and Jenny Pickerill. 2012. The difficult and hopeful ethics of research on, and with, social movements. *Social Movement Studies* 11(2): 133–43.
Goel, Sharad, and Matthew J. Salganik. 2010. Assessing respondent-driven sampling. *Proceedings of the National Academy of Sciences* 107(15): 6743–47.
Goodenough, W. 1956. Componential analysis and the study of meaning. *Language* 38: 195–216.
Greaves, Thomas, Ralph Bolton, and Florencia Zapata. 2010. *Vicos and beyond: A half century of applying anthropology in Peru.* Lanham, MD: AltaMira Press.
Greene, Jennifer C., and Valerie J. Caracelli. 1997. Defining and describing the paradigm issue in mixed-method evaluation. *New Directions for Evaluation* 1997(74): 5–17.
Greene, Jennifer C., Valerie J. Caracelli, and Wendy F. Graham. 1989. Toward a conceptual framework for mixed-method evaluation designs. *Educational Evaluation and Policy Analysis* 11(3): 255–74.
Grillo, R. 1985. Applied anthropology in the 1980s: Retrospect and prospect. In *Social anthropology and development policy,* ed. R. Grillo and A. Rew, 1–36. London: Tavistock Publications.
Guarnaccia, Peter J., Byron J. Good, and Arthur Kleinman. 1990. A critical review of epidemiological studies of Puerto Rican mental health. *The American Journal of Psychiatry* 147(11): 1449–56.
Guarnaccia, Peter J., Pertti J. Pelto, and Stephen L. Schensul. 1985. Family health culture, ethnicity, and asthma: Coping with illness. *Medical Anthropology* 9(3): 203–24.
Guarnaccia, Peter J., Maritla Rubio-Stipec, and Glorisa Canino. 1989. Ataques de nervios in the Puerto Rican diagnostic interview schedule: The impact of cultural categories on psychiatric epidemiology. *Culture, Medicine and Psychiatry* 13(3): 275–95.
Guba, E. G., and Y. S. Lincoln. 1989. *Fourth generation evaluation.* Newbury Park, CA: Sage Publications.
Guimarães, Jean Remy Davée, and Donna Mergler. 2012. A virtuous cycle in the Amazon: Reducing mercury exposure from fish consumption requires sustainable agriculture. In *Ecohealth research in practice: Innovative applications of an ecosys-*

REFERENCES

tem approach to health [Insight and innovation in international development], ed. Dominque Charron, 109–18. New York: Springer.

Gusterson, Hugh. 1997. Studying up revisited. *PoLAR: Political and Legal Anthropology Review* 20(1): 114–19.

Hahn, R., and M. Inhorn, ed. 2009. *Anthropology and public health: Bridging differences in culture and society, 2nd edition.* New York: Oxford University Press.

Hamilton, G., et al. 2001. National evaluation of welfare-to-work strategies: How effective are different welfare-to-work approaches? Five-year adult and child impacts for eleven programs. Manpower Demonstration Research Corporation, U.S. Department of Health and Human Services.

Heath, S. B. 1970. *Ways with words: Language, life and work in communities and classrooms.* New York: Cambridge University Press.

Heath, S., et al. 2009. *Researching young people's lives.* Thousand Oaks, CA: Sage Publications.

Hettiarachchy, T., and S. Schensul. 2001. The risks of pregnancy and the consequences among young unmarried women working in a free trade zone in Sri Lanka. *Asia-Pacific Population Journal* 16(2): 126–40.

Hill-Burnett, J. 1979. Anthropology in relation to education. *American Behavioral Scientist* 23 (2): 237–74.

Hodgkin, Suzanne. 2008. Telling it all. *Journal of Mixed Methods Research* 2(4): 296–316.

Homer, J. B. 2006. System dynamics modeling for public health: Background and opportunities. *American Journal of Public Health* 96(3): 452–58.

Hunt, Geoffrey, et al. 2005. Asian American youth, the dance scene, and club drugs. *Journal of Drug Issues* 35(4): 695–732.

Inda, J. X., and R. Rosaldo. 2008. *The anthropology of globalization: a reader, 2nd edition.* Malden, ME: Blackwell Publishing.

Israel, Barbara, et al. 2006. Challenges and facilitating factors in sustaining community-based participatory research partnerships: Lessons learned from the Detroit, New York City and Seattle Urban Research Centers. *Journal of Urban Health* 83(6): 1022–40.

Johnson, J. C. 1998. Research design and research strategies in cultural anthropology. In *Handbook of method in cultural anthropology*, ed. H. R. Bernard, 131–72. Walnut Creek, CA: AltaMira.

Johnson, R. B., and L. A. Turner. 2003. Data collection strategies in mixed methods research. In *Handbook of mixed methods in social and behavioral research*, eds. A. Tashakkori and C. Teddie, 297–319. Thousand Oaks, CA: Sage.

Johnson, R. Burke, and Anthony J. Onwuegbuzie. 2004. Mixed methods research: A research paradigm whose time has come. *Educational Researcher* 33(7): 14–26.

Johnson, R. Burke, Anthony J. Onwuegbuzie, and Lisa A. Turner. 2007. Toward a definition of mixed methods research. *Journal of Mixed Methods Research* 1(2): 112–33.

Kallis, G. 2007. Socio-environmental co-evolution: Some ideas for an analytical approach. *International Journal of Sustainable Development and World Ecology* 14(1): 4–13.

Kaplan, A. 1964. *The conduct of inquiry: Methodology for behavioral science.* Scranton, PA: Chandler.

Kemper, R. V., and A. P. Royce, ed. 2002. *Chronicling cultures: Long-term field research in anthropology*. Walnut Creek, CA: AltaMira.

Kostick, K. M., et al. 2010. Treatment seeking, vaginal discharge and psychosocial distress among women in urban Mumbai. *Culture, Medicine & Psychiatry* 34: 529–47.

Kretzmann, J., and J. L. McKnight. 1993. *Building communities from the inside out: A path toward finding and mobilizing a community's assets*. Evanston, IL: Institute for Policy Research.

Kuhn, T. 1996. *The structure of scientific revolutions, volume 2*. Chicago: University of Chicago Press.

Kuznar, L. A. 2008. *Reclaiming a scientific anthropology*. Lanham, MD: AltaMira Press.

Laidler, Karen Joe, and Geoffrey Hunt. 2001. Accomplishing femininity among the girls in the gang. *British Journal of Criminology* 41(4): 656–78.

LeCompte, M. D. 1996. What if you organized a reform and nothing changed? The fate of culturally compatible curricula in an American Indian public school district. In *Debating dropouts: Critical policy and research perspectives on school leaving*, ed. J. Gaskell and D. Kelly. New York: Teachers College Press.

LeCompte, M. D., and D. Aguilera. 1996. Year three final product/process evaluation report of the Phoenix Indian Center's learning circle program: A partnership between the Osborne School District and the Phoenix Indian Center, Phoenix Indian Center.

LeCompte, M. D., D. Aguilera, M. E. Wiertelak, et al. 1998/2000. Re-estableciendo y reforzando los lindes de identidad cultural: El Circulo de Aprendizaje. (*The Learning Circle Program for urban Native Americans: Improving achievement by privileging indigenous culture*). In *Nuevos paradigmas, compromisos renovados; Experiencias de Investigacion Cualitativa en Educacion*, Mexico, D.F, 1998/2000. Universidad Autnonoma de Mexico. Proceedings of the (Mexican) Congress of Educational Research, Universidad Pedagogical Nacional, Mexico, D.F.

LeCompte, M. D., and K. Bonetti. 2010. Notes from Ground Zero: Budgetary crises and academic freedom at the University of Colorado. *Theory in Action* 3(2): 7–11.

LeCompte, M. D., and J. Preissle. 1993. Ethnography and qualitative design in educational research. New York: Academic Press.

LeCompte, M. D., and J. Schensul. 2010. *Designing and conducting ethnographic research, volume 1*. Lanham, MD: AltaMira Press.

———. 2012. *Analyzing and interpreting ethnographic data, volume 5*. Lanham, MD: AltaMira Press.

Lewellen, T. C. 2002. *The anthropology of globalization: Cultural anthropology enters the 21st century*. Westport, CT: Bergin & Garvey.

Limbu, Ramyata. 2000. Development-Nepal: Street plays to alert people to AIDS/HIV threat. Inter Press Service News Agency. http://www.ipsnews.net/2000/10/development-nepal-street-plays-to-alert-people-to-aids-hiv-threat/.

Loeffler, Agnes Gertrud. 1998. Memories of difference: From Lur to anthropologist. *Anthropology and Humanism* 23(2): 146–56.

Logan, T. K., Jennifer Cole, and Carl Leukefeld. 2002. Women, sex, and HIV: Social and contextual factors, meta-analysis of published interventions, and implications for practice and research. *Psychological Bulletin* 128(6): 851–85.

REFERENCES

Lopez, William D., et al. 2012. "No jobs, more crime. More jobs, less crime": Structural factors affecting the health of Latino men in Detroit. *Journal of Men's Health*.

Lover, Andrew, et al. 2011. An exploratory study of treated-bed nets in Timor-Leste: Patterns of intended and alternative usage. *Malaria Journal* 10(1): 199–211.

Ludwig, S. A. 2006. "Making fast the thread": Cultural maintenance and transmission by Maya women who weave on backstrap looms. Doctoral dissertation, School of Education, University of Colorado-Boulder.

Mangai, A. 1998. Cultural intervention through theatre: Case study of a play on female infanticide/foeticide. *Economic and Political Weekly* 33(44): 70–72.

McGoodwin, James R. 1993. Applied anthropology: Small-scale fishery development: Sociocultural perspectives. *John J. Poggie and Richard B. Pollnac. American Anthropologist* 95(1): 170–71.

Mertens, Donna M. 2011. Mixed methods as tools for social change. *Journal of Mixed Methods Research* 5(3): 195–97.

Mertens, Frédéric, et al. 2005. Network approach for analyzing and promoting equity in participatory ecohealth research. *EcoHealth* 2(2): 113–26.

Merton, R. K. 1967. *On theoretical sociology: Five essays old and new*. New York: Free Press.

Miles, M. B., and A. M. Huberman. 1994. Data management and analysis methods. In *Handbook of qualitative research*, ed. N. K. Denzin and Y. S. Lincoln, 428–44. Thousand Oaks, CA: Sage Publications.

Milgram, S. 1974. *Obedience to authority*. New York: Harper and Row.

Mooney, C. 2005. *The Republican war on science*. Cambridge, MA: The Perseus Books Group.

Morse, Janice M. 1991. Approaches to qualitative-quantitative methodological triangulation. *Nursing Research* 40(2): 120–23.

Mosack, Katie, et al. 2006. High-risk women's willingness to try a simulated vaginal microbicide: Results from a pilot study. *Women & Health* 42(2): 71–88.

Mosher, Heather I. 2010. Participatory action research with Dignity Village: An action tool for empowerment within a homeless community. Doctoral dissertation, Psychology, Portland State University.

Muhr, T. 2004. *ATLAS.ti Version 5*. Berlin, Germany: Scientific Software Development.

Nader, L. 1974. Up the anthropologist: Perspectives gained from studying up. In *Reinventing anthropology*, ed. D. Hymes, 284–311. New York: Vintage Books.

Nastasi, B. K., and S. L. Schensul. 2005. Contributions of qualitative research to the validity of intervention research. *Journal of School Psychology* 43(3): 177–95.

Nastasi, Bonnie K., et al. 2007. Mixed methods in intervention research: Theory to adaptation. *Journal of Mixed Methods Research* 1(2): 164–82.

Nelson, Cary. 2010. *No university is an island: Saving academic freedom*. New York: University Press.

Nowotny, H. 2005. The increase of complexity and its reduction: Emergent interfaces between the natural sciences, humanities and social sciences. *Theory Culture & Society* 22(5): 15–31.

Oakley, Ann. 1998. Experimentation and social interventions: A forgotten but important history. *British Medical Journal* 317(7167): 1239–42.

OBSSR. 2001. *Qualitative methods in health research: Opportunities and considerations in application and review.* Bethesda, MD: Office of Behavioral and Social Sciences Research, NIH.

Okoko, B. J. 2005. Acquisition of bed-nets, sleeping-habits, and control of malaria in the Gambia: Sociocultural dimension. *Journal of Health and Population Nutrition* 4: 388–89.

Oliva, Rogelio. 2003. Model calibration as a testing strategy for system dynamics models. *European Journal of Operational Research* 151(3): 552–68.

Oliver-Smith, Anthony. 1996. Anthropological research on hazards and disasters. *Annual Review of Anthropology* 25: 303–28.

Oliver-Smith, Anthony, and Roberta E. Goldman. 1988. Planning goals and urban realities: Post-disaster reconstruction in a third world city. *City & Society* 2(2): 105–26.

Pelto, Pertti, and G. H. Pelto. 1978. *Anthropological research: The structure of inquiry.* Cambridge, UK: Cambridge University Press.

Pelto, Pertti, and Rajendra Singh. 2010. Community street theatre as a tool for interventions on alcohol use and other behaviors related to HIV risks. *AIDS and Behavior* 14(0): 147–57.

Pérez-Escamilla, Rafael. 2007. Evidence based breast-feeding promotion: The baby-friendly hospital initiative. *The Journal of Nutrition* 137(2): 484–87.

———. 2009. Dietary quality among Latinos: Is acculturation making us sick? *Journal of the American Dietetic Association* 109(6): 988–91.

Peshkin, A. 1986. *God's choice: The total world of a fundamentalist Christian school.* Chicago: University of Chicago Press.

Peyton, J., et al. 2011. Determination of the nicotine metabolites cotinine and trans-3'-hydroxycotinine in biologic fluids of smokers and non-smokers using liquid chromatography–tandem mass spectrometry: Biomarkers for tobacco smoke exposure and for phenotyping cytochrome P450 2A6 activity. *Journal of Chromatography B* 879: 267–76.

Radda, Kim E., et al. 2003. Assessing Human Immunodeficiency Virus (HIV) risk among older urban adults: A model for community-based research partnership. *Family & Community Health* 26(3): 203–13.

Redfield, Robert. 1930. *Tepoztlan, a Mexican village: A study in folk life.* Chicago: University of Chicago Press.

———. 1956. *The little community.* Chicago: University of Chicago Press.

Reed, D. B., and G. C. Furman. 1992. The 2 x 2 matrix in qualitative data analysis and theory generation. Paper presented at the Annual Meeting of the American Educational Research Association. San Francisco, CA.

Rein, M., and D. Schon. 1977. Problem setting in policy research. In *Using social policy research in public policy making*, ed. C. Weiss. Lexington, MA: D.C. Heath.

Rhodes, Tim, et al. 2005. The social structural production of HIV risk among injecting drug users. *Social Science & Medicine* 61(5): 1026–44.

Rylko-Bauer, Barbara, Merrill Singer, and John Van Willigen. 2006. Reclaiming applied anthropology: Its past, present, and future. *American Anthropologist* 108(1): 178–90.

REFERENCES

Sansthan, Muktakash Natya. 2006. Street plays in rural, remote and urban areas, http://muktakashtheatre.blogspot.com/.

Schensul, Daniel M. 1998. Participatory action research: The Summer Youth Research Institute, Department of Sociology, Columbia University, BA Honors Thesis.

Schensul, Jean J. 1989. *AIDS knowledge attitudes and behaviors survey in multi-ethnic neighborhoods of Hartford.* Hartford: Institute for Community Research Publication, Phase II.

———. 1998. Community based risk prevention with urban youth. *School Psychology Review* 27(2): 233–46.

———. 2006. Life at the crossroads. *NAPA Bulletin* 26(1): 163–90.

———. 2010. Engaged universities, community based research organizations and third sector science in a global system. *Human Organization* 69(4): 307–20.

———. 2011. Building an applied educational anthropology beyond the academy. In *A companion to the anthropology of education*, ed. B. A. U. Levinson and M. Pollock, 112–34. Wiley-Blackwell.

Schensul, Jean J., M. Berg, and S. Nair. 2012. Using ethnography in participatory community assessment. In *Methods for community based participatory research for health, 2nd edition*, ed. B. Israel, E. Eng, E. Parker, and A. Schulz, 161–88. San Francisco: Jossey-Bass.

Schensul, Jean J., S. Diamond, et al. 2005. The diffusion of Ecstasy through urban youth networks. *Journal of Ethnicity in Substance Abuse* 4(2): 39–71.

Schensul, Jean J., Maria Gonzalez Borrero, and Roberto Garcia. 1985. Applying ethnography in educational change. *Anthropology & Education Quarterly* 16(2): 149–64.

Schensul, Jean J., and Margaret D. LeCompte, ed. 1999. *The ethnographer's toolkit.* Seven-volume paperback boxed set. Lanham, MD: AltaMira Press.

Schensul, Jean J., Judith A. Levy, and William B. Disch. 2003. Individual, contextual, and social network factors affecting exposure to HIV/AIDS risk among older residents living in low-income senior housing complexes. *JAIDS Journal of Acquired Immune Deficiency Syndromes* 33: S138–S152.

Schensul, Jean J., S. Nair, S. Bilgi, et al. 2012. Availability, accessibility and promotion of smokeless tobacco in a low-income area of Mumbai. *Tobacco Control.*

Schensul, Jean, K. Radda, et al. 2009. Multi-level intervention to prevent influenza infections in older low income and minority adults. *American Journal of Community Psychology* 43(3): 313–29.

Schensul, Jean, and Edison Trickett. 2009. Multi-level community based culturally situated interventions. *American Journal of Community Psychology* 43(3): 232–40.

Schensul, Stephen L. 1978. Commando research. *Practicing Anthropology* 1(1): 13–14.

———. 1980. Anthropological fieldwork and sociopolitical change. *Social Problems* 27(3): 309–19.

———. 1985. Science, theory, and application in anthropology. *American Behavioral Scientist* 29(2): 164–85.

Schensul, S. L., J. J. Schensul, and M. D. LeCompte. 1999. *Initiating ethnographic research: Models, methods, and measurement.* Lanham, MD: AltaMira Press.

Schensul, Stephen L., G. Oodit, et al. 1994. *Young women, work and AIDS-related risk behavior in Mauritius*. Washington, DC: International Center for Research on Women.

Schensul, S. L., J. J. Schensul, G. Oodit, U. Bhowon, and S. Ragobur. 1994. Sexual intimacy and changing lifestyles in an era of AIDS: Young women workers in Mauritius. [doi: 10.1016/0968-8080(94)90085-X]. *Reproductive Health Matters* 2(3): 83–93.

Schensul, Stephen L., N. Saggurti, et al. 2009. Multilevel perspectives on community intervention: An example from an Indo-US HIV prevention project in Mumbai, India. *American Journal of Community Psychology* 43(3): 277–91.

Schensul, Stephen L., and J. Schensul. 1978. Advocacy and applied anthropology. In *Social scientists as advocates: Views from the applied disciplines*, ed. G. Weber and G. McCall. Beverly Hills, CA: Sage Publications.

Schensul, Stephen L., J. Schensul, G. Oodit, et al. 1994. Sexual intimacy and changing lifestyles in an era of AIDS: Young women workers in Mauritius. *Reproductive Health Matters* 2(3): 83–93.

Schensul, Stephen L., J. Schensul, G. Oodit, U. Bhowon, and S. Ragobur. 1994. Sexual intimacy and changing lifestyles in an era of AIDS: Young women workers in Mauritius. [doi: 10.1016/0968-8080(94)90085-X]. *Reproductive Health Matters* 2, no. 3: 83–93.

Schensul, Stephen L., R. K. Verma, and B. K. Nastasi. 2004. Responding to men's sexual concerns: Research and intervention in slum communities in Mumbai, India. *International Journal of Men's Health* 3(3): 197–220.

Schneider, M., and M. Somers. 2006. Organizations as complex adaptive systems: Implications of complexity theory for leadership research. *Leadership Quarterly* 17(4): 351–65.

Shulman, S. 2006. *Undermining science: Suppression and distortion in the Bush administration*. Berkeley, CA: University of California Press.

Singer, Elyse Ona, and Jean J. Schensul. 2011. Negotiating Ecstasy risk, reward, and control: A qualitative analysis of drug management patterns among ecstasy-using urban young adults. *Substance Use & Misuse* 46(13): 1675–89.

Singer, Merrill. 2012. Studying hidden and hard to reach populations. In *Specialized ethnographic methods: A mixed methods approach, Book 4, Ethnographer's Toolkit*, ed. J. J. Schensul and M. D. LeCompte. Lanham, MD: AltaMira Press.

Singer, Merrill, and Scott Clair. 2003. Syndemics and public health: Reconceptualizing disease in bio-social context. *Medical Anthropology Quarterly* 17(4): 423–41.

Singer, Merrill C., P. I. Erickson, et al. 2006. Syndemics, sex and the city: Understanding sexually transmitted diseases in social and cultural context. *Social Science & Medicine* 63(8): 2010–21.

Singer, Merrill, and M. Weeks. 2005. The Hartford model of AIDS practice/research collaboration. In *Community interventions and AIDS*, ed. E. J. Trickett and W. Pequegnat. New York: Oxford University Press.

Smith, Jeffrey M. 2003. *Seeds of deception*. Fairfield, IA: Yes! Books.

Snow, R. W., et al. 1988. A trial of bed nets (mosquito nets) as a malaria control strategy in a rural area of The Gambia, West Africa. *Transactions of the Royal Society of Tropical Medicine and Hygiene* 82(2): 212–15.

Sosu, Edward M., Angus McWilliam, and Donald S. Gray. 2008. The complexities of teachers' commitment to environmental education. *Journal of Mixed Methods Research* 2(2): 169–89.

Sosulski, Marya R., and Catherine Lawrence. 2008. Mixing methods for full-strength results. *Journal of Mixed Methods Research* 2(2): 121–48.

Spradley, J. P. 1979. *The ethnographic interview.* New York: Holt, Rinehart and Winston.

Strauss, Anselm, and Juliet Corbin. 1994. Grounded theory methodology: An overview. In *Handbook of qualitative research,* ed. N. K. Denzin and Y. S. Lincoln, 273–85. Thousand Oaks, CA: Sage Publications, Inc.

Stringer, E. T. 1996. *Action research: A handbook for practitioners.* Thousand Oaks, CA: Sage Publications.

Sunderland, N., et al. 2012. What does it feel like to live here? Exploring sensory ethnography as a collaborative methodology for investigating social determinants of health in place. *Health Place* (Online May 2012).

Sutton, Constance R. 1998. "Motherhood is powerful": Embodied knowledge from evolving field-based experiences. *Anthropology and Humanism* 23(2): 139–45.

Tanasescu, Mihaela, et al. 2000. Biobehavioral factors are associated with obesity in Puerto Rican children. *The Journal of Nutrition* 130(7): 1734–42.

Tashakkori, A., and C. Teddlie, ed. 2003. *Handbook of mixed methods in social and behavioral research.* Thousand Oaks, CA: Sage Publications.

Tomkins, S. 1987. Script theory. In *The Emergence of personality,* ed. J. Arnoff, A. I. Rabin, and R. A. Zucker, 147–216. New York: Springer Publishing Company.

Trotter, R. T., J. Schensul, and K. Kostick. 2012, in press. Research methods in applied anthropology, 2nd edition. In *Handbook of methods in cultural anthropology,* ed. H. R. Bernard. Walnut Creek, CA: AltaMira.

van Willigen, John. 2002. *Applied anthropology: An introduction, 3rd edition.* Westport, CT: Bergen and Garvey.

van Willigen, J. 2005. Community assets and community-building process: A historic perspective. In *Community development in the 21st century,* eds. S. Hyland and L. Bennett, 25–44. Santa Fe, NM: School of American Research Press.

Varjas, Kris, et al. 2005. Using ethnographic methods for development of culture-specific interventions. *Journal of School Psychology* 43(3): 241–58.

———. 2006. Using a participatory culture-specific intervention model to develop a peer victimization intervention. *Journal of Applied School Psychology* 22(2): 35–57.

Verma, A. 2001. Street plays to create awareness of AIDS. *Times of India*, August 23, 2001, http://articles.timesofindia.indiatimes.com/2001-08-23/lucknow/27230361_1_spread-awareness-state-aids-control-society-abhishek-verma.

Verma, R. K., and S. L. Schensul. 2004. Male sexual health problems in Mumbai: Cultural constructs that present opportunities for HIV/AIDS risk education. In *Sexuality in the time of AIDS,* ed. R. K. Verma, P. J. Pelto, S. L. Schensul, and A. Joshi, 327–54. New Delhi: Sage Publications.

Wang, Yu, et al. 2008. Acceptability of hypothetical microbicides among women in sex establishments in rural areas in southern China. *Sexually Transmitted Diseases* 35(1): 102–10, 10.1097/OLQ.0b013e31814b8546.

Washburn, J. K. 2005. *University inc.: The corporate corruption of American higher education.* New York: Basic Books.

Wasson, Christina. 2006. Making history at the frontier. *NAPA Bulletin* 26(1): 1–19.

Wasson, Christina, M. Odell-Butler, and J. Copeland-Carson, ed. 2011. *Applying anthropology in the global village.* Walnut Creek, CA: LeftCoast Press.

Watters, John K., and Patrick Biernacki. 1989. Targeted sampling: Options for the study of hidden populations. *Social Problems* 36(4): 416–30.

Weeks, Margaret, M. Convey, et al. 2009. Changing drug users' risk environments: Peer health advocates as multi-level community change agents. *American Journal of Community Psychology* 43(3): 330–44.

Weeks, Margaret R., J. Schensul, et al. 1995. AIDS prevention for African-American and Latina women: Building culturally and gender-appropriate intervention. *AIDS Education and Prevention* 7(3): 251–64.

Weidlich, W. 2005. Thirty years of sociodynamics. An integrated strategy of modelling in the social sciences: Applications to migration and urban evolution. *Chaos Solitons & Fractals* 24(1): 45–56.

Weisner, T., ed. 2005. *Discovering successful pathways in children's development: Mixed methods in the study of childhood and family life.* Chicago: University of Chicago Press.

———. 2012. Mixed methods should be a valued practice in anthropology. http://www.anthropology-news.org/index.php/2012/05/01/mixed-methods-should-be-a-valued-practice-in-anthropology/.

Weller, S. C., and A. K. Romney. 1988. *Systematic data collection.* Newbury Park, CA: Sage Publications.

Werner, O., and G. M. Schoepfle. 1987. *Systematic fieldwork: Ethnographic analysis and data management.* Newbury Park, CA: Sage Publications.

White, D., and U. Johansen. 2005. *Network analysis and ethnographic problems: Process models of a Turkish nomadic clan.* Lanham, MD: Lexington Books.

Willett, Jerri. 1995. Becoming first graders in an L2: An ethnographic study of L2 socialization. *TESOL Quarterly* 29(3): 473–503.

Winder, N. 2007. Innovation and metastability: A systems model. *Ecology and Society* 12(2).

Yin, R. K. 1991. *Case study research: Design and methods.* Newbury Park, CA: Sage Publications.

Yosso, Tara. 2005. Whose culture has capital? A critical race theory discussion of community cultural wealth. *Race, Ethnicity & Education* 8(1): 69–91.

Zulaika, Garazi, and Joseba Zulaika. 1998. "Daddy, let's talk." *Anthropology and Humanism* 23(2): 118–20.

INDEX

Note: Page numbers of figures and tables are italicized.

the abstract, 46–48
abstraction, levels of, 5, 90–*91*, 105, 130–31, 134–*35*, 137–42, *145*, 162
activities, 13–14, 16–17, 107, 124, 168–70
Add Health study, 182, 187
adolescents, 8, 119, *146*, 182, 183, 187, 189. *See also specific topics,* e.g., Summer Youth Research Institutes
advocacy, 39, 61–62, 123, 179, 194, 199, 208, 214
age, 27, 94, 123. *See also* demographic information
AIDS-related research, 40, 64–65, 70, 118, 124, 161–62, 180, 194. *See also* HIV; Mauritius study
aims. *See* goals
analysis. *See* data analysis
analytic frameworks, 90
ANTHROPAC (software), 52, 77
Anthropology and Public Health (Hahn and Inhorn), 191
applied research, 19–20, 24, 34, 103
approvals, formal, 55–57
a priori assumptions/categories, 6–7, 16, 43, 115, 134, *157*, 194
archival data, 56, 150, 182–83
ArcInfo (software), 52, 77
Arts Focus study, 121–22
assets-mapping approach, 206
associations, 7, 9, 84, 91, 97, 99, 115–16, 119, 125, 130, *146*, 166, 203
associative model, 186

ATLAS.ti (software), 52, 54, 77
attitudes, 3, 13–15, 90, 120–22, 124, *147*, 160, 169, 180, 196, 201, 203; quantitative data on, 177; the researcher's, 96
attributes, 144, 152
audiovisual observation/recording, 8, 88

baggage, 29
Balaiah, Donta, 47
basic research, 19–20, 34, 75
behavioral health problems, 212
behavioral management programs, 207
behaviorism, 16, 104
behaviors, 3, 23–24, 27–28, 41, 75, 81, 120, 124, 137–38, 142; association and, 99; locally specific, 129; modeling, 141; and motivation, 104; reported or observed, 13–17, 88; theories explaining, 84–86; variables, 164–65. *See also specific topics,* e.g., intervention research; risk-taking behavior
beliefs, 3, 14–15, 17–18, 27, 81, 97, 180; changing, 175; intervention programs and, 196, 198, 201, 208; of researchers, 3, 18–19, 60, 82, 105
Berg, Marlene, 63, 206
Bernard, H. R., 134
bias, 5–6, 18, 27–28, 82, 92, *158*
bivariate relationships, 115
bivariate statistical procedures, 52

229

Borda, Fals, 189–90
bottom up construction, 104–9, 131, 134–35, 137–38
boundaries, 97, 133, 159
bounding, 133
Brault, Marie, 184
Bronfenbrenner, Uri, 10
budgets and budgeting, 71–74

calibration, 84, 163, 187, 192
Cambodia, 64–67, 95
Caracelli, Valerie J., 157–59
causality; causal associations/factors, 27, 98, 110, 186, 193, 195, 198, 203; and hypotheses, generating, 129; resolving dilemmas posed by, 206–7
Centerline Middle School. *See* Arts Focus Study
Centers for Disease Control (CDC), 8, 179, 181
challenges, preparing for, 45–79
change, social. *See* social change
Chicago, 36, 39, 61
class. *See* socioeconomic status
closed-ended questions/responses, 8, 54, 141, 152
codes; coding systems, 52–54, 78, 138, 142, 165–66
colleges and universities, 26, 37–38, 55
comadrona, 197
communities; community-based research, 10, 37, 40–42, 156, 178–79, 193; community life, 27, 35, 89, 164; as dynamic, 84; gaining access to, 60–65; interventions in, 193–98. *See also* populations
community-based organizations (CBOs), 61, 63, 212
comparison studies, 19, 33, 42, 54, 100
complementarity, *158*
"componential analysis," 137
computers, 59, 71–72, 76–77
concepts, 17, 56, 82–84, 89–91, 95, 137, *139*–40, *145*; cultural, 172, 212; and formative model construction, 101,
103, 106, 108; guiding, *93*; hypotheses and, 115; measures for, 156; mixed methods, 160, 171; tree diagram, *148–49*
"conceptual bins," 135
conceptual definitions, 134–37
conceptual frameworks, 90, 119, 152
conceptualization, 8, 51, 68, 82, 105, 110, 130–31, 142, 185
conceptual levels, 105–6, *164*
conceptual models, 21, 83, 87, 115, 126, 169, 171, 191
confidentiality, 28, 55
"configurational" associations, 98
congruence, 33
Connecticut. *See* Hartford, Connecticut; University of Connecticut
consensus; consensus analysis, 52, 54, 138, *150*, 163–64, 173
contacts, 29, 42, 57
contextual factors, 41, 48–49, 120, 159, 189
contraception, 105, 120, 124, 200
convergent designs, 173–75
cover terms, 163, 199
Creswell, J. W., 157, 172–73
critical events, 71, 174
critical theory, *93*
Cronbach's alpha, 166
cross-sectional research, 50, 110–11, *157*, 181, 186
"crunching" data, 52, 166
cuarentena, 197
cultural "capital," 206
cultural domains, 81, 104–5, 118
cultural experts, 3, 163
cultural hook, 172, 196–97, 212
culturally defined interventions, 198
cultural patterns, 3, 133
culture variables, 164–65
"cycle of science," 4–5

Darwin, Charles, 104
data, 46, 76–77. *See also* qualitative data; quantitative data; secondary data; *specific topics*, e.g., dissemination

INDEX

data, coding. *See* coding systems
data analysis, 46, 51–54, 74, 76, 91, 138, 161, 182; preliminary, 59, 77–78. *See also under* qualitative data; quantitative data
databases, 35, 135, *150*
data collection, 8, 76–77; conceptual levels and, *164*; exploratory, 124; matrix, 51; semistructured, 141; stages in, 149–53; structured approaches to, 9, *150*. *See also under* qualitative data: collection; quantitative data: collection
data crunching/reduction, 52, 166
data entry, 13, 72
data sets, 8, 54, 161, 163, 167, 177, 182–84, 187
deductive approach, 4–7, 104–5, 131, 134, 139, *157*
Demographic and Health Surveys (DHS), 8–9, 181, 183
demographic information, 63–65, 123, 177, 182, 199
dependent domains, 83, *111*–19, 143, 145–*47*, *149*–51, 153, 160–62, 164–65; and formative model construction, 105, 110–28, 131; intervention research and, 186–88, 207, 214
dependent variable domains, 116, *118*, 153, 161, 164; intervention research and, 188, 193, 199, 207, 214
dependent variables, 27, 145–46, 160–62, 168, 170; and formative model construction, 110–11, 115–16, 120–21, 125–26, 128; intervention research and, 186–88, 199–*201*, 203–4, 210
depression in older adults, study, 93–*94*
descriptions; descriptive theory, 9, 16–18, 86, 97–98, 166, 171
design. *See* research design
de Silva, M. W. Amarasiri, 118, 121, 124
Detroit, MI, 179
development (mixed methods approach), *158*
Deyhle, Donna, 187

diagrams: creating, 103–4; diagramming and modeling, 125–28. *See also* tree diagramming
digital recordings/photos, 77
direct relationships, 111–12, 116, 125
discovery, 6–7, 41, 82, 84, 86, 130, *150*–51; and qualitative research, *157*, 171, 184; and representativeness, 14–16
dissemination, 18, 178, 185, 187–88, 214
domains; domain level of abstraction, 108–9, *135*, 138–40, *143*–48, 160–65; cultural, 81, 104–5, 118; mediating, 110–12, 125; and model construction, 110–*27*, 129–30; "unpacking," 135, 139, 151, 160, 162, 164–65, 174. *See also* dependent domains; independent domains
drug use/abuse, 8, 23–26, 32–34, 40, 103, 151, 177–78, 180; intervention research and, 189. *See also* substance abuse; *specific topics*, e.g., Ecstasy study

ecological model/approach, 10, 27, 85, 92–*93*, 120, 196, 204
economic factors/activities, 11, 17, 69, 143, 165, 181; intervention studies and, 190, 193, 195, 197, 213
Ecstasy, qualitative study of, 33, 165–66, 178
educational interventions, 189
elicitation; elicitation techniques, 48, 56, 76, 137, *150*, 171
embedded designs, 173, 176–77
emic perspective, 96, 137
empathy, 18, 75
empirical sociologists, 189
equipment, 59, 66, 71–72, 74, 88
ethical considerations, 30–32, 35, 55–57, 190
ethnicity, 27–28, 31–34, 39–40, 42, 92, 94, 123, 130. *See also* demographic information
ethnographers (researchers): baggage, personal, 29; communities' prior experience with, 30–31, 42–43;

first job of, 83; funding, obtaining, 37–42; identity, 23, 27–34; individual, 58, 60; institutional affiliation, 37–42; interests and history of, 24–27; judgment, 137; novice, 1, 83; positionality, 34–37; responsibilities of, 76; self-reflection, 92–93; and the study population, 42–43; as theorists, 81–101; training, 1, 72, 74–76, 85, 89, 157. *See also specific topics*, e.g., bias
Ethnographer's Toolkit, 3, 8, 51–52, 157, 163, 165, 171, 177, 215
ethnography; ethnographic research, 1–21, 27–28, 41, 68, 91, 131, 157. *See also* research projects; *specific topics*, e.g. applied research; basic research; formative research
etic perspectives, 21
evaluation, 63, 70, 97, 99–100, 189, 192, 197–98, 213; data, 53, 176; program-oriented ethnographic, 20; researchers, 43; studies, 121–22
existing theories, 82, 84–85
exo level/approach, 10
expansion (mixed methods approach), *158*
expenses. *See* budget
experimentation, 188
explanatory and exploratory approaches to research, 95, 104, 124, 150–53, 200

face-to-face interaction, 2, 8, 10, 59, *157*
factors; factor level of abstraction, 108–9, 129–30, *135*, 138–40, *143–48*, *147*, 151, 162–64, 174; analysis at, 54; coding at, 165–66; subfactors, 105, *109*, *135*, 138–41, *143–45*, 151
facts, 84–85, 88, 90–91, 91, *135*, 142
family activities, *148*
family fieldwork, 58
family relationships, 140, 142
feedback, 104, 137, 141
fellowships, 157
field experience, 2–6, 21

Field Methods (journal), 156
field notes, 14, 77, 88
fieldwork, 65–68, 131
focus groups, 25, 78, 119, *150*, 163
"folk taxonomy," 137
Fordemwalt, Beth, 168, 170
formative research; formative model, 2, 19–20, *70*, 82–83, 95, 101, 139, 162, 203; communities, working with, 191–92; constructing, 103–31, 144–45, 150–51; dependent and independent domains, 110–25; developing, 104–9, 150–51; diagram, creating, 103–4; diagramming and modeling, 125–28; independent domains, categorizing, 122–23; modifying, 128, 150, 162; operationalization and measurement, 133–53; testing, 188; top down/bottom up construction, 104–9. *See also* research model
formative theories, 83, 86, 89, 95, 124–25, 134; building, 93–100; guidelines for, 131. *See also* theories
frameworks, 17, 83–84, 134, *147*, 171, 191, 198. *See also* conceptual frameworks; theoretical frameworks
free lists/listing, 52, 77, 137–38, *150*, 173
Freire, Paulo, 189–90
frequency, 155, *157*, 167
funding sources, 37–42, 45–46, 48, 50, 57, 71–72, 92, 94, 113, 145

Garcia, Jose, 32
Garcia, Roberto, 191
gatekeepers, 35, 63, 65, 78, 192
gender, 16, 27, 97, 174–76, 182, 212; the researcher's, 92. *See also* demographic information
gender equity scale (GES), 175
generalizability, 15, *157*
geography; geographically defined areas, 23–24, 56, 77, 123, 199
global processes and theories, 10–12, 17–18, 23, 85

goals, 46, 48–55; research model and, 145–49. *See also under specific topics*, e.g., intervention research; mixed methods approaches
Gonzalez Borrero, Maria, 63, 191
government, 35, 45, 72, 190, 195, 199, 213
Graetz, Dylan, 183
Graham, Wendy F., 157–58
"grand theory," 83, 85, 92, 104
grants, 7, 32, 37, 40, 65, 68, 70, 72–73, 157. *See also* funding sources
Greene, Jennifer C., 157–59
"grounded theory," 104
"ground up" inductive approach, 82
group projects. *See* research partnerships
Guarnaccia, Peter, 26, 160
Guatemala, 30–31
guiding concepts, 93
Gupta, P. C., 47
gupt rog, 172–74, 180, 212

Hahn, R., 191
Hartford, CT, 32, 62–63, 93, 178–80, 187. *See also* Institute for Community Research
Hartford Model of AIDS Practice/Research Collaboration, 180
health research/studies, 179, 190. *See also specific studies and topics*, e.g., malaria study; reproductive health
Heath, Shirley, 23, 187
"helicopter" researchers, 42
Hettiarachchy, Tilak, 106–7
hidden populations, 159
hierarchical relations/systems, 86, 137–39, 163. *See also* taxonomies
Hispanic Health Council (Hartford, CT), 63, 179–80
HIV research, 7, 25, 27, 29, 40–41, 62–65, 120, 151, 195; spousal violence and HIV risk, 167, 180. *See also* Mauritius study; Mumbai: sexual risk/HIV prevention studies

holistic approach, 27, 195–96. *See also* ecological approach
homophily, 33
horizontal modeling/movement, 104–9, 130, 144, 161–62, 164
housing, 57–60
Huberman, A. M., 83, 86
human subjects, 31, 46, 55–56, 78
Hunt, Geoffrey, 177
hypotheses, 5–8, 16–17, 19, 51, 82–84, 91, 95, 152; and formative model construction, 115, 119; generating, 129–30; intervention research, 203; mixed methods, 182; modifying, 130; research model and, 145–49; testing, 16, 54, *150*, 160, 183

iatrogenic effect, 200
ideas, 5–6, 41, 82–83, 92, 94–96, 104, *106*, 152
identity, 23, 27–34, 36, *93*, 199
IIPS, 62–63
illegal activities, 32–34, 208
immersion, 3–4, 10, 14, 30
incentives (respondent), 71–72, 74
included terms, 163
independent domains, 83, 99, 110–26, 128, *146–47*, 151, 160, 165
independent research, 37
independent variable domains, *116*–18, *117*–18, 161–62, 164, 169; intervention research and, 188, 193, 199, 201–3, 205, 207, 209–10, 213–14
independent variables, 110, 115–16, 121, 168, 183; intervention research and, 187, 194–95, 199, 201–4, *206*, 212, 214; linking resources for change to, 204–10
in-depth interviewing (IDI), 8–9, 13, 36, 54, 70, 77–78, 85, 153; formative model construction, 108, 119; mixed methods, 159, 163–64, 175, 177–78, 181, 184

India, 9, 12, 13, *69. See also* Mumbai, India
indices, 138, 140, 144, 165
indirect, 72
the individual, 9–10, 17, 189, 196, 207
individual researchers, 58, 60
inductive approach, 4–7, 18, 82, 104–5, 134, 137, 139, *157*
informants, 128, 137–38, 140. *See also* key informants
information sources, 209–10
Inhorn, M., 191
initiation (mixed methods approach), 71, *158*
innovation, 27, 39, 50–51, 195, 208
"insider perspectives," 137
Institute for Community Research (ICR), Hartford, 32, 40–41, 60, 63, 85, 89, 93, 99, 164, 180
institutional affiliation, 24, 37–42, 60–68
Institutional Ethics Committees (IECs), 55
Institutional Review Boards (IRBs), 31, 55–57, 68
insurance, international, 59–60
interdisciplinary methodological pluralism, 184
interdisciplinary partners, 81
interdisciplinary studies and projects, 41
International Institute for Population Studies (IIPS), 62–63
international work, 38, 57
the Internet, 12, 23, 57–59, 209
interpretation; interpretive frameworks, 18, 53, 74, 84, 151, 153, *157–58*
intervention research/studies, 41, 188–94, 214–15; in communities, 193–98; culturally defined, 198; ethnographic intervention designs, 192–93; focus of, establishing, 194; formulation of, 206–7; goals, 197, 210–12; guidelines for modeling, 193–98; key to development of, 193; mission of, 210; modeling, 185–215; modifying, 20, 193–94; objectives of, 210–13; operationalizing the intervention model, 210–14; "prevention," 194–95; and qualitative data, 161; steps in designing, 198–204; systems approach, principles of, 195–96; "treatment," 194–95
interviewing, 7–8; structured approaches to, 138, *150*; unstructured, 121, 125, 168. *See also* in-depth interviewing; key informants: interviewing; semistructured data collection: interviewing
intimate partner violence, 9, 167, 174–77, 180, 212
items; item level of abstraction, 56, *91*, *135*, 137–44, 151, 160, 163–67, 173, 175; coding at, 53–54
iterative process. *See* recursive process

Johnson, J. C., 150–52
Johnson, R. Burke, 155–57, 171–73, 176, 178
The Journal of Quantitative Anthropology, 155–56

key informants, 3, 30, 35, 37, 51, 63, 76–78, 118, 128, 140, 192; interviewing, 7–8, 70, 76–77, 97, 120, 131, 142, *150*, 163–64, 172; key informant activities (KII), 69–70
kinship, 16
knowledge, 13–15, 120, 124, *148*, 155, 201, 209; advancing/generation of, 20, 33, 208, 211–12; cultural, gaining, 58; gaps in, filling, 77, 90, 196; hypotheses, 129; intervention programs and, 196–97, 203–4; mixed methods research and, 155, 181; new, accommodating, 84; the researcher's/prior, 4–6, 21, 42, 84, 96, 104, 137
knowledge-based assessment instruments, 100
Kretzmann, J., 205–6
Kuznar, L. A. (Kuznar's model), *4*

INDEX

languages, 3, 11, 28, *150*; acquisition, child, 187; global, 76; local, 29–31, 58, 74, 76
Learning Circle study, 168–70
LeCompte, Margaret D., 38, 90–91, 157, 177, 191; Arts Focus study, 121–22; Learning Circle study, 168–70
legislation, 12–13, 194
levels of abstraction. *See* abstraction, levels of
Li, Jianghong, 27
Likert scale, 167
Lima, Peru, 114
linear associations, 98, 110, 130
linear modeling, *87*
literature review, 49–51
local level/approach. *See* micro level/approach
locally situated participatory interventions, 191
local model. *See* formative model
local theories, 17, 21, 83, 92–93, 100, 104; building, 93–100; guidelines for generating, 131
location. *See* research site
logistics, 57–60
longitudinal research design, 50, *157*, 186–87
Longitudinal Study of Adolescent Health, 182, 187
Ludwig, Sherri, 30–31, 42
Lusaka, Zambia, 29, 64–65
Lwendo Moonzwe, 29, 64–65

macro level/approach, 5, 10, 17, 83, 85, 92, *157*, 198
Maharashtra, India, 12, *69*
malaria study, 25–26, 121, 195
mapping, 12, 48, 76–77, 85–86, 128, 206
Marisela, Dona, 31
marital relationships, 47, 173–75, 212. *See also specific topics*, e.g., spousal violence

marital status. *See* demographic information
material culture, 52, 56
material style of life (MSL), 124, 144, 165–66
matrices, 51, 172, 177
Mauritius sexual behavior/sexual risk study, 14–15, 97–98, 105, 108–9, 123, 142–43, 146–*48*
Maya people; Mayan language/culture, 12, 30–31, 42
McKnight, J. L., 205–6
MDMA, qualitative study of, 33, 165–66, 178
measurement, 113, 128, 133–53, 156, *158*, 160, 165
media, 13, 90, 96, 110, *146*, 199, 201
mediating domains, 110–12, 125
"member checking," 78, 172
men, "secret illness" of. *See gupt rog*
Merton, Robert, 17, 95
meso level/approach, 10
methodologies, 2, 19–20, 27, 49–51, 54, 78; "interdisciplinary methodological pluralism," 184; methodologists, 155, 157, 163; multiple, relating or sequencing of, 171–81; "third methodological paradigm," 161
methods. *See* research methods
micro level/approach, 5, 10, 17, *157*, 198
Microsoft Word software, 54
midpoint, 104, 135
midrange/middle-range theory, 16–17, 83, 85–86, 93–96, 101, 104, 134–35
Miles, M. B., 83, 86
mixed methods research, 1–2, 8, 12, 49, 155–84; convergent designs, 174–75; data collection and, 171, *192*; different approaches to, *158*; embedded designs, 176–78; fundamental principle of, 156; goal in/ideal, 166–67; integrated, 153, 184; models, methods, case examples, 171–81; multiphase designs, 42, 178–

81; parallel stages of data collection/organization, 174; qualitative and quantitative methods, 159–70; recursive process and, 162; relating or sequencing of, 171–81; research, definitions of, 156–58; secondary data, role of, 181–84; sequential designs, 171–73; simultaneous and multiphase designs, 173–81
models. *See* research models
modes of operation, *91*
Moonzwe, Lwendo, 29, 64–65
Morse, Janice M., 172–73
motivation, 104
moving horizontally/moving vertically, 105–6
multimedia data, 52
multinational corporations, 11, 13
multiphase research/designs, 42, 171, 173–81, 187
multivariate regression model, 186
multivariate statistical procedures, 52
Mumbai, 36–37, 40, 167, 172, 174–77, 180, 184, 195; anemia study (Graetz), 183–84; gaining access in (S. Schensul), 62–63; sexual risk/HIV prevention studies, 9, 172, 174–77, 180–81, 212; smokeless tobacco study, 12, 47–48, 53

Nader, Laura, 10, 35
Nair, Saritha, 12–13, 47, 206
national data sets, 8, 183, 187
National Family Health Survey (NFHS), 9, 183
National Health and Nutrition Examination Survey (NHANES), 8, 182, 187
National Institute for Research in Reproductive Health (NIRRH), 40, 47, 49
National Institutes of Health (NIH), 7, 47, 50, 71–72, 157, 179

National Longitudinal Study of Adolescent Health, 182, 187
Native American communities, 56, 168–69, 177
Navajo study, 187
negotiation, 40, 43, 60–61, 72
nested stages of data collection/organization, 174
network analysis, 77
nongovernmental organizations (NGOs), 61, 63–66, 123, 175
nonprofit organizations, 26
notes. *See* field notes
numerical studies. *See* quantitative research
NVivo (software), 52

objectives, *150*. *See also under specific topics*, e.g., intervention research: objectives
objectivity, 18–19
observation, 5, 14, 48, 84, 89–91, 98, 111, 130, 138, 142, 192; empirical, 95, 144; ensuring consistency in, 134; face-to-face, 8; modes of, 90–91; participant, 10, 96, *150*; qualitative research, 16, 48; selecting the best, 19; semistructured, 8, 140, *150*, 159, *163*–64, 171; sites, 35; structured, *150*, 171; training in, 76; unstructured, 120–21, 125, *150*, 168
older adults, 7, *70*–71, 93–*94*, 114, 160, 174, 180
Onwuegbuzie, J., 155–56, 171–73, 176, 178
Oodit, G., 97–98, 105
open-ended participant observation, 96
open-ended questions, 152
operational definitions, 134–37
operationalization, 133–45, *150*–51, 153, 160, 162, 210; from the bottom up, 137–38; conceptual vs. operational definitions, 134–37; from the top down, 138–45

INDEX

operational models, 126, 200–201
oral health intervention study, *70–71*, 160
organization, 199
organizational dependent variables, *201*
organizational domains, 124, *126–27*
organizational independent variables, *202*, *204*, *206*, 209
organizational resources, *204–9*, 214
outcome, objectivity and, 18–19
outcome problem, 110

Pacific Institute for Research and Evaluation (PIRE), 41
paradigms, 5, 16, 18, 83, 90–93, 104, 128, 130, *158*, 161; guiding, 85; selecting, 92–93; "third," 155
parallel stages of data collection/organization, 174
participant observation, 10, 96, *150*
partnerships, research. *See* research partnerships
patterns; pattern level of abstraction, 5–7, 9, 16, 41, 48–49, 53–54, 89, *91*, 182, 194; constructing, 144; cultural, 3, 81, 133; demographic, 177; mixed methods approach, 166–67; numerical characterization of, 166; pattern recognition, 166; predicted/observed, 86; qualitative work and, 177–78
Pelto, G. H., 17, 86, 90–91, 95, 134, 155
Pelto, Pertti J., 17, 62, 86, 90–91, 95, 134, 155, 212
permissions, obtaining, 55–57
personnel/staff, 45, 55, 65, 68, 71–72, 78, 213; hiring and supervision, 74–76, 78. *See also* teams
Peru, 114, 187
phenomena, 7, 82, 90, *93*, 96–98, 133–37, 141–42; and formative model construction, 103–6, 113; intervention research, 186, 189, 193; local, 10, 96; mixed methods, 155–57, 159, 161, 171, 181, 184. *See also* social phenomena

photographs, 12, 14, 31, 77
pilesorts, 52, 77, 89, *150*
place of residence. *See* demographic information
population dependent variables, *201*
population independent variables, *202*, *204*, *206*, 209
population level domains, *127*
population resources, *204–6*, 208–9, 212, 214
populations, 199; domains of relevance to, 124; target, 122–24, 152, 159, 208–9. *See also* study populations
positionality, 34–37
predictive model, 186, 188
predictive statements, 129–30
predictors, *94*, 114–15, 162, 164, 174, 176, 183, 193, 212
pregnancy, 9, 24, 89, 108, 113, *147–48*; post-partum practice, *cuarentena*, 197; and prenatal care, *111–12*; pre-pregnancy health status, 111–12; prevention vernacular, 14–15; smokeless tobacco and, 47, 152; teenage, 27, 89, 99, 164, 200
preparatory work, 1, 21, 78–79; "preparation triangle," 43–44
"prevention," 194–95
primary data collection, 128
principal components analysis (PCA), 166
principal investigator (PI), 54, 74
privacy (confidentiality), 28, 55
"problems," 3, 27, 83, 103, 194–98
project director/principal investigator (PD/PI), 54, 74–75
proposals. *See* research proposals
propositions, 85–86, 90–91, 121, 129, 134, 152
Puerto Rican community studies, 26, 32, 62–63, 197
purposes. *See* goals
purpose statements, 48, *146–47*

qualitative data, 7–9, 52–54, 78, 152–53, 160–65; analysis, 52–54, 76, 138, 160–61, 163, 165; coding systems, 54, 78, 138; collection, 2, 8–9, 51, 152, 155–56, *164*, 168, 171–81; convergent designs, 174; crunching, 166; domains/factors, linking with, 163–70; focus of, 162; and interventions, 161; mixed methods approach, 167–70
qualitative models, 163
qualitative research/methods, *157*, 159–70; objective of, 16; when to use, 159–60
quantitative data, 8–9, 52, 86, 152–53, 160–*64*, 166–68, 184; analysis, 52, 76, 138, 144, 161; collection, 152, 156, 163–*64*, 177, 181; convergent designs, 174; mixed methods approach, 167–70
quantitative models, 84
quantitative research/methods, *157*, 159–70; objective of, 16; when to use, 160–61
questionnaires, *150*. See also surveys
questions, 2, 19, 51–52, 82–84, 90, 146, *150*, 152–53; defining, 93–100; structured, 141. See also closed-ended questions

race; racial identification, 30, 39, 42, 61, 130. See also demographic information
range of variation, 152
rapport/relationship-building, 2–3, 18, 28, 33–34, 36–37, 56–57, 74–76; and gaining entry/access, 61–63
raw data, 182
reality, 5, 7, 17, 84, 86, 129, 163
Reclaiming a Scientific Anthropology (Kuznar), 4
recording, 8, 76–77, 88
recursivity; recursive process, 89, 105, 108–9, 162, 165, *192*–94, 198, 214
Redfield, Robert, 10
regulations; regulatory agencies, 45–46, 123, 199, 201

relationships, building. See rapport; trust
reliability, establishing, 52, 134, *157*
religion; religious identity, 27, 33, 36, 67, 92
report writing, 70
representations, 104–5, 201
representativeness, 14–16
reproductive health, 9, 14, 40, 47–49, 115, 176, 183–84, 200, 208
research design, 51, 75, 85, 92, 121, 128, 145, *149–50*; constructing ("domain, factor, and variable" framework), *147*; cross-sectional or longitudinal, 186; mixed methods, 156, 171, 176; stages in, 149–53
researchers. See ethnographers
research methods, 3, 37–38, 41, 51, 75, 82, 85, 149–*50*, 155
research models, 6–7, 51, 78, *150*, 167; calibration of, 84, 163, 187, 192; construction of, 110, 112–13, *126–27*; creating, 86–*87*; domains in, 139, 144; experimentation and, 188; framing goals/objectives/hypotheses, 145–*50*; guidelines for, 131; intervention and, 188, 193–94, 214; preliminary, 82; and qualitative/quantitative research, 161; "recalibrating"/adjusting, 82, 84; selection of, 92; systems analytic approach, 199; testing, 153; verification of, 186–88. See also conceptual models; formative models; theoretical models
research partnerships, 24, 96, 118, 142. See also team-based research
research process, 28, 82, 119, 140, 152–53, 185, 188, 192–93; initiation of, 6, 89
research projects, 16, 41, 43, 84; components of, 45–55; end product of, 186; starting point for, 83. See also ethnographic research
research proposals, 45–56, 68, 72, 78, 81–82, 131, 145, 157, 185; for interventions, 210

INDEX

research questions. *See* questions
research results, 17, 82, 96; interpreting, 84; preliminary, 77–78; usefulness of, 2, 37, 45–46, 185
research site, 49, 55, 57, 59, 107, *150*, 164–65, 187; selecting, 23–44; sponsoring institutions in, 60–68
research topic, 43, 88, 90, 96–100, 113
resources, 204–9, 212, 214
respondent-driven sampling, 27
results. *See* research results
retesting, 5, 84, 187
risky behavior, 33, 47, 49, 165–66, 187, 195–96

safed pani study, 9, 174, 176
sampling, 9, 15–16, 51, 56, *150*, 157–58, 160, 166; respondent-driven, 27
Sandelowski, Margarete, 178
SAS (software), 52
scales, 13, 53, 138, 140, 144, *164*–65, 166, 173
schedule. *See* timelines
Schensul, Jean J., 13, 38, 54, 58, 91, 95, 97–100, 118, 157; Ecstasy study, 33, 165–66, 178; fourth-grade diet/nutrition/gardening program study, 100; intervention research, 187, 191, 206; Lima, Peru study, 114; Mumbai studies, 12, 174–75; Sri Lanka study, 124. *See also* Institute for Community Research; Mauritius study
Schensul, Stephen L., 54, 105–9, 118, 159; Chicago's West Side Mexican American community research, 39, 61; gaining access to populations, 61–63; intervention research, 47–48, 186, 190–91; Lima, Peru study, 114; Mumbai studies, 172, 174–75, 180–81, 212; Sri Lanka study, 7, 106–7. *See also* Mauritius study
schools: educational interventions, 189. *See also specific topics/studies,* e.g., Learning Circle Study; Teach Cambodia

secondary data, 35, 52, 95–96, *150*, 172, 181–84
"secret illness." *See gupt rog*
selection of, 203–4
self-reflection, 92–93
semistructured data collection, *150*–53, 169; interviewing, 8, 53, 76, 140–42, *150*–53, 163–65, 168, 171, 173, 177; observation, 8, 140, *150*, 163–*64*, 171
sequential designs, 171–73
sex (demographic variable). *See* demographic information
sexually transmitted infections. *See* STIs
sexual risk behavior/studies, 54, 106–8, 118–19, 167, 172–75, 180–81, 187, 212; among adolescents, 113, 124; in Sri Lanka, 7, 106, 113, 118, 124. *See also* AIDS research; Mauritius study; Mumbai: sexual risk/HIV prevention studies
shantytowns, 114
Silva, K. Tudor, 118, 124
simultaneous and multiphase designs, 173–81
Singer, Elyse Ona, 165–66, 178
Singer, Merrill, 159, 180, 195
Singh, Rajendra, 212
site. *See* research site
Skinner, B. F., 104
Skype, 59
slum communities, 174, 183
smokeless tobacco, 12–13, 47–49, 53, 79, 152
smoking; stop-smoking programs, 103, *126*–27, 160, 201, 204, 206, 208, 210–11
social change, 37, 42, 64, 184, 190, 213–14
social class. *See* socioeconomic status
social desirability scales, 13
social ecological model, 10
social justice researchers, 37, 63
social network analysis, 77
social phenomena, 2, 133–34, 137

sociocultural norms and practices, 28, 190
socioeconomic status, 27–28, 30, 34–37, 65, 76, 92, 120
software, 52, 54, 71–72, 77
spatial data, 8, 52, 77
sponsoring institutions, 60–68. *See also* institutional affiliation
spousal (intimate partner) violence, 9, 167, 174–77, 180, 212
Spradley, J. P., 163
SPSS (software), 52
Sri Lanka studies, 7, 106, 113, 118, 121, 124
staff. *See* personnel
stages in research design/data collection, 149–53
stakeholders, 42, 203
status. *See* socioeconomic status
STIs (sexually transmitted infections), 15, 47, 62, 98, 108, 172, 181, 212
story, 168
structured observation, *150*, 171
structures; structure level of abstraction, 5, 35, 53, 89, *91*, 135, 144
studies, ethnographic. *See* ethnographic research; research projects
study populations, 15, 24, 28, 34, 55, 76, 78, 96, 124, 129; intervention research, 191, 193, 198, 214; mixed methods research, 159–61, 171–72, 174–75; perspectives/needs/priorities of, 42–43
subfactors. *See under* factors: subfactors
subjectivity, 18–19. *See also* bias
substance use/abuse, 41, 55, 187, 211. *See also* drug use/abuse
summative theories, 96
Summer Youth Research Institutes (ICR), 85, 89, 99, 164
supplies, 59, 71–72, 74
surveys, 5, 8–9, 14–16, 19, 47, 49, 52–54, 76–77, 85, 89, 96, 107, 187; construction of, 138; mixed methods, 155–56, 163–67, 176–78, 181–84; operationalization and measurement, 141, *150*, 152–53; results, interpreting, 152, 170–73; structured, 54, 169
"syndemic" factors, 195
systems analysis; systems analytic approaches, 195–96, 198–204; as the "2 × 2 table," 204–10

target populations, 122–24, 152, 159, 208–9
taxonomies, 134, 137–40, 142, 144, *147–48*, 151, 162, 173
Teach Cambodia, 64–67, 95
teams; team-based research, 12–13, 28, 36, 39, 54, 57–58, 71, 74–78, 87; interdisciplinary, 41. *See also* personnel; research partnerships
teens. *See* adolescents; *specific topics*
terms, hierarchies of. *See* taxonomies
testing, 5, 84, 134, 146; and retesting, 5, 84, 187. *See also under* hypotheses: testing; validity, establishing
text-based data. *See* qualitative data
theoretical description, 88
theoretical framework/paradigms, 16, 18–21, 50, 85, 92–93, 100, 128, 192
theoretical orientation, 5–6
theoretical propositions, 121, 134
theoretical questions, 19
theoretical research model, 5–6, 85–86, 90, 93–95, 115, 139, *146*, 153; intervention research, 185, 200–201, 214
theoretical sociologists, 189
theoretical statements, 5, 89
theories, 16–18, 81–101; applying, 85; building, 84, 89, 93–100, 130, 134; concept of, 83; ethnographer as theorist, 83–91; existing, use of, 82, 84–85; generating, 85; "grand," 83, 85, 92, 104; importance of, 88; locally situated, 92; modification of, 82, 84–85, 89–90, 95; paradigm, selecting, 92–93; and research questions,

defining, 93–100; summative, 96; as tool of science, 90; two primary functions of, 84. *See also* formative theories; midrange theories
timelines, 68–71, 74, 78
tobacco. *See* smokeless tobacco; smoking
top down construction, 104–9, 131, 134–35, 138–45
topic. *See* research topic
training researchers. *See under* ethnographers: training
transcription, 53, 76–77
travel/transportation, 58, 60, 64, 71, 72, 74
"treatment," 194–95
tree diagramming, 54, 139, 144, *148–49*
trends, 160, 166, 177
triangulation, 9, 14, 156, 158, 161, 167–68, 172, 174
Trickett, Edison, 191
trust, building, 3, 28, 30–35, 56, 66
Turner, Lisa A., 156

UCINET (software), 77
Uganda, 11, 190
units, 91, 135, 144, 151, *157*
univariate statistical procedures, 52
universities, 26, 37–38, 55
University of Connecticut, 26, 32, 62, 64, 71, 179
"unpacking," 200, 211. *See also under* domains: "unpacking"
unstructured observation/interviewing, 120–21, 125, *150*, 168
U.S. National Institutes of Health. *See* National Institutes of Health (NIH)

USAID (U.S. Agency for International Development), 8–9, 11, 181
Ute study, 187

validity, establishing, 13, 53, 133, *157–58*, 188, 191–93
variables; variable level of abstraction, 8, 108–9, 129–30, *135*, 137–40, *143–48*, 163–66, 174. *See also* dependent variables; independent variables
variation, range of, 152
Verma, R. K., 172, 181, 212
vertical modeling/movement, 87, 104–9, 130, 139, 144, 162
Vicos Project (Peru), 187
videos, 14, 32, 49, 71, 110
violence, 55, *148*, 180, 189. *See also* spousal violence

Weeks, Margaret, 27, 180, 191
Weisner, Thomas, 157, 184, 187
Wellington, Yuri, 64–67, 95
White, Douglas, 187
white discharge study, 9, 174, 176
Wilks, Sandra, 168, 170
women. *See specific topics*, e.g., pregnancy
Women's Structured Survey (WSS), 176
Word software, 54
write-ups, 77–78

Yosso, Tara, 206
youth. *See* adolescents; *specific topics*

Zambia, 29, 64–65
Zegarra, M., 114

ABOUT THE AUTHORS AND ARTISTS

Stephen L. Schensul, a medical anthropologist, is professor in the Department of Community Medicine, University of Connecticut School of Medicine, and the director of the Center for International Community Health Studies. His teaching focuses on research methods and international- and U.S.-based community health for medical, Masters in Public Health students, and international health professionals. His early work focused on community health development through applied research, and his work in Chicago resulted in one of the classic applied social science research community development case studies. Later community development efforts in Hartford, Connecticut, resulted in the founding of the well-known Hispanic Health Council and other community-based institutions. Since the mid-1980s, he has turned his research attention to the prevention of HIV and other sexually transmitted diseases in developing countries, primarily in the Indian Ocean area. He is a consultant to a number of international agencies on community health research, and he has written more than one hundred peer-reviewed publications, including papers on action research and community development, public health, and factors contributing to HIV risk and HIV prevention in Sri Lanka, Mauritius, and India. Among his books are two seminal publications, *Sexuality in the Time of AIDS*, one of the first published on sexuality and HIV in India, and the first authorship of *Essential Ethnographic Methods, Book 2* of the *Ethnographer's Toolkit, First Edition* (Schensul, Schensul, and LeCompte 1999). He is the recipient (with Jean Schensul) of the American Anthropological Solon Kimball Award for research influencing policy, of the Provost Award for Engaged Scholarship (University of Connecticut), and the Career Achievement Award of the Society for Medical Anthropology.

Jean J. Schensul, founding director and now full-time senior scientist, Institute for Community Research, Hartford, is an interdisciplinary medical/educational anthropologist. Born in Canada, she completed her BA in archeology at the University of Manitoba and her MA and PhD in anthropology at the University of Minnesota. From 1978 to 1987, as deputy director and cofounder of the Hispanic Health Council in Hartford, Connecticut, she built its research and training infrastructure. In 1987, she became the founding director of the Institute for Community Research, an innovative, multimillion-dollar community research organization, conducting collaborative applied research in education, cultural studies and folklore, participatory action research, and community intervention research in the United States, China, and India. Dr. Schensul's research cuts across the developmental spectrum, addressing contributions of ethnography to disparities and structural inequities in early childhood development, adolescent and young adult substance use and sexual risk, reproductive health, and chronic diseases of older adulthood. She is the recipient of more than twenty National Institutes of Health research grants, as well as other federal, state, and foundation grants. In addition to conferences, workshops, over eighty peer-reviewed journal articles, many edited substantive special issues of journals including *Anthropology and Education Quarterly, AIDS and Behavior, American Behavioral Scientist*, and the *American Journal of Community Psychiatry*, her collaborative work in research methodology is reflected in a book (with Don Stull) titled *Collaborative Research and Social Change*, the widely celebrated seven-volume series, the *Ethnographers' Toolkit*, with Margaret LeCompte, and in other articles and book chapters on ethnography and advocacy, community building, and sustainability of interventions. She has served as president of the Society for Applied Anthropology and the Council on Anthropology and Education and is an elected board member of the American Anthropological Association. In recognition of her work as a scholar-activist she has been awarded two senior anthropology awards, the Solon T. Kimball Award for anthropology and policy (with Stephen Schensul) and the Malinowski Award for lifetime contribution to the use of anthropology for the solution of human problems. Dr. Schensul holds adjunct faculty positions in the departments of Anthropology and Community Medicine, University of Connecticut, and she is co-director of Qualitative Research and Ethnography component of the Interdisciplinary Research Methods Core, Yale Center for Interdisciplinary Research on AIDS.

Margaret LeCompte received her BA from Northwestern University in political science, and after serving as a civil rights worker in Mississippi and a Peace Corps volunteer in the Somali Republic, she earned her MA and PhD from the University of Chicago. She then taught at the universities of Houston and Cincinnati, with visiting appointments at the University of North Dakota and the Universidad de Monterrey, Mexico, before moving to the School of Education at the University of Colorado-Boulder in 1990. She also served for five years as executive director for research and evaluation for the Houston Independent School District. She is internationally known as a pioneer in the use of qualitative and ethnographic research and evaluation in education. Fluent in Spanish, she has consulted throughout Latin America on educational research issues. Her publications include many articles and book chapters on research methods in the social sciences, as well as her cowritten (with Judith Preissle) *Ethnography and Qualitative Design in Educational Research* (1984; 1993) and coedited (with Wendy Millroy and Judith Preissle) *The Handbook of Qualitative Research in Education* (1992), the first textbook and handbook published on ethnographic and qualitative methods in education. Her collaborative work in research methodology continues with this second edition of the *Ethnographer's Toolkit*. Dr. LeCompte is deeply interested in the educational success of linguistically and culturally different students from kindergarten through university, as well as reform initiatives for schools and communities serving such students. Her books in these areas include *The Way Schools Work: A Sociological Analysis of Education* (1990, 1995, and 1999) with Kathleen Bennett deMarrais and *Giving Up on School: Student Dropouts and Teacher Burnouts* (1991) with Anthony Gary Dworkin. Her diverse interests as a researcher, evaluator, and consultant to school districts, museums, communities, and universities have led to publications on dropouts, artistic and gifted students, school reform efforts, schools serving Native American students, and the impact of strip mining on the social environment of rural communities. Her most recent research involves explorations in the politics and finance of public universities. A Fellow of the American Educational Research Association, the American Anthropological Association, and the Society for Applied Anthropology, she also was awarded the Spindler Prize for advances in the field of anthropology and education by the Council on Anthropology and Education of the American Anthropology Association, an organization that she also served as president. She has been editor of the journals *Review of Educational Research* and *Youth and Society*. A founding member and the first president of the University of Colorado-Boulder chapter of the American Association of

University Professors (AAUP), she also served as vice president of the Colorado Conference of the AAUP and was active in faculty governance at the University of Colorado. As professor emerita, she continues to use action research strategies in the service of improving the intellectual life in higher education.

A fiber artist, quilter, teacher, curator, and lecturer, **Ed Johnetta Fowler-Miller** is acknowledged to be one of the most creative and colorful improvisational quiltmakers in the United States. Widely exhibited in the United States and internationally, her quilts can be found in many important museums, corporate and private collections including The National Gallery of the Smithsonian Institution in Washington, D.C.; Nelson Mandela's National Museum in Cape Town, South Africa; Wadsworth Atheneum Museum of Art in Hartford, Connecticut; and the Rocky Mountain Quilt Museum in Golden, Colorado. Her home state of Connecticut awarded her its most prestigious artistic award, The Governor's Art Award, as well as the Wadsworth Atheneum Museum of Arts first Presidents Award; Leadership of Greater Hartford's Arts and Cultural Award, Vision Award for Arts; and Cultural and Capital Community College Heritage Award. The Home and Garden Station featured Ed Johnetta on the Modern Masters series; she appeared on Debbie Allen's series *Cool Women*, Public TV, Tokyo, Japan; and her woven creations were worn by actress Phylicia Rashad on *The Cosby Show*. The Sunday *New York Times* featured her in the Best of the Best series, and most recently, she appeared on HGTV's *Simply Quilts*. In 2009 Ed Johnetta represented the United States and the Women of Color Quilters Network at the largest quilt festival in the world in Yokohama, Japan, and in 2010 she represented the United States in Costa Rica, where she lectured and taught workshops. She has exhibited her work across the United States and lectures and offers workshops in New England, elsewhere in the United States, and worldwide. More information can be found at http://www.edjohnetta.com.

Graciela Quiñones-Rodríguez is a gourd carver/lutier/multimedia artisan/performer and Master Teaching Artist. She draws most of her inspiration from indigenous and traditional Puerto Rican imagery and symbols to create *higüeras* (gourds), clay/wood figures, and folk string instruments (*cuatros*, *tiples*, and *bordonuas*). She has been a resident artist in numerous schools and libraries throughout Massachusetts, Connecticut, and New York. She has received fellowships and awards from the Commission on the Arts, the New England Foundation for the Arts, and the National Endowment for the Arts. Her works have been on exhibit in Puerto Rico, the Smithsonian Institution, University of Massachusetts, Wisconsin, New York, and several exhibit sites throughout Connecticut. She is a member of Urban Artists Initiative and the Connecticut Cultural Heritage Arts Program. Graciela Quiñones-Rodríguez is a licensed clinical social worker, currently working at the Storrs campus of the University of Connecticut.